CW00839914

YOU CAN'T DO THAT HERE! THIS IS THE BBC!

Or one man's odyssey around the fringes of radio broadcasting...

By

Lawrence P. Lettice

Copyright © Lawrence P. Lettice 2016
This book is sold subject to the condition that it shall not, by way of
trade or otherwise, be lent, resold, hired out, or otherwise circulated
without the publisher's prior consent in any form of binding or cover
other than that in which it is published and without a similar condition
including this condition being imposed on the subsequent publisher.
The moral right of Lawrence P. Lettice has been asserted.
ISBN-13: 978-1523764679
ISBN-10: 1523764678

This book is dedicated to the memory of many ex-BBC friends and colleagues who have now all sadly passed away.

Gone they may be, but forgotten, they certainly aren't.

So here are just a few of the names from that time:

Peggy, Dorothy, Alex, Catherine, Frank, Tom, Jean, Bill, Harry, George, Donald, Edith, Pat, Douglas, and last but not least – Fraser, a good close friend, who laughed almost as loud as myself, at some of the antics we witnessed.

This is a work of creative nonfiction. While all the stories in this book are true, some names and identifying details have been changed to protect the privacy of the people involved.

CONTENTS

Acknowledgments

Whether you ever yielded a microphone, an editing blade, a typewriter, a telephone, a sweeping brush, a teapot, or a soup ladle, you deserve to be remembered with distinctive affection, within these pages.

And for those past offspring of "Auld Granny Beeb" (whether legitimate... or otherwise) who provided endless entertainment (whether intentional... or otherwise) for audiences (whether outraged... or otherwise) this book is gifted for you to enjoy... or otherwise.

Inspirations

Looking for some form of subliminal inspiration in writing this book, I looked instantly towards the examples of a few select learned men and accomplished writers, whose work has made me laugh, and equally at the same time, has also made me think.

Chief amongst them were Hollywood star *David Niven*, whose memoirs and reminiscences produced two much loved books (*The Moon's A Balloon* and *Bring On The Empty Horses*) in which he took a wry, humorous and affectionate look back on his life. Very few did it better.

Other literary inspirations included writer *Robert Sellers* with his hilariously outrageous study of four great actors and boozers in *"Hell-raisers"*, the equally funny *"Hampden Babylon"* by BBC Scotland's *Off The Ball* presenter *Stuart Cosgrove*, the diaries of *Richard Burton*, the comic observations of *Ricky Gervais* and *Stephen Merchant*, and finally the writings of two BBC men who I have long admired and had the great fortune of meeting and conversing with – *Barry Norman* and *Michael Palin*.

All of the above gentlemen whose combined intelligence of words, insightful expressions, sharp-edged humour and colourful descriptions, has made me want to open up a word document, start typing furiously and follow (however cautiously) in their elevated footsteps.

For that, I thank them all.

Cast of Characters

Bob L - *Commissionaire & Noel Coward style man about town*

Miss Wilson - *Administration Assistant, elegant lady boss, stickler for protocol*

Bob P - *Commissionaire & gruff ex-army type*

Bob - *House Attendant, Clarinet playing Storm trooper, Demolition Man*

Hamish - *Mailroom Assistant & Don Juan figure with narcissistic tendencies*

Robin - *Mailroom Assistant, manic drummer & aspiring pop idol*

Harry - *House Attendant, Religious Theologian &, connoisseur of fine beverages*

Frank - *House Electrician, Burma Veteran, Purveyor of Artistic Literature*

Donald - *Television News Editor, frequent visitor to Frank's Library!*

Mac - *Commissionaire, House Foreman, ex-Scots Guards, waspish tongue*

Richard - *Mailroom Assistant, Audio Engineer, History Student, Arts Producer*

Mr Snax - *Sound Engineer, TV Camera Man, Curry King of Scotland, Bon Vivant*

Tom - *General handyman, ex-RAF, carries a large & adaptable sonic screwdriver*

Fraser - *Mailroom Assistant, object of frustrated male desires*

Bella - *Administration Assistant, former Art Student, Wine connoisseur*

Dot - *News Room Secretary, Party Animal, Funny Lady*

Eileen - Receptionist, Switchboard Operator, Cliff's Number 1 fan
And a visitor from Leith - Lawrence

Some Supporting Players

The Security Men - The original men in black

The Audio Crew - Heavy Metal Merchants & Sound men all…

The Cleaners - The ladies who wielded the mops and drank the booze!

The Catering Staff - Food from the gods, and the goddesses

The Radio Producers - Some Good, Some Bad, Some Downright Obnoxious!

The News Journalists - Cigarettes and whiskey and wild, wild women

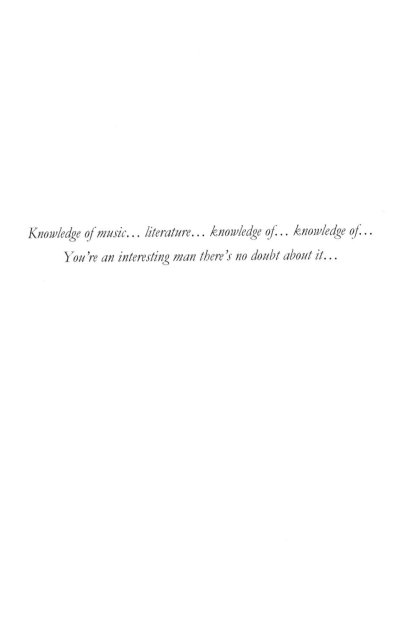

Knowledge of music... literature... knowledge of... knowledge of...
You're an interesting man there's no doubt about it...

PREFACE

"If they ask me, I could write a book..."

I was thinking and reflecting (something I do a lot of these days) that I should sit down in front of my PC during a quiet period and write. But I thought to myself, what should I write about?

Yet a learned scribe once told me: "Always write about what you know, what you've seen, what you've heard, what you've observed, and what you've experienced."

So, with those few pearls of wisdom and encouragement still ringing in my ears, I thought I would start banging away (so to speak) on the keyboard.

*

A long, long time ago, in a broadcasting galaxy far, far, away (I thought that would be a good start) I once found myself working at the illustrious and prestigious establishment that was once the BBC Radio Scotland offices and studios, based at 5 Queen Street in Edinburgh.

Sadly, although the building is still very much intact and still very much in evidence, the BBC has long since vacated the premises. In fact it was fifteen years ago when the powers that be (not too sure at the time if it was London calling the shots, or Glasgow, or a combination of both?), decided that Scotland's capital city no longer needed – or required – a major broadcasting centre.

From what I discovered, from several reliable sources at the time, it was getting far too expensive to maintain, and the advancement in modern broadcasting technology was creeping up fast. So good old "Auntie Beeb" decided in their all-knowing wisdom, to close the place down, and deprive Scotland's capital city of an important major centre for broadcasting. Replacing it instead with a cosy wee broom cupboard, situated somewhere alongside the new Scottish Parliament, down near Holyrood.

But here, I am getting a little too far ahead of myself…

*

So, to begin at the beginning (where have I heard that before?), my initial aim was to write down some of my memories, observations, and anecdotes about the various individuals, personalities and events that I witnessed and experienced. Purely for my own self-interest and more importantly, to give myself a right good laugh! As well as hopefully perhaps, the enjoyment of a few good friends and some former colleagues, who will possibly appreciate and recognise of whom I might be referring to during the course of my story.

Yet this exercise has also given me the opportunity to give my memory bank a thorough energetic workout, as well as offer up the opportunity to laugh out loud at some of the more outrageous and astonishing things that went on. I guess that I consider myself a little bit lucky, in as much as I appear to still possess (even considering that I am now well advanced into my mature years) a reasonably photographic memory regarding the past. Yet not only that, but the facility to instantly recall quirky and offbeat conversations and scalding dialogue exchanges from numerous individuals – as if they were characters straight out of an old Hollywood movie! This advantage has helped me enormously in the telling of my many tales, as you will soon find out.

However, it is important not to forget that many of these events happened some 20/30/40-odd years ago. So apologies if I have managed to exclude, or omit any names, individuals, or important details during this sidestepping comedic journey through Scottish radio-land.

2

In truth, I am not out to slander or embarrass anyone (apart from myself!), and if I have managed to cast aspersions on the character of any of the individuals alive, or deceased in the course of my story, then I offer my sincerest apologies. That is certainly not my intention.

In writing this memoir (Memoir? That makes me sound more like a disgraced former Tory MP, or an ageing Shakespearean thespian), I am really hoping to paint a bizarrely impressionistic, and maybe even slightly exaggerated and surreal portrait of a particular time and place.

During my years working for BBC Scotland, we played host to writers, actors, academics, musicians, scientists, politicians, philosophers (even the odd bullshit philosopher – no names mentioned!) men and women of letters, deep thinkers – and even on the odd occasion, big stinkers! So it's safe to say that at one time or another, we had the tall, the talented, and the tossers – though not necessarily altogether at the same time!

*

My honest intention with this book, is to display affection mixed with bewilderment, humour mixed with shock, and above all, friendship mixed with gratitude.

Like so many of my former friends and colleagues who shared with me this moment in time, it was probably the defining period of our lives.

Although one or two have questioned my motives in putting down in print what they perceive as a fairly critical view of the BBC, nothing could be further from the truth. Again, just to emphasise, what I have written about is not the BBC in Edinburgh as it is now, but a BBC in Edinburgh that no longer exists. It's gone, disappeared, vanished, nothing but a sepia-toned, soft focus memory of a place that is no more. Lost in the distant mists of time, while being accompanied by the faint echo of clinking empty wine and beer bottles, along with much raucous and bawdy laughter!

Yet I am acutely aware that quite a few of my ex-colleagues could relate far more hilarious stories of working within the BBC studios at 5 Queen Street, so much better than me, and with probably far greater insight and intelligence than my meagre efforts presented here. Of that, I am totally convinced.

With that in mind, I must also add that I do not feel remotely qualified regarding the detailing of programmes, productions, or in any way probing and delving into the more creative and technical side of BBC Edinburgh. That can be well taken care of by individuals much more knowledgeable and experienced than my own good self. So if you were looking for a complete, detailed, definitive history of the BBC in Edinburgh, its programmes, productions, and artistic creations within radio and TV, you would be best placed in looking elsewhere, as this certainly isn't it!

In fact a recent publication written by that fine and much respected gentleman (who I had the privilege to know quite well) *Mr David Pat Walker* (along with Mike Shaw), wrote a fairly exhaustive and informative history of the BBC in Scotland called (not surprisingly) *The BBC in Scotland*. In which Edinburgh's broadcasting origins are discussed and analysed with a great deal of depth and well-researched detail.

But my more modest attempts (unvarnished, uninhibited, and revealing a good deal more that you might possibly realise, or expect) sheds light upon a more light-hearted and alternative view of the BBC in Edinburgh – a "Lord Reithian Comedy of Errors" perhaps? Although I'm not quite sure what the BBC's founding father would have thought about some of the antics that went on.

I am plainly sticking to what I know, as well as viewing proceedings from a more plebeian (a great word that *Andrew Mitchell* might well approve of!) angle. A worm's eye view if you like, as I surveyed and observed all manner of things that made me giggle out loud, while shuddering with shock at the differing conversations and images that still rattle about in my memory to this very day.

My time at the BBC was shaped by the ordinary, the mundane and the routine. As *William Holden* once described himself in the film *The Bridge on the River Kwai* – "I'm just an ordinary swab-jockey, second class!" That pretty much sums up what I was. In other words, I was looked upon as nothing more than a pen pushing, envelope opening box-shifter! Not much exciting glamour about that, but certainly plenty of laughs – whether it was intentional, or otherwise.

To use a further analogy, I had decided to place myself within the shoes of the likes of *Nick Carraway, Ishmael, Addison DeWitt*, and the *Emperor Claudius* – celebrated observers, witnesses and chroniclers to strange events and unusual individuals encountered, that often left one gasping with a sense of numbing incredulity. So it's fair to say that in my day job, I probably didn't learn all that much about broadcasting, but I certainly learnt a lot about life – in all of its myriad colours and forms.

However – just as a warning – this was also a time of gross and course sexual innuendo, blatant religious bigotry, unrestrained homophobia, and very un-PC language and attitudes that in today's society would be deemed totally inappropriate and unacceptable. Whilst if you look at it another way – you may discover more "groping, grabbing and gripping" than you would experience at an all in wrestling bout! Or (allegedly), a recording of *Top Of The Pops!!*

With all that in mind, I have attempted to modify the use of swear words, and so I have blanked out many of the more offensive ones.

Although the proliferation of swearing was a daily occurrence in such a place, I have retained the odd expression and expletive, if only to add a bit of necessary spicy authenticity to the humour of a specific story. As someone once said – you cannot airbrush history. This is how they were – and this is how they spoke.

*

I have absolutely no intention in attempting to alter what has gone before, or delete what went before. I just wanted to relate my story – warts and all.

I have also decided to omit some (not all) of the surnames of many of the leading characters. Perhaps as protection to their anonymity (and myself from potential lawsuits??) but again to reaffirm that my sole intention is not to be scurrilous or to be personally damaging, but to bring back to life a period that I and many of my former colleagues and friends lived through.

I feel the need to be nostalgic and just to chuckle within myself at the absurdity of individual personalities I worked alongside and situations that I witnessed. This is really what went on behind closed doors – or in some circumstances, what came off, behind closed doors!

*

In conclusion, I ultimately and sincerely hope that all I have written is perceived by potential readers as humorously affectionate, gently tongue in cheek, and non-malicious, reflecting a vastly different time. I do hope you enjoy them, and for the benefit of many of my former colleagues, I also hope they may stir a few fond memories and manage to give you the odd laugh or two! It made me laugh!

The rest, as they say, is history…

CHAPTER 1

It's Better Than Working For Murphy's The Builders!

"When the legend becomes fact…print the legend."

As the writer *LP Hartley* once wrote: "The past is a foreign country. They do things differently there." Very wise and profound words, particularly in relation to the story (and stories) that I am about to unfold.

*

Long, long before the thought of a "career" with BBC Scotland ever entered my mind, I found myself enduring the perils and joys of boyhood, living within the Pennywell/Muirhouse area of north Edinburgh.

I moved there with my parents just prior to the dawn of "the swinging sixties", with one of my earliest memories being that of observing the slow construction of the once infamous Martello Court (later dubbed "Terror Tower" by the tabloids) as it rose from the ground like a monolithic 20th-century version of the *Tower Of Babel*.

This was the very same scheme (once demonised and dubbed faintly notorious during the 1970s for its level of drug problems and gang violence) that gave the world the likes of Scotland footballer, and later manager *Gordon Strachan*, as well as the acclaimed author, *Irvine Welsh*.

Being only a few months older than myself, *Gordon Strachan* was someone I knew reasonably well, as we both attended the same primary and secondary schools, and he also happened to live just along the road. In fact, I tend to often boast (to anyone who bothers to listen?) that I once played football with him. Albeit, it was almost 50 years ago, when attempting to prise the ball from his quick, nimble, and tricky feet was deemed an almost almighty and impossible task!

Even at a very young age (and when playing alongside footballers slightly older than himself), I vividly remember him displaying a unique and precocious talent on the football pitch, marking him out as someone very special. Not surprisingly, here was a young player who could go a long way in his chosen sport if he showed equal amounts of dedication and commitment. Which he eventually later did with a great deal of success, both as a player, as well as a manager.

As for *Irvine Welsh*, I must confess that I don't recall him at all during my early years growing up in the Muirhouse area. Despite him frequently mentioning the place (and its tawdry and criminally tinged drawbacks) in his books.

More likely we attended different schools? But our paths never crossed – even though we were living in roughly the same scheme and with both of us holding an affinity for the same Edinburgh football club – the one that normally plays in green and white.

As everyone knows, *Mr Welsh* has written extensively, successfully, and lucratively about the corrosive drug culture in Muirhouse – often from a very personal perspective.

However, from my own perspective, the only memories I have of "Shooting-Up in Muirhouse", derives from my pretence as an imaginative five-year-old, pretending to be *John Wayne*, as I roamed the rugged badlands of (no, not *Arizona, Texas, or Durango*) Pennywell Gardens!

Alongside close pals such as *Graham Allan* and *Dane*

Harrison, as well as my young brother Gary, we bravely confronted such imaginary foes as Apache warriors, Zulu impis, Mexican bandits and Japanese snipers, while applying the concentrated true grit of an underage Pennywell soldier!! Those were sunnier, seemingly far happier days, in which the dark, malevolent forces of lowlife drug dealers had not as yet slithered from beneath the ground, and hence did not feature, or figure anywhere within our toy pistol, or plastic rifle range!

Ah, the innocence of youth.

*

It's a funny thing, but during the period running up towards my final departure from my secondary school, and before I found myself walking through the front glass doors of BBC 5 Queen Street for the very first time, I don't recall anyone ever discussing my future with me.

No one, from teachers, employment and career advisors, not even my own parents, ever sat me down and discussed in any great detailed length, long term plans regarding where my skills/abilities/talents best lay in the world of employment.

I was in no way regarded as the Dux of the school (a term, position, and status that I was totally ignorant of, and was only explained to me just recently by a couple of friends) but I like to think that I was modestly intelligent with a reasonably enquiring and inquisitive mind.

Yet for me at this time, there were no lengthy discussions investigating the potentiality of a place at university, college, or any style of further education planted within my brain.

And who knows, maybe in retrospect, the intellectual world of academia turned out (for me, anyway) to be ultimately irrelevant?

I was simply and unequivocally left to my own devices.

In other words – find myself a job and start earning a wage!

*

Looking back, perhaps I wasn't alone in that respect, as probably thousands – if not millions – faced a similar situation during those nervous, edgy, and uncertain times between the end of school days and the beginnings of a working career.

After all, in the grand scheme of things, I wouldn't have been gifted with the experience of working for some considerable years within such a lively, fun-packed environment such as the BBC. One full of wacky, bohemian and unconventional characters!

Something that further down the line, has now presented me with the ripe opportunity of writing all about the place and the people I met and encountered.

Life certainly does move in mysterious ways.

*

However, it was during the early summer of 1974, that I began my time at the *BBC* in *5 Queen Street* as a rather callow youth of 16. I had not that long finished my education at secondary school, while achieving the astounding total of 4 'O' Levels, with very little else besides. When I used to mention to people that I had in fact achieved 4 'O' Level passes (which I thought at the time, wasn't all that bad?) the usual reply was something like "'O' Levels? They're nothing special, as they normally give these out in cornflake packets!" Talk about feeling deflated!

What I really strived for (at least at that time in my imagination) was a career in the cinema (or the movies, or motion pictures!) but at 16 I wasn't entirely sure as to how I would go about it, and more importantly, how to gain a foothold into that magical world.

Looking back at that time, and if memory serves me correctly, it was my mother who spotted an advert in the *Edinburgh Evening News* for an office junior to start at the *BBC*

Radio Studios in 5 *Queen Street.*

This, I thought, would be a role that would ideally suit a school leaver like myself, and the first rung in again what I thought (more fool me!) would be a substantial career within the entertainment and media industry.

And who knows, possibly a doorway that might lead towards my eventual ambition of getting involved in some level with film.

This was what was buzzing in my brain at the time, and it's funny how your imagination makes you think such bizarre thoughts at such a young and tender age.

*

So, I arrived for my interview, all smartly turned out with jacket, shirt, and tie, as I stepped into the main reception area to await my interview with the Glasgow-based Personnel Officer. He was a gentleman by the name of *James Littlejohn,* who had travelled through from the west to conduct the interviews that day.

Thinking back, I believe I was amongst about half a dozen aspiring applicants, all very eager to become part of this prestigious home of Scottish radio broadcasting.

I remember arriving at the reception, where I was told to take a seat and to await my call for the interview. I immediately noticed a large glass case on my left that featured a number of books and BBC publications that included *Alistair Cook's America,* as well as a special summer edition of the *Radio Times,* that was advertising the forthcoming World Cup in Germany. This would be the famous one that Scotland was participating in, and solely representing the UK during the summer of 1974, since England and the rest of the home nations had failed to qualify. What a shame.

*

Well, the interview must have gone ok, as I received word to start the following Monday at 9am.

Excitement merged with anticipation at gaining my first job, my first proper wage, and particularly within an organisation of the status of the *BBC*.

I was one lucky guy – or so I thought?

Yet as one of my late uncles shrewdly observed when I told him of my good news: "Well, it's better than working for Murphy's the builders!"

Before I proceed any further, I must add my apologies for any unintended slight to any existing company that are called *"Murphy's the Builders"*. My late uncle's remark may have appeared comically flippant, but he was just illustrating a point. With the point being that my new job would prove a far more appropriate and conducive working environment for me, than slogging away on a cold, bleak and punishing building site!

*

From the outset, I never felt any strong affinity, or desire to work in either the audio, or engineering side of broadcasting, for I realised straight away that my interest and brain movements just weren't wired up in any way towards that direction.

The thought of finding myself lost amongst valves, tubes, copper wiring, microphones and cables wasn't something that I aspired to. Not that I didn't have great respect for the guys who spent hours of their working lives immersed in the technical side of life. I just always knew that it wasn't for me.

Which then left my options slightly limited. So I just carried on regardless, did what I was told (most of the time), kept my head down, caused no ruptures, and eventually found a small niche for myself as a guy who could prove to be (for the most part) versatile, adaptable, and amenable. But that lay further up ahead.

Well, my very first impressions of the interior of 5 Queen Street were that of viewing a musty building from a bygone era. Not quite *Dickensian*, but it had a uniquely quaint Caledonian atmosphere that felt straight out of a novel by *John Buchan, or Arthur Conan Doyle.*

From where I was standing, this wasn't "Auntie Beeb" – but more like "Auld Granny Beeb".

I suppose a good many of the companies and businesses that occupied offices within Edinburgh's New Town during this time must have had a very similar décor, style, and layout in that respect. This was the 1970s after all.

Although in saying that, I suppose you could say that the old building possessed a certain quaint old world charm and character, that helped make it quite unique as a centre of broadcasting.

It may well have creaked and groaned a bit with age here and there, but at least there was nothing bland or soulless about it.

I had also been reliably informed (whether it was true, or not) that BBC Edinburgh was then the oldest broadcasting building in the entire UK.

While glancing around, I wouldn't have disputed that fact.

Certainly from my own limited perspective, the offices, studios and corridors had a slightly stuffy, dusty, antiquated feel, looking as if they had all been frozen in time since the early 1930s. With some of the staff (as well as many of the elderly visitors and contributors) closely resembling cast members from either *"Whiskey Galore"*, or *"Dr Finlay's Casebook"*!

*

During my initial couple of years working in the place, I did feel a slight sense of inferiority, coming as I did from a basic working-class background; with the majority of the staff all appearing (at least in my eyes) as very much middle-class in their outward demeanour.

From where I was standing, they all emanated a staid Morningside aura that was generally reflected in their speech, manner and attitude.

Yet in saying that, the vast majority of them were friendly and welcoming and I never really felt that they looked down on me.

I guess what with Edinburgh being a much smaller building (than say Glasgow), it possessed a much more intimate (maybe too intimate in certain quarters?) atmosphere to it. This made it far easier for staff, as well as the differing departments, to move amongst one another with a greater degree of comfortable ease.

On the distaff side (as I would much later learn), it also made it far easier for stories, gossip and snippets of dodgy news to gallop rampantly throughout the building like a virulent outbreak of plague!!

∗

The normal reaction I would receive when telling people that I now was working for BBC Edinburgh, was: "I never knew there was a BBC Edinburgh. I was always under the impression that it all came from Glasgow?"

In such circumstances, I had to provide a little education on that score.

∗

If my memory is not deceiving me, among the main departments that were around during my first few years, included the likes of:

TV News (providing pieces for *Reporting Scotland*)

Radio Features (including *12 Noon*), *Studio Bookings,*

Music, Arts, Religion, Radio Education

The Schools Broadcasting Council for Scotland

Audio & Engineering

Hope I have not left anyone out?

*

We also had a Tele-printer room, a switchboard (complete with switchboard operators, as you do), a mailroom, a stationery store, a canteen/restaurant, a main control room, a small green room (with comfy seats and a large TV), workshops for the house electrician and handyman, an audio crew room, an engineering maintenance room, and a rest room for the house staff (a.k.a. The Howff).

Not forgetting the boardroom, a cloakroom, a furniture store, a listening room and sound archive (complete with record decks), a small TV studio and of course three radio studios, which I suppose would come in handy, considering this was in fact, a radio broadcasting station.

We also had a First Aid Room, but as you will soon find out, that very special and much-loved room, deserves a chapter all of its very own!

Then by the beginning of the 1980s (with the coming of Radio Scotland), we would be bolstered by the arrival of *Good Morning Scotland, News & Current Affairs, Radio Drama*, and even more studios. But much more of that later…

Despite the rich amount of entertainment generated within the studios, it's a fair contention to state that there was equally just as much entertainment going on among darkened basements, shadowy corridors and other faintly hidden places around the building. With the majority of those being accidental, unintentional and not surprisingly, un-broadcastable. But again, much more of that later…

Away from 5 Queen Street, the BBC also leased another building, just a few minutes down the road at Abercromby Place. This was the main headquarters for both the Schools Broadcasting Council, as well as the majority of the Radio Education department.

As well as the above, Abercromby Place also had a large

registry office, situated in that building's basement floor. Running that department was *Gary Lugton*. Gary would turn out to be one of my closest friends during my first few years there. A young man who possessed a vast intellect and was someone whose abilities were absolutely wasted in that dry, dull basement environment, full of musty old files, full of musty old contracts for musty old contractees. Gary deserved much better. Just entering conversation with him, I became aware that he was without any shadow of a doubt, a far more intelligent individual than many of the programme makers that were around during that time in BBC Edinburgh.

Here was a guy who was one prime shining example of a bright, creative mind that BBC Scotland had on their books, and for one reason or another, simply wasted.

*

The staff at Abercromby Place would be based there for a number of years, before eventually moving out (perhaps the rent had increased considerably?) and then taking up residence elsewhere – this time further up the road at Thistle Street.

This building would eventually become a temporary home for the entire staff during the latter half of the 1980s. But once again, more of that later…

Well, apart from myself, there was one other new starter, who like me had successfully overcome the interviewing process and would be my new work colleague. He was called Hamish. He appeared to be slightly older than me (or so he acted) but was most definitely far more worldly and mature in his outlook on life – and with women in particular. As for me, I was as green as a freshly laundered Hibs Strip!

At this time, my mind was still full of old western movies, and his, well it seemed to dwell on females – lots and lots of busty and available young females. Not that my mind didn't venture into that tender territory on the odd occasion too, but Hamish gave the impression that he had a PhD on the subject.

He possessed a somewhat obvious and spurious charm that appeared to effortlessly work with smooth success upon many a female he encountered. I suppose he was likeable in his own way, and we got on reasonably fine despite our very different backgrounds. Yet I always had the impression that despite his many alleged conquests, the mirror reflected where his true affections lay!

Hamish also used to talk regularly about his horses. I naively thought at first (owing to the fact that my father also used to talk excitedly about his horses – the ones that usually featured on the newspaper racing pages) that he was discussing his daily visits to the local bookmakers.

In fact, I couldn't be more wrong.

When waxing lyrical about his horses, what Hamish was really doing was telling me that his family – *did indeed own horses*. So with that being the case, I quickly figured that he obviously came from a reasonably wealthy and comfortable background. One that owned land and with that, of course, horses!

It's funny now, but when I come to think about it, what with Hamish's love for all things equestrian, coupled with his amorous nocturnal activities, BBC Edinburgh had in its very midst, their very own *Midnight Cowboy*!

It was no exaggeration to state that Hamish moved around the building with the overconfident aura of a strutting, swaggering, narcissistic stud! In fact someone once commented that he reminded him of (and I quote) "a walking erection!" Which come to think of it, might well have been a bit awkward and painful for the poor guy!

Yet his often-lurid descriptions of bedroom athletics (whether real, or imaginary?) left me green with envy, as well as presenting me with a deep feeling of inadequacy.

Mac (of whom there is much more later) even colourfully described Hamish as "throbbing cock".

And he casually looked upon most women as easy and inevitable conquests, who would fall readily into his arms and into his bed.

Apologies if I am being a little unfair on the guy, as I recently discovered that far away from his humble BBC beginnings, he has managed to carve out a fairly successful career in broadcasting – so I guess that it all worked out fine for him in the end.

Over the subsequent decades, it's safe to say that Hamish would have any number of serious rivals or contenders for that much sought-after title of *Stud in Residence!* With several athletically primed individuals all too eager in the coming years in providing ample evidence of their versatile seduction skills (along with deeply etched bed notches) that may (or may not?) enhance their burgeoning CVs!

*

Well, aside from the sexually assured Hamish, there was one other part of the team, that I was yet to meet. This was Robin, he was again slightly older, and a guy who was destined for greater and higher things. Or so he kept telling us, on more than one occasion.

Robin was a drummer – but not your ordinary, regular, everyday, run-of-the-mill drummer – he was a drummer in a pop band.

At first glance he seemed to be full of excessive energy, like a human version of "the animal", straight out of *The Muppet Show!*

He would use tables, desks, chairs, cabinets, anything in fact that was lying or standing around, in order for him to bang away with his drumsticks. His group, he assured us, was due to hit the heights and achieve worldwide domination.

Something again that he would tell us over and over again, with increasing degrees of regularity and monotony.

His navigation to pop superstardom was being

masterminded by none other than the Prestonpans Svengali – *Tam Paton*. This was the very same man who had just recently unleashed the *Bay City Rollers* upon an unsuspecting public.

When Robin used to tell us that he was being "managed and handled by *Tam Paton*" that statement would reverberate many years later in my memory, with a chilling connotation that I didn't fully realise at the time.

Being a part of *Tam Paton's* "stable of boy artistes" (for want of a better phrase), Robin would often tell us of his band's frequent visits to his manager's luxury pad, situated just outside Edinburgh. No doubt to discuss "music strategy", their inevitable assault on the pop charts, or something vaguely along those lines?

"Me and the guys were all up at Tam's place over the weekend for a party," he expressed to me one Monday morning, adding with a laugh in his voice, "It was f*****g wild man, f*****g wild!" I bet it was – as I shudder still at the thought of what was going on in those parties! Certainly not blind-man's buff, or postman's knock – although, you never know?

A philosopher once said, "There are some experiences in life that are best left well alone and undiscovered..." with *Tam Paton's* wild parties by all accounts, being one of them!

Perhaps it was wise on Robin's part that he never divulged too much information about what actually occurred during those, ahem, "parties".

Maybe just as well.

*

One day Robin brought in an album that he wanted to listen to. So he headed off down to the listening room during a quiet spell in order to play it. The album was by the 70s glam rockers *The Sweet* and Robin was particularly enamoured by the ferocious drum playing of *Mick Tucker*.

He put the album on the turntable and set the volume

19

control to – its absolute limit! To say it was blaring loud was a bit of an understatement! The roof was in danger of blowing off! Yet, not only that, but he left the room's door wide open, so the booming sound of *The Sweet* could now be heard throughout the main part of the building.

It didn't take long for the assistant operations manager to pop down to investigate the noise.

He then (once he could be heard, that is) calmly, but firmly instructed Robin to tone it down, as it was affecting the recording that was taking place next door in Studio 3!!

Robin just laughed, and cried out as the manager quickly departed up the stairs, "What a f*****g machine man, what a f*****g machine!"

Then he carried on banging away with his drumsticks, oblivious to the constant noise he was causing.

From memory, he was always hyper, always high, and always assured that the day of his band getting their big break on *Top Of The Pops* was only a few, fleeting moments away.

Nobody took him all that seriously – least of all Bob and Harry.

*

Bob and Harry (along with another guy called Jimmy, who would soon leave following a bust up with the Admin Assistant) were Queen Street's two hard-working (I think?) House Attendants. To those who encountered them at close quarters during this time, they tended to view them as being – *Mad, Bad & Dangerous To Know!* This may be a slight exaggeration perhaps – but then again, maybe not?

Their jobs involved virtually any odd labouring task that was required around the building, such as moving furniture, cleaning up, setting up the studios, as well as fulfilling the odd stint on the Reception desk.

It was perhaps fair to say that Bob and Harry tolerated

each other, rather than them being the best of buddies, by just getting used to the fact of working in tandem. Even so, it was not unusual for thinking that they might verbally stab each other in the back, if the right situation arose. Which did happen fairly frequently.

Yet for most of the time, you could usually find Bob and Harry wandering around the building in their distinctive brown working jackets, mumbling, grumbling and moaning, while using a wide variety of expressive and descriptive profanity, as they constantly complained about their lot in life.

Usually when he wasn't around, Bob often referred to Harry as *Ray Milland*, alluding to the fact that in his eyes, he closely resembled the Hollywood actor's Oscar winning performance of a man fully in the firm and shackled grip of an alcoholic dependency, while adrift in his own *"Lost Weekend"*.

I often thought that if they ever made a film of Harry's life (however fantastical that may sound) the perfect title would be not so much *Days Of Wine & Roses* – but more likely *Days Of Whiskey & Woodbines* instead.

There was one specific regular event that was guaranteed to turn Bob and Harry into a couple of grouchy, grumpy old men ("What? You mean they weren't that already?" I hear you say?) and that was the monthly Studio 1 Lunchtime Chamber Music Concerts. Both gents were fairly scathing as to their mystifyingly popular appeal, as well as to their musical validity and let it be known as to their opinions on the matter whenever questioned. Bob often wondered as to why they didn't put on a lunchtime concert that featured jazz and swing music instead. "The place would be packed, for who wants to hear all that f*****g crap music!" Bob was now referring to the archaic sound of several classical compositions (string quartets, piano concertos, etc.) that originated from the 18th and 19th centuries, that they were being forced to endure on a monthly basis – whether they liked it or not! Unfortunately, the overall effect of this musical cultural feast inevitably also sent the majority of the audience into a sound slumber.

"Look at all those poor buggers," Harry added as he observed a steady troop of shuffling pensioners heading into the main studio for the recording. "Ye' ken' they only come in here for a f*****g heat and a sleep!" he confirmed for anyone listening, just as the shivering poor old souls began to slowly take their seats prior to the beginning of the concert.

"What they need is a quick loud blast of f*****g Benny Goodman to wake the poor bastards up!" Bob announced, just as he finally closed the studio door shut.

Harry was the sort of man who didn't possess what you would describe as a fanciful outlook on the mysteries of life. For instance, if the conversation dwelt upon subjects such as UFOs, extra-terrestrials, the Loch Ness monster, the Abominable Snowman, and the existence of faeries at the bottom of the garden, his face would sternly scowl and then he would grunt and growl at you, by saying something unmentionable and equally unprintable.

Bob's way of an explanation to this attitude, was that someone like Harry, with his background cemented in a small East Lothian "one-horse town" purely lacked any form of inquisitive imagination regarding certain aspects of life. What he truly believed in was not any imponderable mysteries, but the far simpler notion of frequenting his local pubs and clubs, filling his glass all night with whisky and then gulping it straight down his gullet.

Maybe a tad harsh, but Bob also added that Harry had experienced something rare and unusual.

When I pressed him about this, and what he meant by this statement, Bob simply said that Harry could well be one of the very few men in Scotland who have witnessed the bizarre sight of not "Pink Elephants", but "Pink Leprechauns" waddling towards him!

A frightening thought no less, but a far less frightening vision for Harry if they had all turned out to be "Green Leprechauns" instead.

With them all carrying lighted candles and wearing Celtic scarfs!! What a frightening, nightmarish prospect that might have been for the poor guy, to have to go through that kind of experience.

The "boys" (as they were sometimes ironically known) once told me that a couple of years before I had started, Edinburgh had hosted the *Eurovision Song Contest,* from our very own Usher Hall. Bob and Harry were called upon to do their bit (whatever that might have been?) up at the venue, as the great and the good, and the powerfully elite of the BBC descended en masse upon Edinburgh.

One man who was present (not surprising since it was being screened live by the BBC) was *Bill Cotton*, then the BBC's Head of Light Entertainment.

From what they told me, Bob and Harry were less interested in the international musical event, as much as they were in helping themselves to *Bill Cotton's* expensive cigars.

This they successfully managed to do when they sneaked into his office when he wasn't around – and without a second glance, or a moment's hesitation, they simply helped themselves. What *Bill Cotton's* reaction to this secretive assault on his cigar box was remains a mystery to this day.

*

Harry was a tall, thin man, with lugubrious features who hailed from one of those chic sophisticated places you would find east of the capital city. He often reeked of stale tobacco and cheap whiskey, and possessed an unusual inquisitiveness as to your personal religious beliefs.

For instance, he often asked me if I was "a Tammy Reekie". To be honest, I had absolutely no idea of what he was talking about. Maybe it was some form of East Lothian expression that I was totally unfamiliar with.

However, once I eventually cottoned on to what he was getting at, I assured him that I had been baptised within the Church of Scotland, if that made him any happier.

I suppose it did in the end. Yet if I had confessed (no pun intended) that my religious affiliations resided elsewhere, he would no doubt have growled obscenities in my direction, as he tended to do to others.

For example, if any new member of staff just happened to have an Irish-sounding name (like Pat, Shaun, or Mick) Harry's orange attuned antenna would immediately spring into action, as he began his forensic investigation, as to what side of the religious fence they originated from. I was left constantly baffled at the time as to why which religion, or church you may, or may not belong to, held such an obsession for him.

Coming as I did from Edinburgh, religious attachments from either side of the ecclesiastical divide were pretty low on my list of priorities, and something that I gave very little thought, importance, or credence to.

In fact despite my being christened in the Protestant Church, I had several relatives who were Catholic.

Yet it made no odds to me, and to be quite honest, I couldn't care less if they had been Eskimos, or Trappist monks!

So being confronted by someone like Harry, whose general tone and manner regarding all things religious was, shall we say, a little bit confrontational, left me a bit baffled and confused.

Harry also had a deep distrust for the gentleman who manned the desk at reception, as he harboured bitter suspicions that they would "drop him in it" at the slightest opportunity. The very idea – although he may well have had a point, as his gruff manner (usually moistened with strong alcohol) sometimes didn't endear him to many of his colleagues.

One afternoon, Harry was trying to figure out how he was going to make a quick getaway, without anyone seeing him. The fact was that on that particular day he was about to go on holiday, and was due to meet up with his wife at the bus station, which was situated around the corner at St Andrew's Square.

"I dinnae want any of those bastards at the front desk seeing me leave. So I'll have to think of a way to get out of here early, as I don't trust any of them."

This was a charming sentiment, and one directed straight towards the Commissionaires on the door.

Well, it was later that same afternoon, with the clock ticking away, that Harry decided to make his break for freedom. He had in his possession a very large suitcase, and was eying (with all the furtive skill of an undercover operator) the window of the room that led out into one of the basements. This would be his perfect avenue to get away without being noticed.

He then slowly opened the window, all the time keeping it ajar with a stick, whilst he carefully (and somewhat awkwardly) climbed out of the window, complete with his over large suitcase. It was a hilarious sight to behold, as it soon resembled a scene from *"The Colditz Story"*. Harry then closed the window behind him, carefully walked up the basement steps, narrowly avoiding any onlookers, and was soon gone into the darkened night.

Funnily enough (alongside Bob), Harry would on the odd occasion find himself manning the front reception desk, whenever the duty commissionaire was on a tea break.

One night, just as I was preparing to leave the building to go home, Harry was grumbling away to himself at reception, when in through the front door stepped a female member of the public, with a particular programme complaint she wished to air.

Well, it didn't take long before an argument flared up, with Harry becoming a little aggravated at the raised voice now being thrown towards his direction concerning a specific BBC programme that had particularly annoyed her.

Finally, Harry had enough.

Instead of saying something along the likes of "Well thank you, madam, for your complaint. I will see that it is passed on to the appropriate department for you," he bellowed out to the shocked complainer, "Away and f**k yerself, ya f*****g old git!!"

The lady was a little shocked at first, but then replied back, "How dare you speak to me like that! I'll report you for this!"

Harry then yelled back at her, as she was finally departing the building, "Away and f**k off and don't come f*****g back!!"

It certainly put a different slant on what you could describe as proper and correct BBC protocol, whenever dealing with members of the public. This is what could easily be described as a genuine JFK moment.

He also shook up my young friend Richard, who Harry confronted one day when he bluntly asked him the question: "Do ye' go tae the church son?"

Richard looked at him equally baffled as to why he was asking this question.

"Do ye' go tae the church son?" Harry enquired again, this time with a slightly more aggressive edge to his voice.

Richard wasn't quite sure as to how he should answer. "Eh, I haven't been to church for a few years. Maybe I went at Christmas time, or to an Easter service, when I was at school," he simply answered, hoping that plain explanation would satisfy his inquisitor.

Harry then thought about his reply, and mulled it over in his mind. "So ye dinnae go to the chapel then?" he asked.

"The chapel?" Richard replied, a little taken aback. "No, I don't go to the chapel."

Harry was now satisfied with the eventual answer he received, as he walked away with a slight smile on his lips.

Looking back, those kinds of conversations must have given him some mystifying sense of satisfaction, which tended to leave many bemused and confused. Richard and myself included.

*

At one time we had an engineer working for a period at Queen Street called Tony Neilson. Tony was a popular, good-natured and cheery character who hailed from the borders region and was known affectionately to all as "The Buffer".

He enjoyed a beer, a laugh, and a party and loved the game of rugby – not too surprising considering where he came from.

Tony was also a devout Catholic and often spoke about seriously about giving up his career as a radio engineer and joining the priesthood. Yet when he heard of this particular snippet of news, Harry was (to put it mildly) apoplectic!

He flew into a rage, with both eyes almost bulging out of their sockets, as he was attempting to digest (for him anyway) this shocking religious revelation.

The irony in all of this was that he quite liked Tony as a person, but the thought of him wearing a dog collar, quoting Latin and lighting candles, was proving to be far too much for his blood pressure!

No doubt if there had been a cat lying around the basement area on that day, Harry's blistering anger would have been aimed directly at the poor creature's backside!

Harry also took a great dislike to two gents who –

although not employed by the BBC – made frequent visits to the building as contracted maintenance painters. They were a father and son business, and (as rumour persisted) gained regular work due to, what can only be described as "a strategically well placed handshake" that had stemmed from a distant Lodge meeting of assembled brothers.

No need to go any further on that score, I think. Their combined skills involved taking a routine painting job that would normally take a couple of days, and as if by magic, they would stretch it to two weeks. Well the BBC was paying generously for it, so why should they worry?

They were indoors out of the cold, getting a regular supply of tea and coffee, as well as filling their ears with the latest BBC gossip.

Harry described them both (not with any great feeling or affection, I might add) as "a right pair o' grippers!" Frank, the house electrician, also used to shake his head in wonder, whenever they made their periodic visits.

He once referred to them as *Pat Garrett* and *Billy the Kid*, no doubt alluding to the fact that he was surprised to see them turn up for work by van – and not by horse? I think he felt, that in his mind, they would have been far better plying their trade *West Of The Pecos*, rather than *West Of The Pentlands*.

Whilst once paying me a visit, my dad – an experienced painter and decorator himself – saw the two "brush artists" at work.

He looked on with a mixture of puzzlement and amazement, and then said to me, "They look like a right pair of cowboys! I've never seen painters like these guys before. How the f**k did they get employed here?" How indeed?

Well, as you can gather, Harry had a drink problem. With his main problem being that working denied him the opportunity to drink even more.

He could often be seen at work, slightly staggering, often

incoherent, and always belligerent in his outlook and attitude. It made him someone to avoid at all costs if he was in this specific mood and frame of mind.

He also possessed the unusual ability to read a newspaper upside down! But that may have been more to do with an extended liquid lunch, rather than a rare and unique talent with the printed word.

Although, on the very rare (and those were very rare) occasions he was "on the wagon" he could be a surprisingly good-humoured and agreeable individual. But that was often akin to the sighting of the Loch Ness Monster bursting into an impromptu highland reel while wearing a kilt!!

*

Bob was, I think, roughly around the same age as Harry, although he looked a good deal younger. He was a feisty, pugnacious character, with dark hair (that I think was dyed), was physically fit and agile, and it was obvious that he kept himself reasonably in trim.

I must admit that I liked him a lot, despite the fact that he was perceived by quite a few at the time, as an almost borderline psychopath. He was someone that you treaded very carefully with, if you valued your health.

Although in saying that, surprisingly, he was also a greatly intelligent, well-read and perceptive man, who taught himself how to play the clarinet with tremendous application, commitment and patience.

He was also (of great surprise to many) an amateur historian of some depth and intellect – although his views on world history could be controversial and alarming at best.

Like the time he freely admitted to myself that he "always admired *Adolf Hitler*" and that he often boasted that he had "killed better Germans than some of the bastards that work in here!"

I was never entirely sure that he said all of those things

purely to shock, or whether he really believed it himself? Perhaps the fact that he once showed me a long-playing record that he proudly possessed called *Marching Songs Of The Afrika Corps*, should have given me some clue.

He also confused a good few people as to his past illustrious war record.

At one point he was in the Navy involved with the evacuation of Dunkirk, then battling the Japanese at both Wake Island and Midway, whilst also storming the Normandy beaches and then (after a short breather and a cup of tea!), standing defiantly against the Werhmacht and several elite SS Panzer divisions during the Battle of the Bulge.

Boy, he must have been exhausted after all that!

I am convinced that he served his country with distinction at some point during WW2, but not too convinced that he could successfully appear in all of those theatres of conflict – all at the same time. Perhaps he was just stretching the historic truth, just a little bit.

Over the many subsequent years that I got to know him, it was safe to say that Bob told more *"Ripping Yarns"* about his heroic adventures on land and sea, than had ever been explored on one of *Michael Palin's* TV comedy shows! Perhaps he was that series true inspiration?

Well both Bob and Harry were fairly contemptuous of any thing that young Robin said, particularly as to his aspirations as a future pop superstar. "Away and f***k yerself," was Harry's usual response.

However, both he and Bob (as well as myself) were stunned into a strange form of silence, when Robin announced his determination to get on *Top Of The Pops* – regardless of what he would need to do to achieve this aim.

I remember (as if it were only yesterday), when he told all three of us, that he was willing to allow a certain disgraced former cigar-smoking DJ with the initials JS, have his wicked way with him!!

I would like to think that he never had need to place himself in that perilous position, and maybe just as well considering all the recent lurid revelations that have erupted into the public domain concerning that much tarnished individual.

*

Both Robin and Hamish would soon depart the *BBC* within a year. Hamish decided that his ambitions pointed him towards pastures new (as well as the prospect of strange new beds to fall out of) and he was soon gone, taking his cocksure swagger with him.

Robin, on the other hand, was beginning to behave much more erratically and eccentric with each passing day. The heady mix of potential pop stardom (coupled possibly with alleged suspected illegal substances) and the glittering visions of his appearances on *TOTP* made his exit predictable.

I recall that he was sacked for gross misconduct, along with the fact that he referred to our venerable senior station manager as "Old Jock", which didn't go down too well, as I remember.

Richard and Pamela arrived and became my two new colleagues, quickly replacing the drummer and the stud. And far more agreeable companions they turned out to be as well.

Then over the next few years we had the likes of Wendy. She was a lovely girl who stirred up a few passions amongst many of the male members of staff – no pun intended.

Then there was Jennifer (a fiery red-haired girl from Macmerry, with a fiery temper to match), Avril (an ambitious girl who would later go on to work in Glasgow, for the Controller, no less), Jane (a lovely, caring, thoughtful girl and a good friend besides).

Not forgetting Suzette (a young lady from Leith, who would eventually become my boss a few years down the line),

Fraser (my good pal, and of more later…), and on the odd occasion a young chap called Scott.

Scott would return frequently over the years to fill a number of positions that were temporarily vacant, and was known endearingly in some quarters as either *"the eternal student"*, or sometimes even *"the student prince"*, depending on whom you spoke to, I suppose.

For Scott, I got the feeling that it was less about working within such a prestigious outfit as the Beeb – and more about expanding his social circle!

Which became quite considerable over the next two decades.

*

Scott had a unique way of addressing the public. For instance, whenever he was manning the reception desk, instead of giving out with the normal greeting along the lines of something like: "Good morning, welcome to BBC Scotland, you are speaking to Scott, how can I help you?"

With no beating around the bush, he just got straight to the point, cut out any extraneous verbiage and as soon as the phone rang, he answered with the simple word of "Yes". That was it. No stretching of the greeting, no mention of BBC Scotland, or BBC Edinburgh, just a simple "Yes".

He had managed to eloquently pare down reception etiquette to its very purest essence. Good on him. I wonder if anyone in the BBC has the nerve to do that nowadays with the same style and aplomb.

*

Richard would eventually become one of my closest and dearest friends over the next few decades. Someone I would share many happy hours drinking, laughing, and discussing complex subjects as dissimilar as politics, history, philosophy, cinema, classical music, *Roxy Music*, and the comic legacy of *Benny Hill!!!*

He would later go on from being an integral member of the audio unit, as well as an arts and features producer responsible for a number of intelligent and wide-ranging programmes.

Richard would also turn out to be an accomplished musician, whose self-penned compositions, influenced by many a techno-electronic innovator (such as *Brian Eno, Kraftwork* and *Midge Ure*) has led to his work being downloaded by music enthusiasts all over the globe.

But I felt very sorry for him, at what turned out to be his initial impressions of life at *5 Queen Street*.

This culminated, when I first introduced him to Bob.

I could write many chapters on Bob alone, as he was one of those characters you meet in life (hopefully just the once) that causes you to tremble with fear and crease yourself with laughter – almost at one and the same time.

No wonder that someone described him thus as "a one-man blitzkrieg gone berserk!" Not far off the truth there.

When I took Richard on a tour of the building so that he could familiarise himself with the place, we popped into "the howff" (an affectionate name given to the room where the house staff relaxed over a cup of tea) to say hello.

Bob was in there himself, reading his paper and muttering away, as he tended to do, from time to time.

"Hi Bob, this is Richard, he's just started with us today." Young Richard said his hellos and quietly sat down, while Bob folded his newspaper and looked coldly at us both.

I can't remember exactly what it was he said, but he then began to get very agitated and started rambling and swearing, for no apparent reason.

I could then sense Richard's unease, and he looked slightly nervous as to what may, or may not happen next.

Then Bob took his teacup and smashed it with fury against

one of the walls! The teapot was next. It was a solid metallic one with the engraved BBC logo imprinted on it. Probably quite valuable these days, although it could very easily have caused a serious injury, as it flew out of his hand and thumped against another wall.

Bob then proceeded to rant and rave, not exactly at us, but just at his life in general, as well as his frustrated anger at the BBC. Richard, by this time, was very anxious to leave for the comparative calm and safety of the ground floor. I too felt that it was time to leave, just in case Bob took it into his mind to throw us through the window!

We said our goodbyes and quickly departed. Although we could hear other various pieces of crockery hitting and smashing against the walls, along with loud, angry swear words, as we moved smartly along the corridor.

Richard often speaks of this event, usually with much laughter, although for a youngster fresh out of school, it must have been a terrifying experience to endure.

Richard would eventually survive this unsettling initiation relatively unscathed, and go on in furthering his *BBC* career as one member of that colourful and illustrious group known as the "Audio Crew".

He then took time out to expand his education at university, and later returned as a very successful arts producer, responsible for a whole range of challenging, entertaining and informative programmes.

*

The Reception Desk (and its staff) would of course be the very first focal point of contact for the public, as well as for the various contributors and participants to the programming output.

When I first arrived at the BBC back in the summer of 1974, the two main men manning the desk (they were addressed during this period with the grandiose title of

Commissioners or Sergeant, for some odd reason) were, well, let's call them Bob Laing and Bob Pape.

Bob L was a small, neat, smartly dressed, fastidious man who revelled in his position as a BBC Commissionaire.

I later found out that he was financially pretty well off, and had no real need to work at his age. But I guess he enjoyed the status, the company, and above all, the gossip.

He could be very welcoming and accommodating, and was ideal for such a prestigious role. However, he could also be waspish, sarcastic and very, very bitchy!!

Bob P, on the other hand, was a much gruffer individual, but both men complemented each other within their roles.

He was a large, solid, bullish ex-army sergeant, whose usual unsubtle war cry when cutting through the thick smog of cigarette smoke that permeated between the main reception and the adjoining mailroom was, "This place smells like a f*****g brothel on a Monday morning!" Subtle – or what?

Bob P didn't stay too long when I first arrived. He was gone within a couple of months, owing to an argument he had with our Admin Assistant (Miss Jean Wilson), which led him to storm out, never to return.

One thing I do remember about him was the time I returned from a short holiday to Morecambe with my folks.

He enquired if during my holiday I had enjoyed a "bunk-up!" I was puzzled as to what he was referring to, thinking at first it must have something to do with bunk beds!

Beds certainly came into his thinking, but not in the way that it made much sense to me at the time. I must have looked very gauche and naive in those far off days!

With Bob P gone, a new man soon replaced him by the name of Mac.

Yes, Mac, the one and only. He was someone who would

become a good close friend, mentor, supervisor and colleague to so many of us during that time.

He was, for the most part, a reassuring, commanding and steady figure, although not without his unusual quirks. Although in fairness, he wouldn't be the only one.

An ex-soldier who had served with distinction in the Scots Guards as a sergeant major, his experience and military bearing, made him an ideal man to have at the front desk. Not long after he had started, he began to receive many a complimentary observation from some of the female production and office staff.

It was mainly all to do with his shirts. Mac took enormous pride in his appearance (all those years guarding Her Majesty down in London sure rubbed off) particularly when it came to the brightness and sharpness of his white shirts.

They gleamed with a form of irradiation that often blinded you.

*

Catherine Smith (who was then the Edinburgh Manager's secretary and personal assistant, and in all the time that I knew her was a lovely, kind, and benevolent woman) once asked him as to how he managed to get his shirt collars so immaculate. "I use starch in my collars," Mac replied. "I always use it because I like my collars to be *extra stiff!*" Not sure what to say about that, but his shirts (not forgetting his stiffened collars) were always much admired. Something you couldn't say about a number of the producers and managers, with a few of them easily cultivating that "just fell out of bed look".

In fact one or two gave the impression (going by their outward appearance) that they had been sleeping rough for a month in some dilapidated cattle shed!

Well Mac and Bob L hit it off immediately, and soon became a bit of a comic double-act, as they attempted to out do each other in their levels of bitchy sarcasm – particularly when directed at some of the members of staff!

Bob L was especially acidic in this.

Each morning he would always warmly greet the technical and office production staff, as they walked through the front door to begin their day's work.

He was charm personified, as he often complimented them, while cheerily pampering their egos as they trooped into the reception, just before they exited up and down the stairs to their respective offices.

Then, just as they were out of range he would (with an insincere smile on his lips) mutter, "F*****g bastards!"

Not everyone would receive this withering appraisal from him, but there were one or two that he could be particularly savage about, when naturally, they weren't around.

One producer in particular he stingingly described as "a wet dream dried up!" Even after all of these years, words still fail me regarding that particular description.

Bob L enjoyed a lively social life and would often boast about hosting a number of exclusive soirees at his penthouse flat. Parties that only those and such as those, were cordially invited, for Bob L was, you could say, a bit of a snob.

One day Robin (he always cheekily referred to Bob L as Bobby, which he loathed) asked him about one of his upcoming social gatherings and what would be happening on the night. Bob answered, "Well, we will have cheese and wine till 12, and then a buffet after midnight." He further added, looking straight towards Robin, "My friends are the cream of society, we enjoy lots of intelligent conversation, good wine, and certainly no f*****g riff-raff!"

Robin laughed at this and then with an equal amount of barefaced cheek, replied: "Well how about if me and the band popped up for a few beers after midnight, Bobby?"

With a look of absolute disdain and disgust now clearly visible on his face, Bob L attempted to deal with this affront to his dignity and hospitality in the following manner. "Do you think that I would want the likes of *you* and all your f*****g stinking, slobby pals in my house? You are very much mistaken. That would be just horrible, horrible, a bunch of uncouth f*****g riff-raff." Robin was beside himself with laughter for winding him up so much and with such a degree of apparent ease.

As for Mac, I always recall with a smile the odd occasion he could be heard singing to himself at times an old soldier's song that went something along the lines of: *"Kiss me goodnight Sergeant Major..."* As far as I know the next lines go something like: *"Tuck me in my little wooden bed..."*

However, Mac tended to subtly alter the lyrics of the second line, which placed a whole new meaning to an uncomfortable image of "lights out in the barracks". A few years later, he also took to singing another ditty from time to time that originated from a hit song originally sung in the 1960s by *Ken Dodd.*

The song in question was called *"Happiness"* and Mac could often be heard cheerily singing this number as if full of the joys of spring.

Unfortunately, his personal version deliberately omitted the first letter of the song's title. Which gave it an entirely different shape and meaning.

Although those of us who heard the lyrics that followed – *"the greatest gift that I possessed..."* were left in no doubt that he meant what he sang!

Mac also used to regale a few of us with a few jaw-dropping and risqué stories of his time as a soldier in the Scots Guards.

One episode in particular I recall laughing at, but one that also left me feeling somewhat uncomfortable at the same time: This festive soldier's tale revolved around a lavish Christmas lunch in the officer's mess, and a pair of disgruntled chefs, both possessing a shared loathing of the officer class.

Their combined contempt for their superiors, led to the addition of a mysterious ingredient to the festive menu that I gathered had never originated from any bottle, jar, packet, or Nigella Lawson's cookbook.

However, you could say, that it culminated in producing an unusual and unique flavour that added just a little bit of extra texture to the brandy sauce! Oh dear!

*

As I said, Bob L was a very smart, neat and tidy man. Immaculately turned out (his taste in clothes always looked very expensive), he would turn up for his shift at the reception desk looking like a latter-day *Noel Coward*.

Yet before he positioned himself to start work, he always disappeared into the mailroom at the rear of reception, where he started to undress.

This was a daily ritual for him, regardless of who was in the room at the time, and despite anyone who might walk in – whether male, or female!

He stripped off right down to his underwear, unaffected as to how this may, or may not, shock any onlookers.

I don't believe that such activity (whether innocent or not?) would be tolerated nowadays, and I got the feeling, like so many at the time, that he was enjoying every minute of it, as I was convinced that he was a bit of a teasing exhibitionist!

Bob L's tenure as a BBC Commissionaire came to an abrupt end about a couple of years later. Rumours and speculation began to circulate as to why he was suddenly gone, with such a degree of haste.

One story I heard was that the management discovered

that he had lied about his real age and that he was so far over the official age to retire, he was forced to leave with immediate effect.

In truth, you could easily have taken him for a much younger man, so neat and smart he was in person. But at the same time the management were not best pleased at his attempts to hoodwink them regarding his real age.

Another rumour floated about simultaneously, stated that he was caught late one night staggering and swaying around the reception area, drunk out of his mind, just as a close friend of the then BBC Chairman walked in the front door, to retrieve a suitcase she had left behind.

By all accounts she was outraged at the unpleasant sight that beheld her, as a BBC member of staff, in an inebriated state of partial undress (apparently he was only in shorts and socks at the time), was found swaying, staggering and leaping up and down, oblivious to any observers.

In addition to this (again, this might only be rumour?), the night security man was mistakenly and unfairly blamed for the event, and summarily dismissed.

His son learned of this grossly unfair treatment of his father, and then threatened the BBC with severe legal action, as well as harnessing the full attention of the press, which would have caused a great deal of embarrassment to all concerned.

Bob L left soon afterwards, and the entire sorry tale was covered up to avoid any unpleasant repercussions. I later learnt of this side of the tale from a pretty reliable source, but it was never discussed or brought up afterwards.

*

On a lighter note, one rather humorous episode happened during my first year at 5 Queen Street, when the building would find itself unexpectedly blockaded and almost invaded by a large number of the then *Gay Liberation Front*.

At first glance the majority of them looked like members of a touring company of *The Rocky Horror Picture Show!* At one point, I even half expected them to burst into a quick chorus of the *Time Warp,* complete with hands on hips and aggressive pelvic thrusts!!!

So what we had assembled outside, were dozens and dozens of colourfully dressed protesters – complete with large placards, banners and assorted handbags and man-bags.

They then began to amass and position themselves right outside the front door.

I was not entirely sure if they were specifically targeting and demonstrating against the BBC during that day, or if they were just attempting to gain massive media publicity and attention for their cause, but they were determined to stay put and make themselves seen and heard – regardless of what anyone thought!

You could say that it was a little like being under siege from *The Village People Appreciation Society!*

Maybe they just mistook 5 Queen Street for the local YMCA?

I suppose if such an event were to happen today (now that we are supposedly living in far more liberal and enlightened times), no one would bat an eyelid. Unless you were living in *Putin's Russia* of course!

However, we are talking about the mid-1970s here, and not surprisingly, there were many groans and gasps of disapproval from some of the older members of staff, who looked upon the fey protestors as if they had just landed from an alien planet!

An instruction was soon issued by our senior manager for the entire staff to stay indoors and not to venture outside of the building – until the time came when the police would eventually arrive to calm things down.

Although, thinking back, I don't think that anyone who

might have dared to walk out would have been in any real physical danger, or possible risk from the demonstrators. Apart from the possibility of being warmly embraced, kissed, and cuddled to death!

In fact the senior Edinburgh manager bravely took the bull by the horns and stepped outside to negotiate with the crowd (without a white flag I may add, though maybe a pink one might have been more appropriate under the circumstances) and stood there for about ten minutes trying to arrange some form of a reasonable negotiable settlement.

About the same time, Bob appeared, all fired up and ready to give his scathing assessment of the situation. "What a bunch of f*****g weirdo freaks! And to think that I fought in three f*****g wars for f*****g bastards like that!"

With those parting words now stinging in my ears, Bob stormed off downstairs to cool his incendiary temper with a hot cup of coffee.

It wasn't too unusual for Bob to regularly emphasise (to anyone around) that he had indeed fought in three wars to help preserve the concept and ideals of freedom.

So I guess it was the supreme irony that due to all his combative efforts on land and sea (while confronting an unyielding fascistic enemy), this would later allow large groups (including the *Gay Liberation Front*) to loudly demonstrate outside of public buildings, without fear of violence, recrimination, and intimidation.

I wonder if he ever gave that very notion a thought, as he was colourfully describing them as… well, whatever he was describing them as.

A few of the other staff, now intrigued at this unusual sight unfolding before our very eyes, began to stare out of the front windows, strangely fascinated at the camp congregation now milling about outside, and congesting at the front door.

Our window curiosity was soon met by loud cries of

"Yooo hooo!" and "Hello darling!" which was accompanied by a combination of loud wolf-whistles and lasciviously blown kisses.

All these displays of sweetly intentioned affection came from gents of various ages in loud shirts, flared trousers, red lips, dark eye shadow and not forgetting droopy moustaches!

And this attention was now being aimed straight towards our direction!

In retrospect, this experience for a young 16-year-old, may well have turned out to be a portent of what lay up ahead over the next 28 years..

CHAPTER 2

A Weapon Of Mass Destruction

"He was the most extraordinary man I ever knew."
"But did he really deserve… a place in here?"

In the previous chapter I gave a brief impression as to a man who was known to all as Bob – the House Attendant. He was truly, without a shadow of a doubt, one of those characters you encounter in your life, who leaves a scorched earth style impression on your mind. Even while looking back, after all those years, his uniquely corrosive personality and his curious blend of profanity and wisdom, still resonate loudly in my imagination.

Well, how could I best describe Bob? Well, for me, he combined the personality characteristics of *Rigsby* and *Rambo!* Sharing the extremely outspoken, archaic and reactionary views of the former, with the explosive destructive tendencies of the latter. He was, for the most part, a fascinating man in many ways, but one with a very short fuse (a colleague once described him as a human hand-grenade with the pin pulled out – or even an incendiary device in human form) and someone who attracted and caused disaster like few others.

Like the time he almost gassed the entire building…

*

Bob decided one day that he was going to give the basement gents' toilet a thorough clean. Nothing wrong with that, but Bob's idea of a thorough clean meant something else entirely.

At the back of the gents' loo that was situated in the far basement, stood a small supply room in which they kept large containers of bleach, disinfectant, carpet wash, and strong industrial cleaner to be used, well, sparingly.

Bob decided that this was a golden opportunity to, let's say, experiment.

I wasn't aware that he had a degree in chemistry, but this day, he decided to challenge the very laws of science.

Bob took it into his head to pour large amounts of all the flammable liquids he could lay his hands on into a very large bucket and then see what bubbled to the surface. I was down in the basement at the time, and could hear him clattering away with cans, bottles and buckets, as he was preparing to clean the floor.

However, I soon became painfully aware of the strong toxic fumes that were now drifting from the toilet into the basement corridors, and slowly and gradually making their way upwards to the floors above.

I began to choke, as the toxic fumes now gripped and caught the back of my throat, making me feel quite nauseous and queasy.

Then, a couple of the audio and production staff stepped out of the nearest studio to see what was going on. They too appeared to be coughing and spluttering as they were trying to catch their collective breath.

One of the engineers ran swiftly up to the reception area and cried out, "Somebody better go downstairs, we're all being gassed!!"

Mac, accompanied by myself and a couple of others, decided to take a deep breath, and venture bravely back down to investigate. We walked into the basement toilet, and there we found Bob washing the floor with what looked like the most disgusting concoction appearing from his bucket.

While at the same time, he was wearing a handkerchief to protect his eyes, face, and nose from the dangerous fumes that were now searing and burning our throats.

I tell you, if someone had been down there at the time with a lighted match, the entire building could have been blown to smithereens!!

Bob seemed oblivious to the consternation he was causing.

"Bob, what the f*****g hell do you think you're doing?" cried Mac as he was simultaneously coughing up his guts.

"I though I would wash the floor," replied Bob, looking now like some demented masked bandit!

The engineer muttered as he walked away, "We'll all end up getting poisoned!!"

Bob then said, "No ye'll no'. I'll open up the windows".

Good sense finally prevailed as Bob opened up as many windows as there were, and fresh air came into the area, clearing what could have potentially been catastrophic for the entire staff. It's amazing to think that all those years ago, we may well have been experiencing an early form of primitive chemical warfare!!

Life was certainly never dull when Bob was in full flow.

One day he incurred the wrath of one of the audio crew, who was busy recording a programme in Studio 3. On that particular day, Bob was busy negotiating the movement of a couple of large rolls of carpet down the stairs towards the basement. Unfortunately, Bob threw them down, as if they were a couple of dead bodies, and they made an almighty thumping thud against the main door of the studio. Just then the engineer stormed out looking none too pleased and with fiery anger in his eyes. He then spotted Bob and loudly complained about the noise interrupting the recording and aggressively pointing his finger straight in his face. Wrong move! Bob just grabbed him by the throat, uttered a few obscenities, and then the engineer gave out with a blank look of frozen fear. No doubt at that moment, he was wishing he were back in the comparative safety of the studio cubicle. Which he soon was, once tempers had finally cooled down and Bob proceeded with his carpet rolls.

*

Bob was also a man who could leave you in a fit of the giggles, with many of the things he came out with (the majority unrepeatable) outrageously funny. One example was when on one particular day we were discussing the classic epic movie *Spartacus,* which just happened to be one of Bob's favourite films. The conversation went something like this:

"Did you watch *Spartacus* again at the weekend Bob?" I enquired.

"Aye I did," he said.

"It's a great film, don't you agree?" as I awaited his inevitable answer.

"Aye it's a great film, but do you think that would have happened in real life?" he asked me.

"What do you mean?" I replied.

"Well for one thing, he's in that cell, all alone, never seen a woman for years and then in comes *Jean Simmons* looking gorgeous and smelling of rose petals, eastern spices and sandalwood." I was not entirely sure in which direction he was now heading. "Then *Kirk Douglas* with his teeth gritted and his dimpled chin jutting out, growls at her – 'I'm not an animal.' Do ye' think that would have actually happened?"

I thought for a second and then replied, "Well, maybe not when you put it like that."

Bob went on, "He would have been up her as quick as a flash! Then after his night of passion with Jean, he would have been too shagged out in the morning to lift his gladiator sword."

I looked at him for a second and then said, "Eh, I don't think they could have got away with that in the film, Bob? At least not back then."

"Aye, but that's probably what really would have happened," he insisted.

Then getting further into the subject, he asked, "What about that bit with *Laurence Olivier* and *Tony Curtis?* What was all that about? And what the f**k were the two of them doing in the bath together?"

"Eh, he was probably giving him a hand in finding the soap," I chuckled back at him.

Bob looked at me with a straight face and then said, "*Spartacus – you Thracian dog!!*" before he started to laugh.

Then Bob began to discuss the famous scene near the end of the film. "See that bit where they all stand up and shout *'I'm Spartacus!!'* well what really would have happened, is the slaves would have all stood up, pointed their fingers straight at *Kirk Douglas* and shouted, 'See that bastard over there – *he's Spartacus!!!*'"

When he first came out with that I was in convulsions of laughter. Now every time I watch the film, Bob's alternative imaginary version always comes flooding back to my mind.

*

If Bob hated anyone in this world (and he particularly didn't care for many people – particularly some of the BBC staff) it was the dreaded traffic wardens.

He described them as either "Hitler's f*****g SS men", or just simply "F*****g scum of the earth!" and he made every effort he could to wind them up, and make their lives a misery. He really despised them with an intense passion that was awe-inspiring!

Bob usually parked his car on Queen Street, not far from the Broadcasting building. But he was always looking out for the men in the black uniforms and the peaked caps who patrolled the street, and who were always hoping to catch out those vehicles that had overrun their allotted time.

I noticed that Bob always had in his possession a large number of metal ring pulls that came from used cans of Coca-Cola.

I was never exactly sure why this was, until he told me one day that they worked a treat on the car meters! This would potentially save him hundreds of pounds, as well as frustrate and annoy the men in the black uniforms.

One day, I looked out of the window and saw him running over the road to his car. From what I could see, he was putting in a number of ring pulls into the meter to give him an extra couple of hours' parking time. But just then, out of his vision, a traffic warden appeared at his side, and seemed to quickly realise what he was doing. I couldn't hear exactly what was being said, but going by the animated and twisted, furious looks on both of their faces, a fierce argument was now ensuing. Bob was pointing his finger at the warden's direction, and was no doubt describing him in the most colourful Anglo-Saxon language imaginable.

After this rant, Bob then ran back over the road and into the building where he stood alongside Mac at the front desk.

I came through from the mailroom and was about to ask him what all that was about, when the warden suddenly appeared at the front door, red of face and with another of his uniformed colleagues.

They were both already poised for an explosive confrontation. The first warden pointed his finger straight at Bob and stated that he had used "foul and abusive language" at him, and he was going to report him to the proper BBC authorities. Bob stood there motionless at first, and then calmly said, "I don't know what you're talking about. I never

49

said anything." This caused the warden to get even redder in the face and even more exasperated and frustrated.

Then he turned his attention to Mac. "You will have to do something about him!"

Mac then snapped back "Me? It's got nothing to do with me."

"But you're his boss, you need to do something about it," the warden asserted.

Mac, by this time, upset at this accusatory response, was beginning to lose the rag with the warden. "Look, it's got nothing to do with me," he said firmly. "What happens outside of BBC property has got absolutely nothing to do with me!!" He further stressed this to the warden, so he would hopefully and finally get the message.

All this time, Bob said nothing, but it was clear that he was chuckling away within himself, at all the fury and commotion his actions had now caused.

The second warden then shrugged his shoulders and motioned his increasingly frustrated colleague to leave the building, as they were simply getting nowhere.

"I've got my eye on you. You won't get away with it another time," the warden said just as he was storming out the front door. Bob then laughed as he departed. Mac looked a bit flustered and then decided to make himself a calming cup of coffee.

"Bob, you shouldn't wind these traffic wardens up, you will get yourself into all sorts of trouble."

Bob just smiled and said, "They're all a bunch of bastards anyway. If I only had a German Schmeisser machine gun, I'd shoot them all. The f*****g bastards!!" One felt that Bob was anything but joking when he uttered such statements. Days like those didn't help Mac's blood pressure any!!

As for Bob, he relished stirring things up, and took great

delight in causing a calamity, particularly for those he intensely disliked. Yet at the same time, you just couldn't help but like him, as well as laugh at some of his more outrageous antics. Just as long as he wasn't trying to thump or poison you!

*

As well as the traffic wardens, Bob had a particular distaste for young, snooty, patronising and condescending radio producers.

Long before the likes of *Jeremy Clarkson* first stepped within the doors of the BBC, Bob may have been amongst the very first individuals who invented that amusing term *Fracas with a Producer*! In fact he may well have owned the original copyright on it?

Although in fairness to Bob, I don't recall if clenched fists were ever involved (apart from his usual morning bouts with *Kenny MacIntyre!*), but certainly fierce verbal volleys were often aimed and fired straight in the producer's direction – in as forthright a manner that only Bob could produce.

As earlier described, one of Bob's consistent war cries, funnily enough, was the fact that he had fought in three major conflicts!

"I was in the 2nd World War, the Korean War and the Malayan War!" he told so many of us, just in case we might have forgotten it!

This was usually followed by, "And to think that I fought in all those wars, seen good men die, for all these f*****g bastards to ponce about up and down these f*****g stairs! It's a f*****g injustice!"

He also told us that as a young man, he served time in the Merchant Navy, as well as a period sailing the rough seas with no doubt an equally rough crew, in various whaling ships.

When telling some of his salty sea tales, he would often bring up and discuss a couple of curious terms known as

"Navy Cake" and "Port Hole Duff".

For me, these were yet another example of unusual and uncommon expressions that I encountered and found myself totally unfamiliar with, during my early BBC years. However, once he went into minute detail by telling me exactly what both expressions meant, I was eternally grateful that I never signed up for a sailor's life on the ocean wave!!

Although he admitted that on a personal level, he did like a number of the older established producers, it was the younger ones who arriving fresh from university, wet behind the ears with numerous letters after their name, and all pumped up with a sense of their own inflated importance, he couldn't abide.

I agreed with him up to a point, as I also found that one or two of them could be very haughty, often unfriendly and occasionally unpleasant, as they tended to look down with undisguised disdain on the manual staff, who were not directly engaged in shall we say, "creative production work".

On one occasion Bob was cleaning up outside one of the radio studios. A recording was in progress, but this didn't deter Bob from loudly banging the hoover at the side of the walls, and the outside door.

Then the studio door flung open, and a youngish, red-faced, posh-voiced producer emerged, looking none too happy.

"Do you realise that we are trying to make a recording in here?" he spouted at Bob.

Bob switched off the hoover and then let him verbally have it with both barrels. "Look, I was asked by my supervisor to clean up this mess here, and that's what I'm f*****g doing!"

The producer then raised his voice slightly (not a wise thing to do I might add) and said, "I will report you for this."

This was like a red rag to a bull to Bob, as he now stared

straight at the producer. "Look you, I was doing this job when you were still at f*****g school!!"

The producer stood back slightly as Bob then developed a manic and demonic look in his eyes that spelt instant danger. So, with that being the case, he no doubt could sense that Bob was not a man to anger. The producer then said, "Oh just forget it!" and stormed back into the studio to complete the recording.

Bob shook his head and said with added venom in his voice, "What an absolute f*****g bastard he is." Further adding, "He wouldn't have last two minutes if he was up against a Panzer regiment!!!"

*

Bob had an unusual and unorthodox way of enduring the various senior managerial meetings we were "persuaded" to attend.

One particular occasion happened during the early 1980s, when the then BBC Scotland Controller came through from Glasgow and assembled the entire staff in the canteen to tell us some extremely important news. It may even have had a little something to do with the proposed new broadcasting centre? But more of that later...

Whatever the subject of the Controller's talk was on the day, it didn't prove all that enthralling, or engaging for Bob to indulge in.

I was sitting right near the back and Bob was sitting directly in the row behind me. Once we had all settled down and as the Controller was in full conversational flow, I soon became aware of someone singing.

Totally uninterested in anything that the Controller was saying (he wasn't saying that much that gripped the audience), Bob started to warble an old *Bing Crosby* number – *"I'm an old cowhand, from the Rio Grande..."*

All this time, the Controller was getting intensely carried

away with his talk, hoping that those attending were taking in all of his information. Going by the uninterested and exhausted looks on the majority of their faces, probably only about five of them.

However, going by the strange, puzzling look that was now slowly appearing on his face, I noticed that he was also becoming acutely aware of the faint sound of someone singing coming from the back of the room.

In between his words, he was now peering through his thick headmaster-style glasses and scanning the room to catch out the guilty party – but he was having no success.

At the same time, I was finding it extremely hard in keeping a straight face and trying not to burst out laughing, while the Controller of BBC Scotland was equally attempting to maintain a dignified pose during his talk, while there was an unexpected *Crosby*-like voice crooning away in the background!

Yet Bob just carried on regardless – *"I'm an old cowhand, from the Rio Grande…"*

The BBC Scotland Controller during this time was a somewhat dour, humourless character. In fact he gave the impression that he was carrying the weight of not just BBC Scotland, but the entire world on his shoulders.

In all the time that I saw him arrive and walk through the front doors of 5 Queen Street, I don't ever recall him smiling, or looking at all happy, or even cheery – not once!

A gruff and almost inaudible "Good morning," was usually the only sound that came from his lips, before he ponderously stomped up the stairs to the Manager's Boardroom.

Then again, from what I could gather during this time, he was a man feeling the big heat of political pressure, as well as something not too dissimilar from his own superiors down south. Being the BBC's Scottish Controller during the majority of the 1980s was, I believe, hardly a bundle of laughs for the poor guy. So no wonder he rarely smiled. In fact he was present when BBC Glasgow were raided by Special Branch in order to remove certain videotapes that had a connection with a controversial programme that in some quarters may have been seen to compromise National Security.

This was better known as *The Zircon Affair* – which made it sound like an old episode from *The Man From Uncle!*

I suppose it was a good job that Special Branch never raided 5 Queen Street looking for videotapes, as they would have been sure of a big surprise!

The tapes that they would have discovered would have raised more temperatures and well, certain other things, than complex political issues.

*

So, getting back to Bob. His activities whenever he was obliged to cover the reception desk also made me chuckle.

He would arrive promptly; complete with his BBC blue jacket (obligatory for house staff whenever they were on reception duty), a mug of coffee in his hand, and carrying his beloved clarinet.

Yes, you heard me correct, his clarinet.

Bob, as it turns out, was very accomplished on this instrument, and more or less, entirely self-taught. He would often entertain all and sundry with a few bars of *Benny Goodman, Artie Shaw, or Acker Bilk.*

And pretty good he was too, with *Acker's Stranger On The Shore* being a particular favourite.

However, it was not expected, or required for him to play a musical instrument simultaneously, whilst also manning the front desk, and answering the telephone during his stint at reception.

Yet this small detail, did not dissuade him.

Many a time when seeing him supposedly on reception duty, supposedly dealing with the public, or the staff, or answering the many phone calls, this all proved to be an inconvenience and a major annoyance, when he simply had clarinet practice in mind.

Early one evening, the reception was being inundated with phone calls from the general public.

The licence fee payers decided to voice their disapproval, as well as their anger and dismay, when it turned out that a film on BBC 2 had been cancelled, due to an overrun of cricket!!

This did not sit well with Scotland's movie lovers, who took great exception to the BBC's preference for the gentle traditional English game of bat on ball, and ball on wicket, at the expense of everything else.

Bob had just arrived when the phone started to ring. He gave the standard answer to the caller that this was just a local radio station, and that we had no control over television scheduling. Which was a true and accurate statement at that time. But still the phone calls continued to persist. By this time, Bob simply had enough.

With an anguished cry of "F*****g bastards!" he simply unplugged the telephone socket under the desk that was connected to the main switchboard, and by doing that, it quickly silenced the calls. So anyone calling the BBC to voice some displeasure regarding a radio, or more likely a TV programme, was met with nothing less than a cold, dead, silent tone.

Bob, then feeling a sense of rich satisfaction, took a swig of his coffee, sat back on the chair, put his feet up on the desk, and began serenading himself with a selection of swing band favourites.

Who cared if the licence fee payers were up in arms, they

could scream and shout on the phone as much as they liked – just as long as it didn't interrupt Bob's music practice. That was far more important to him.

One of Bob's own particular musical favourites from his vast repertoire was a jazzy, bluesy number, that conjured up images of sleepy hamlets way down south in Dixie, smoky bar-rooms and sultry hot nights. He used to play it regularly and I got to recognise its opening bars straight away. I once asked him: "Bob, what's the name of that piece? It's got a lovely texture and feel to it."

Bob paused for a few seconds, put down his clarinet and said, "That's called 'Darkies Dreamland'. Do you like it?"

I hesitated for another few seconds and then said, "Eh, it's good. Although I'm not too sure about the title!"

Suffice to say, this languid musical treat is one that I have never heard since. No doubt it doesn't feature prominently on the Radio 2 playlist!

*

The furniture store was situated deep within the bowels of the building. In fact it lay directly underneath the vast arena that was the old Studio 1. Now it's better known as that popular venue for lively dancing and live music – *The Jam House*.

Unfortunately, there are some who I've heard describe it solemnly as "a desolate haunt for desperate women".

I suppose that could be viewed as another story entirely, and something that I wouldn't want to delve into, or possibly comment upon!

Anyway, returning back to the main story. Within that furniture store was an entire variety of, well, furniture, but including amongst it was also found many pieces of rare antiques that were frequently used for a number of BBC Drama productions. Funnily enough, also situated within the same area was – a boat!

A bizarre thought and sight to see a longboat lying almost derelict below the stairs. It had been purchased a few years back using BBC Club funds, for club members to use ostensibly on some water. But for some unaccountable reason, it had been unceremoniously dumped in the basement.

I thought at first glance it bore an uncanny resemblance to the original *"African Queen"*, lying in wait for the inevitable remake?

It certainly looked as if it had been through some fairly choppy waters, but it was all rather sad that it had now ended up rusting away below Studio 1, lying just outside the furniture store.

One day Bob had been given instructions to "tidy up the furniture store", not a euphemism, in case you were wondering, but a reasonable routine assignment you would think for a man of his capabilities. One in order to keep him busy and out of harm's way. Or so we thought.

However, this was Bob we were talking about! I am led to believe that earlier that very same week, this elderly student of military history had devoured a very large book on the life and times of one – *Genghis Khan*. Now you might very well be asking yourself what the connection is.

Well, the great Khan, along with his all-conquering descendants and their marauding hordes, were known to have laid waste to most of Central Asia, the Russian Steppes and Eastern Europe, leaving utter devastation and catastrophic turmoil in their wake. Which made it inevitable that on this occasion, Bob was now about to take on the mantle of the mighty *Temujin* and lay waste to the furniture store!

This, as you can imagine, he did with enormous glee and enthusiasm, and a rapacious appetite for sheer destruction that was simply breathtaking.

Tables, chairs, desks, bookcases, cabinets, all quickly

became twisted, splintered, and broken as they smashed against the wall in bits and pieces. I always felt that perhaps in another life, Bob had indeed been one of the mighty Khan's most favoured generals, someone who led his armies on a journey of decimation, committing numerous atrocities, whilst playing the odd tune on his clarinet.

Bob was now like a madman, almost foaming at the mouth, as he took out his frustration and anger (that always seemed to be bubbling deep within him) on some very rare antiquities that unfortunately would no longer grace the soundstages of a BBC television drama.

As far as I can recall, following this specialised task, no repercussions were forthcoming, and Bob managed to skilfully dispense of his "work" without too many people knowing about it.

It's perhaps a good job that at that particular time, BBC Scotland were not planning on producing a lavish historical programme on the lines of *"Down-Town Abbey"*, requiring the presence of fine antique furniture.

Because what they would have had as a replacement, would have been piles of crunched up wooden remnants that wouldn't have been out of place at a pre-bonfire party.

On another occasion, Bob decided that he didn't like the look of a particular light shade that was hanging from a ceiling light, down in his basement room. He leapt up and singularly punched, it smashing the glass shade into smithereens, and then calmly sat back down and took a gulp of tea.

A little while later, he walked through to the electrician's workshop where old Frank (the house electrician) was working, told him that an accident had occurred regarding the shade (he told him that it had fallen down of its own accord?) and that it now needed replaced.

Frank popped along to see the debris lying all over the floor. He shook his head and at first couldn't understand how it had fallen from the light fitting.

He mumbled away to himself as he realised that owing to Bob's somewhat reckless reputation, he must have had something to do with it.

Bob then sat down, picked up his newspaper and began to read, as he waited for Frank to return with a new light shade.

I am convinced that after reading his original BBC contract, Bob must have misinterpreted some of the wording as giving him a free licence to systematically attack and destroy the buildings property – like a one man *Operation Barbarossa!!!*

Talking of *Operation Barbarossa*, one frequent and distinguished visitor and contributor to a number of radio programmes, was the noted military historian, *Professor John Erickson.*

This hugely intelligent man had written extensively on the brutal and annihilating conflict between Nazi Germany and Soviet Russia during WW2, making him one of the world's foremost authorities on this subject.

This also made him a fascinating figure – particularly for Bob.

Whenever *Professor Erickson* popped into the building to conduct an interview, Bob always made it his point to engage him in detailed conversation concerning the devastating war on the Eastern Front.

Bob had devoured both his hefty volumes dealing with this topic: *The Road to Stalingrad* and *The Road to Berlin,* and had nothing but the highest respect for him, as a writer and as a historian. He even told me that *Prof. Erickson* was greatly impressed by his own vast knowledge on this specialised subject. As well as amazed at how much he knew about the various battles and military leaders, from both sides.

You could say that great minds were now thinking very much alike!

While looking at them both deep in animated discussion, I was left in no doubt that Bob was truly in his element. As together they were inevitably dissecting the strategies of *Field Marshal Zhukov, Field Marshal Von Paulus* and the decisive, bloody Panzer and T-34 tank movements during the *Battle of Stalingrad*.

Away from the carnage of the Russian front, Bob had a very unique way of handling a Hoover. To give you an example: the house staff often during their daily duties had to use a Hoover to clean up the Studio 1 lounge area, as well as the interiors of many of the other studios.

I was amazed at the time that in fact they were still using Hoovers that appeared, in my mind, to be extremely outdated and antiquated.

They were heavy cumbersome pieces that looked as if they had been left over from the pre-Edwardian era. I often felt that they might also have been potentially dangerous to use, and that they could easily break down and even self-combust, owing to their age. Although it was usually Bob that self-combusted – with or without his Hoover!

Whenever the Hoover bags were required to be emptied, Bob now displayed a skilfully unique way in handling the item. Instead of unclipping the bag from the side and emptying the dusty contents into a refuse bag, Bob physically upended the considerably heavy piece of domestic equipment, and shook the contents into a waiting black bin bag. This was taking a very long route, when a shorter one was much more preferable and far easier.

Yet it wasn't just the sight of him grappling and almost wrestling with the Hoover that caused so many raised eyebrows, it was the mess that the exercise was causing.

This often occurred around the main reception area when usually there were guests, visitors and a small audience in attendance.

During Bob's procedure of "emptying the Hoover bag" was in progress, the main reception area would soon became engulfed in a large *Hiroshima*-style mushroom cloud, complete with dust, grime, and grit that spread throughout the entire reception like a thick fog – straight out of an old *Sherlock Holmes* movie!

Soon, everyone in the vicinity was coughing, spluttering, and choking, as they inadvertently consumed the unpalatable contents of the Hoover bag, while Bob seemed completely oblivious to the alarm he was causing.

*

Apart from being a furniture destroying, warden abusing, clarinet playing, military historian, Bob possessed one other talented string to his bow. He was a dab hand at cleaning windows!

Complete with large bucket, soapy water and leather sponge, this would prove to be a lucrative wee sideline for him, in order to augment his paltry BBC salary. Because, as he always stressed (to those who would listen?) the BBC was simply not paying him enough! Usually followed by his claims that the BBC was also overpaying certain celebrity TV and radio presenters, far too much money!

Maybe Bob should have been working for the tabloid press?

In fact, one of his regular window-cleaning customers turned out to be the main Salvation Army headquarters that was based down at the old Grass-Market.

I don't recall if the BBC ever asked him to clean their windows, although (as part of his usual duties) he regularly put out and raised the BBC flag on the flagpole.

This flagpole was placed in a very high position, near the top of the building, just outside the old control room, and to have it tied properly, involved a very elaborate and somewhat risky procedure.

I had to laugh at how he used to handle that very special flag, which proudly declared *Nation Shall Speak Peace Unto Nation.*

In Bob's roughened hands this symbolic and noble fabric – that was once emblazoned with the BBC's grandiloquent motto – soon began to resemble an old rag that Bob would usually polish his windows with!!

*

Bob would often tell me that he was a frequent visitor to a well-known establishment based in the heart of Edinburgh's new town, near Stockbridge.

He was referring to a building that was situated in Danube Street, and was commonly described as either "a house of ill-repute", or "a house of joy", depending on how you viewed it, I suppose.

Bob would tell me that the lady who ran the place was an old and dear friend, who catered for the demands of the city's male population with a degree of good humour, as well as equally a degree of sound business acumen. He also told me that (on his regular visits there) he would often bump into one or two of the BBC engineering staff, as well as certain gentlemen of the clergy. On one occasion he popped along to the house, accompanied by a member of the Edinburgh audio crew. Unfortunately, according to Bob, the audio engineer's much anticipated evening of bliss was quickly over before it had even started. As he reached that inevitable moment of no return, just as he was removing his trousers!

Bob also explained to my youngish ears, that during the week of the General Assembly of the Church of Scotland, the house was always guaranteed to be bursting at the seams with loosened ecclesiastical dog collars and trouser buttons.

While all the time cash registers were constantly ringing, with business going through the roof towards the clouds where the angels watched over their flock! No doubt the elderly gentlemen were just giving the employees a little taste of what is commonly known as "that old-time religion." If it was good enough for *Elmer Gantry* – it was good enough for them.

Bob however, had his tender moments as well. He loved his dog Hannibal with a passion. In fact I often remember him heading out to his car and returning about ten minutes later with a large black bin bag tucked under his arm.

The funny thing was, the bag was moving, as well as making a slightly growling and moaning noise. This was in fact his dog Hannibal, being secretly smuggled into the building in a black bin bag, with the hope that no one would see him.

This was simply because Miss Wilson had banned all dogs from the interior of the building during working hours. However, this proved a particular challenge for Bob, who was going to get his dog indoors, one way or another.

He then rushed quickly by the reception desk, making no eye contact with anyone, and with his faithful hound, tucked under his arm, he ran down the stairs into the basement. You knew that his dog was in the black bag, owing to the fact that its long waggly tail was sticking out of the end.

I am led to believe that Miss Wilson was ignorant of this fact all during her time in charge.

I also remember Bob told me that on one night when he was doing a night shift, his dog, stubbornly and doggedly (no pun intended!) refused to venture anywhere near the top of No. 6 building. To be more specific, for those unaware of this, BBC 5 Queen Street was in reality three buildings merged together – 4, 5, and 6.

Number 6 building featured a narrow winding staircase that went almost up into the attic area where some production offices lay.

This included one in particular near the very top, in which

a very high profile arts producer was caught out by one of the early morning cleaners, in a rather compromising situation (on the desk no less!) with his secretary! Let's just say that she wasn't taking down dictation – at least not in the traditional manner!!

A very embarrassing position for all concerned, not least the poor cleaner who didn't know where to look and soon required a calming cup of tea and a taxi home in order to soothe her shattered nerves!!

Well I'm sure that this wouldn't be the first (or last) occasion in which some senior members of staff would be accidentally discovered by an early morning cleaner – as they were minus trousers, skirt, dignity – or all three!

Anyway, I am getting away from this old shaggy dog story… so to speak.

When checking that particular part of the building very late one night, Bob's faithful hound refused to budge, and venture anywhere near the narrow stairs that led to the top.

According to Bob, he whined and growled, and never moved a paw, determined not to go towards a room or a floor that may, or may not have harboured a deep dark secret from the past.

Bob was convinced that many, many years ago something terrible had occurred in that part of the building, one that made animals fearful of going anywhere near it. Who knows if there was any truth in the rumour?

But I often heard others saying that strange things had been felt and experienced at that part of the building, particularly late at night.

Although I am perhaps more convinced that it may have been either the consumption of strong drink, or more likely stronger primal desires that often brought about the same results!

We will hear more of the First Aid Room later.

One day Bob looked in a particularly foul mood. I decided to act with a degree of bravery and ask him what the matter was. "Did you read in the paper about Elton John?" he asked. For a second, I wasn't quite sure where this conversation was leading. "He's a F*****g poof!" he snarled before I could answer his query.

"Oh that's right," I laughed, "I did read it the other day. The paper stated that he's decided to come out of the closet, as he's been struggling with his sexuality for a number of years."

"What the f**k was he doing in a closet?" Bob shouted back at me.

"No, you don't understand, Bob. That's just a term that's often used when somebody announces that they're gay," I informed him.

"Well, I'll tell you what I did the other night." Bob was now about to tell me something I wasn't sure I wanted to hear.

"I took all of his f*****g records, and I threw the lot of them, right in the f*****g bucket!!"

I must admit I wasn't a bit surprised at that. Yet, what was more surprising to me (once I digested his blunt announcement) was the fact that he apparently owned some of *Elton John's* records in the first place!

Considering his background, I suppose, at the time, with him being a man of a certain age and generation, it wasn't too unusual to find him curtly describing gays as either "Nancy Boys" or "Sodomites."

Maybe he was just channelling a little bit of the old *Marquis of Queensbury* philosophy into his outlook on life?

*

On another occasion, we had that distinguished Irish actor of stage and screen *Cyril Cusack* visiting us. He was participating in a Studio 1 radio drama production during this time. Bob in his usual friendly manner went along to have a chat with him, during a short break in the play.

He returned after about fifteen minutes, and I asked him what Mr Cusack was like. Bob stood there for a few seconds and said, "Aye, he's alright. But the bastard called me love!!" I had to stifle a laugh, as I tried to explain to him that after all, he was an actor, and that's what certain actors who have been long established in the grand thespian manner, usually tend to say.

I suppose, what with Bob coming from one of the rougher schemes of old Edinburgh, he wasn't used to a man addressing him in such an affectionate and effete tone. "Bastard called me love!" Bob was heard to mutter again to himself, as he wandered of back down the stairs.

*

Around the mid-1980s Bob would encounter a new sparring partner in the shape of the late lamented *Kenny Macintyre*. Kenny originally hailed from the Isle of Mull and became one of BBC Scotland's most respected political and industrial journalists, and for a time he did his reporting in Edinburgh, before moving back through to Glasgow.

Kenny sadly passed away in 1999 at the tragically young age of 54.

For the brief time he was based in Edinburgh, he made an indelible impression on all who knew him, worked with him, laughed with him, fought with him and played football with him. Kenny gave the impression that he just never halted, or took breath. In all the time that I used to see him, he never appeared to be a man who relaxed, or took things easy. He was always in his absolute element, frantically pursuing a red-hot story to fill the airwaves, or hit the TV screens.

When he passed away I noticed one day in BBC Glasgow, a large memoriam book set aside near reception as a tribute to Kenny's memory.

I recall writing something along the lines of: "To Kenny – you were the best football captain I ever had."

*

As I said, Kenny was a terrific character and much liked by everyone. He was always cheery and up for a laugh (I am led to believe that along with one of the news editors, they both, for a joke, grabbed a fellow reporter by the name of *Ninian Reid* and hung him over the banisters by his ankles!).

Kenny was also a good footballer (he became one of my Thursday night soccer buddies), yet he took particular malicious delight in winding Bob up as much as he could.

This could very well prove to be a dangerous course of action, and would usually manifest itself early in the morning when Kenny was in the newsroom and Bob was on an early shift.

As I arrived early in the morning, I became acutely aware of some very loud noises and animated scuffles that were echoing from the newsroom interiors.

One of the guys on reception would inform me that "Bob and Kenny are at it again!" As I listened more closely, not wanting to step into the gladiatorial arena of the newsroom myself, all I heard now was the continuing sound of loud thumps, banging cabinets, and cries of "Take that Macintyre, ya f*****g bastard!!" from Bob.

Then all of a sudden Kenny would rush out of the newsroom, running through the corridor, with Bob hot on his tail, cursing and blinding as only he could, and then Kenny would collapse in a heap on the floor, in convulsions of laughter, just as Bob laid into him again with his fists!

While reading all of this you might be under the impression that a serious physical assault was taking place. However, you couldn't be more wrong.

This was just Bob and Kenny's usual morning antics to get them fired up for the day. This usually started off with them

68

aiming a few well chosen swear words, curses and insults towards each other. This usually culminated in thumps, punches and chases that were redolent of an old episode of *Batman!*

Kenny would then slowly get up on his feet, while holding his ribs, and start laughing again as he made his painful journey back to the newsroom. Bob later confessed to all "That f*****g bastard Macintyre. I'll get him again tomorrow!" This regular morning ritual of fisticuffs and insults between Bob and Kenny would prove far more entertaining than anything that was being screened on Breakfast TV.

In fact there was one incident where Kenny bravely attempted to push Bob into one of the large bins that were lying in the newsroom. I think he received a few more thumps in the ribs for that piece of audacity.

Funnily enough, this, as many believed at the time, was just Bob and Kenny's strange and bizarre way of showing friendship and affection towards each other.

*

Sadly tragedy touched Bob's life in the early 1980s when his beloved eldest daughter took seriously ill and passed away in hospital. She was still a young woman, with a young family and Bob was understandably shocked and grief stricken.

I felt for him during this time, as his family meant everything to him, and to have to go through an experience like that of seeing his own daughter die, must have been horrendous. This was something that truly engulfed him with momentous grief and made him even more consumed with anger at the world.

Along with Mac, I attended his daughter's funeral and I can still recall the look of unimaginable pain and sadness that was marked upon Bob's face during this bleakest of days.

Bob was particularly aggrieved when he felt the BBC was trying to get rid of him. To be honest, he was fast approaching his pension years, and the times they were a-changing within the corporation. However, he was one angry man (not too difficult when it was Bob we were describing) as he felt he still had a few good more years to give.

"The BBC has no f*****g right to make me retire!" he would often say.

I suppose in one way he may have felt a little justified, as for a man nearing his mid-sixties, he was still physically pretty fit and could still do a job that required some physical effort.

Yet on the other hand, could the BBC afford to keep him on in a changing and more modernistic environment? And what about all that new furniture that was recently installed in the refurbished building?

What exactly would have happened to it, and would it have remained intact, once Bob had been set loose?

The feeling was that once Bob had fully got into his stride, it might not have remained brand new for very long!

Overall, it's maybe a great pity that the staff who would arrive during the early 1990s, never had the opportunity of experiencing at first hand, Bob's explosive *Patton*-like presence and his "Smash & Thump" style of personality! Although on second thoughts, perhaps not, as I'm not entirely sure just how a new generation of assorted producers and programme makers, would have reacted to such an individual.

*

So the time had come for him to depart, which was for me a little sad, as he had provided so much needed colour and unintentional entertainment into the place over the past few years. When Bob finally left, it was truly the end of an era, and BBC Edinburgh was never quite the same again.

Yet when he did finally leave the BBC, Bob would achieve

his lifetime's ambition. He would be playing his beloved clarinet as part of a jazz/swing band – on a cruise ship, no less!

So, dreams can come true, even for someone in the most unlikely of circumstances.

Now he could put the past bitter memory of having the odd fracas with a producer, far behind him.

One of the last times that I ever saw Bob was about a dozen years ago. I happened to bump into him on Princes Street one day whilst I was out browsing the shops

He was looking good, considering he was probably well into his seventies at that time. He seemed genuinely pleased to see me, as I was of him, but I had a feeling that his old pent-up belligerence towards life and its injustices were still burning very much alive within him.

The spirit of *Robert De Niro's Taxi Driver* and *Charles Bronson's Death Wish* vigilante was still very much in evidence when we started to talk.

He told me in fact that not so long ago, he had managed to get himself lifted by the police. This news didn't really come as any great shock to me, considering all that he had done in the past. But a bit alarming, what with him now being well advanced into his pension years.

"What happened?" I innocently asked, dreading to hear exactly what he had done to incur the wrath of the law.

Bob then began his story. "Do remember there was an anti-war and an anti-American demonstration near the mound not that long ago?" He asked me.

"Yes, come to think of it, I do recall reading about something like that in the Evening News."

Bob then began to give me the gritty details about what had happened that precise day. "There was this f*****g Arab bastard shouting against America. He was screaming at the top of his f*****g voice calling for all Americans to die and to get out of Iraq and go home." With this description of the event, I now knew exactly as to where this conversation was ultimately heading.

Bob then (getting himself more fired up) growled, "So I grabbed the bastard and shouted back at him, 'See you, ya f*****g git, if hadn't been for the Americans in 1944, you wouldn't f*****g be here!!'"

Whilst at the same time pointing straight towards Edinburgh Castle, he further added, "I told him as well, 'See that up there? If it hadn't been for the Yanks during the war, that would have been f*****g SS headquarters and we would all be under the f*****g Nazi jackboot!! And as for you, ya f*****g git, you would have been the first bastard put up against the wall and shot!!!'"

I suppose, in some ways, he did have a valid point.

Although some might say that he did put it across somewhat crudely.

Anyway, he said that following the angered exchange with the dark skinned, foreign demonstrator, all hell suddenly broke loose, and the police quickly moved in to diffuse the heated situation.

Bob was then taken away to a nearby police station, probably in order for him to cool down, before he was released and left to go home.

I don't think that I am stretching the truth in saying that Bob was, unapologetically, a man of his time and generation. In fact the term "Political Correctness", figured absolutely nowhere within his personal lexicon. In fact he would scoff at such an expression.

Race, religion, sexuality, politics, the monarchy, celebrity, and pretty well everything in between, felt the full force of his corrosive scattergun explosion of opinions and attitudes. And he felt all the happier for having expressed them.

I often think of Bob as possibly "the last angry man", someone who displayed no hesitation in venting his furious anger at what he perceived as life's cruel injustices. This was usually reserved for many a BBC producer, union representatives, traffic wardens (especially traffic wardens), and various figures of managerial authority.

Much of what he said over the years did occasionally carry a tiny grain of truth, as well as a touch of validity. In all the time I knew him he was never slow to rouse himself to anger, or shout from the rooftops, as what he saw as society's unfairness.

Yet, many (including myself from time to time) attempted to try and duck out of his firing line when he was on the warpath. Which happened a lot, particularly when something or other was annoying and angering him.

In spite of his somewhat combustible personality, I look back with an immense degree of fondness for the man, who despite his apocalyptic nature and simmering dark moods (that often threatened all kinds of mayhem) he often displayed the occasional bit of unexpected kindness.

Not forgetting that he gave not only me, but countless others, so much laughter over so many years.

CHAPTER 3

Ooh Matron – I Need First Aid!!!

Arguably the most popular, well-used, and most frequented room in the entire building of 5 Queen Street turned out to be, not perhaps one of the various radio studios, nor even the canteen – but the First Aid Room!

Ah, the First Aid Room. Even the brief mention of its name conjures up a world of strange goings on, unusual sounds and an entire variety of lurid images – not many dealing with actual first aid!

Although on the other hand, maybe I am being a bit premature… so to speak.

*

The true meaning of a First Aid Room is one that should bring comfort and relief to the suffering. Well, I suppose that was true in many ways.

It can also provide rest, respite, and a sanctuary for the ill and the injured. This was a room situated far away from the hustle and bustle of feverish production creativity, and one full of peace, tranquillity and much-needed calm. Maybe that is why the mere mention of its name makes a number of former staff members go all misty eyed with nostalgia. But I am led to believe that this very same room harboured a secret, one known to only a privileged few, and whose walls would soon echo with the sounds of, well, let's say, lots of physical comfort, complete with some ultimate blessed relief!

*

I first became truly aware of the First Aid Room's alternative existence, one day when we received our regular monthly visit from the BBC nurse. Let's call her *Sister Ann*, and she resided mainly in Broadcasting House in Glasgow. Each month she would travel through from the west, to check on all health matters relating to the Edinburgh staff.

Normally, this would involve the likes of blood tests, blood pressure readings, eye tests and the like. Nothing out of the ordinary, but all part of the BBC's obligation to make sure that all staff members were reasonably fit and healthy. And it was more often than not, that the fit and the healthy would make good use of the room – particularly the bed!

Anyway, Sister Ann arrived at reception and said her usual hellos to Mac, who was on duty at the desk on this specific day.

She was a large, quite formidable looking woman, and you instantly felt that she was someone not to be trifled with, or to upset in any way. She collected the keys, and then smartly walked towards the First Aid Room that was situated through a corridor towards the ground floor level of building number 6.

Then, about two or three minutes later she returned – with a face like thunder! Looking uncannily like *Hattie Jacques* in a very bad mood!

"Who has been using that room??" she bellowed at Mac, who was taken aback and slightly startled at her vocal ferocity, as well as her now heightened purple face.

"What do you mean? What's wrong?" Mac replied, slightly quizzical as to what she was referring to.

"The First Aid Room! Someone's been in there and made a hell of a mess!! It's an absolute disgrace!"

By this time, she was getting more and more angry and Mac must have been thinking, *How I am going to cool the situation and calm this very upset woman down?*

"I have no idea," Mac said. "The keys are always kept behind the desk, and only ever given out in a medical emergency."

"Well somebody's been using it!!" she barked back. "The bed looks as if a herd of elephants have trampled all on top of it. And as for the state of the sheets…" By all accounts, the sheets in question had quickly gone from crisp pristine white – to fifty shades of grey, virtually overnight! I am convinced that if she had caught whoever it was, she would have given them a blistering tongue-lashing, to say the least. Then again, the idea of more lashings, might not have worried the pair in question? We will never know?

Well she was simply exploding with rage, as Mac tried to alleviate the situation by offering her the inevitable soothing cup of tea. This as expected, was to no avail.

She then with steely emphasis, gave out with her order. "Under no circumstances, has that room to be used for anything other than First Aid!! And only in emergencies." She then stormed up the stairs to make her anguished report to the Administration Officer, Miss Wilson. I would have loved to be a fly on the wall when that conversation took place. No doubt it would have been worth the price of admission alone just to see the look on Miss Wilson's face, when the full sorry, sordidly salacious saga of the First Aid Room was relayed to her in full gory detail!

An investigation was quickly begun to track down the "guilty parties" and to have them severely disciplined. Although I had a feeling that both the mysterious individuals involved, must have already been indulging in a form of severe discipline of their very own.

It wasn't too long for word to soon get out amongst certain members of staff as to the First Aid Room's regular availability for illicit meetings, amorous encounters and secret couplings of all sorts. Just as long as anyone in managerial authority were kept firmly in the dark and remained unaware, and ignorant as to what was actually going on. As I'm sure that they would not have been best pleased as to what was happening – under their very noses.

That availability usually involved late-night physical and emotional assignations. Not forgetting the odd (and sometimes very odd) non-staff visitor who might gain a rare invite to test the room's unusual ambience. It also soon became apparent, that you could book the room well in advance, almost as if you were booking seats for a West-End Musical! From the stories I heard (from a variety of sources) – it was always continuous performances, opening with a rapturous overture, followed by a brief intermission (for a well deserved breather), then ending with a climactic crescendo that almost shook the walls and broke the bed! Talk about a "wow" finish!

This is what is generally now known as exhaustive entertainment.

Word soon spread that the room often hosted late night "pyjama parties!" Although it was later confirmed, that pyjamas were – more often than not – absent from the activities.

So it wasn't all that long that the First Aid Room became freely known as a "nocturnal knocking shop", and soon became viewed as an unofficial clubroom for late night rest and, ahem, relaxation.

On one particular day, Bob came over to me and asked an enquiring question: "I've just heard a rumour. Is it true that the First Aid Room is getting used as a f*****g knocking shop?"

By the way, just in case you were unfamiliar with the term "knocking shop", this was a common slang expression that usually describes a house (or in this case a room) in which much sexual activity could be found. At least I think that's what it means? It's also a phrase much used by soldiers and sailors of older generations, when stationed abroad and far from their wives and sweethearts!

Getting back to Bob's original question, I tried to look just a little surprised at what he was asking and innocently replied, "Well, I really couldn't say, Bob. Although, as you said, there are a number of rumours floating about."

Bob grinned slightly and then shook his head. "For f**k sake – what a f*****g state of affairs. What is this place coming to?" He then added thoughtfully, "Well, I hope they change the f*****g sheets from time to time."

As he then wandered off, no doubt wondering why he was missing out on all the frisky fun!

I must confess that from what I could gather the bedsprings must have been made of some very durable and flexible metal, considering the athletic overuse it had to deal with.

My own experiences of lying in the First Aid Room coincided with my suffering from that dreaded affliction known as labyrinthitis (a term I was unfamiliar with, and at first, I thought was the name of some long-departed Roman Emperor).

This was an extremely unpleasant infection involving the inner ear that once it grips you, makes you dizzy, nauseous and disorientated. Not something I would wish on my worst enemy.

Often I would retreat to the sanctuary of the room to rest until the attack receded, enough for me to return to normal work.

So if anyone passing the room at that time, heard mysterious moans, groans and sighs, unfortunately, they were all emanating from me, all on my own, and with no willing accomplice lying alongside.

*

Over the years, the First Aid Room became a much-beloved place that attained near mythical and legendary status, bringing, ahem, bodies and souls together for a great deal more ecstasy than agony.

I vividly recall one cheeky individual quipping that the sheets possessed an almost sacred aura that demanded that they should be carbon-dated, just like some ancient religious artefact!

Sadly, the room as well as its all-embracing reputation has disappeared far into the mists of time. Although I often wondered whatever happened to the bed, when the building was eventually sold off.

Perhaps it landed up in Sotheby's and fetched several thousands of pounds at auction. Then again, maybe it was donated to the Scottish Museum as an important historical relic? Although I am totally convinced that the bedsprings alone were deserving of a special place, maybe even for intensive scientific study, considering the amount of wear and tear they had to endure, over a considerable period of time.

In fact one active (some might even say overactive) participant was affectionately known to one and all as "Miss Bedsprings" – for very obvious reasons.

But whatever the end result turned out to be, one thing is for certain, the room and especially the bed, provided a great amount of endless enjoyment for so many people. Fun, frolics and consummations that were devoutly to be wished occurred almost nightly, amongst the hallowed walls of this much-missed room. You can't ask for more than that – can you?

Funnily enough, I am often reminded of the First Aid Room whenever I watch the classic *Michael Caine* thriller *Get Carter.*

There is a scene near the beginning of the film when he books into a seedy boarding house and is given a first look at his rather underwhelming and tatty room. He tests the mattress on the bed and with a wry smile says, "I bet that's seen some action." I rest my case.

*

You may well be thinking that life within the walls of BBC Edinburgh was now beginning to closely resemble the activities of a "Carry On" film?

Well, you might not be too far off the truth.

One shining example concerned a request I received from Miss Wilson (the Admin Assistant). At that time, part of my responsibilities concerned supplying and looking after the stationery store for the staff.

However, I was due to go on two weeks leave, and so a temporary replacement was sought to hold the fort for the time I was absent. Miss Wilson called me into her office to discuss the issue, and what best to do to keep things ticking over while I was away.

We had at the time two young girls working within the mailroom, and so one was selected to keep an eye on things for the duration of the two weeks. Miss Wilson said the best way in order for the girl (I shall refrain from exposing her identity in order to spare her blushes. Unfortunately, it's too late to spare mine!) to gain the sufficient knowledge and experience was for me to take her downstairs, then take her into the storeroom and in her own words (and I quote) "Ram as much as I possibly can into her!!!"

Well, I tell you, I didn't know where to look, although Miss Wilson appeared to be innocently, and blissfully unaware as to the possible implications of her request. I swear to you, at that very moment, I'm sure I could hear faint echoes around me of *Kenneth Williams ("Ooh Matron!!")*, as well as the sound of *Sid James's* leery, lecherous laugh.

*

It wasn't only the First Aid Room that brought emotional contentment for the staff. We also had a fully functioning Green Room that would also become an active (some would say very active!) area for guests and VIPs to rest and relax, prior to stepping in front of the microphones during a particular show in Studio 1.

However, it was also a room that the odd presenter and "close friend" could find some downtime to get, well, better acquainted, before the show began.

One particular well-known radio presenter was caught (not alone, as you can well imagine) in a somewhat embarrassing position when the door of the Green Room was suddenly swung wide open when he least expected it.

There, facing the naughty couple, were some of the production staff.

So instead of red wine all round, it was more likely red, flushed faces all round!

Yet, the show still went on – what a professional.

*

Incredibly, for a brief period during the early 1980s we had a switchboard operator (in the days when we had a separate switchboard that was connected to the offices, studios and reception) who ran a successful Escort Agency from the confines of 5 Queen Street!

The lady responsible for bringing kindred spirits and lovelorn souls together was called Muriel.

Unfortunately, she didn't last too long as an employee in Edinburgh, and yet she was instrumental in setting up meetings and introductions to those seeking love, long before the Internet encroached upon this particular territory.

The only issue was that she was doing all of this, almost simultaneously while she was supposed to be doing her normal job.

Perhaps that's why she was swiftly moved along, to avoid embarrassment, when management discovered that she was utilising BBC time, money, and equipment in setting up liaisons with those seeking love, or perhaps more accurately, a bit of frisky fun! A bit harsh you would say, for someone who was only attempting to bring a bit of uncomplicated passion into the lives of the unloved and the lonely!

Suffice to say that the management would eventually look upon it somewhat differently, considering that she was paid to do a job that (no doubt according to her contract at the time) didn't involve affairs of the heart.

She even attempted, on the odd occasion, to try and pair up one or two of the staff with her, ahem, clients.

Peggy, who at one time worked in the canteen, and later became the print-room operator, had been widowed for a few years.

Muriel (perhaps thinking that she was doing Peggy a bit of a favour) suggested to her that she could be instrumental in "fixing her up" with a lonely sailor who was currently on her books, and who just happened to be home that weekend on extended leave!

Peggy was black affronted, outraged, and rightfully indignant that no way did she want to be "paired up" with a saucy sailor looking for some weekend "nookey"! Once she had made her point crystal clear, she then stormed out of the switch-room, taking her cup of tea with her.

Muriel just shrugged her shoulders and then carried on setting up dates and assignations, while the switchboard was almost red-hot and ablaze with production staff vainly trying to get an outside connection!

*

I always felt that the goings on in the First Aid Room (and the Green Room as well) were deserving of a song. Something to remember it by when its memory drifts off into the far distance.

An up-tempo swinging hip/jive number put together by a riot of a band something like *Swing That Thing* (of more later) would have been ideal.

So, how about this for the first few verses:

The joint was jumping,
The bed was bouncing,
The springs were squeaking,
The sheets were sweating,
The sink was shaking,
The pillow was pounding
"Oooh baby, I need First Aid…"

CHAPTER 4

Is That Who I Think It Is? Close Encounters with Famous Faces

Working within BBC Edinburgh would often give you the privileged opportunity to encounter and meet so many famous and successful people from the stage, the screen, the arts and politics. And this I managed to do over much of the duration of my time there. We didn't enjoy too much in the way of "perks" (well, apart from a free copy of the Radio Times), so I suppose meeting and having the opportunity for a brief chat with the great and the good, the rich and the famous, the legendary and the obnoxious, was an added perk in itself.

It's safe to say that the vast majority of the visiting celebrities and show business personalities were for the most part, fascinating and delightful in equal measure.

Yet it's not incontestable to also say that there were the odd few who turned out to be somewhat less than delightful. In fact, some were even downright rude at times – although maybe they were just having a bad hair day?

The very first famous celebrity I ever encountered during my first year at 5 Queen Street was one of the biggest names in British show business – *Frankie Vaughan*.

"Mr Moonlight" himself turned up, accompanied by his wife Stella, to do an interview, which was going to take place in the old Studio 3 (which had a red door and not a green

YOU CAN'T DO THAT HERE! THIS IS THE BBC!

door – as Frankie used to sing about!)

As befitting a man of his stature, he was immaculately attired with a very smart (and no doubt very expensive) grey checked jacket. He seemed smaller in person than what I imagined him to be, but he was without doubt at that time, one of the greatest names in British entertainment. A giant on stage and in cabaret, as well as a man who possessed tremendous humanitarian qualities, as I'm sure those troubled teenagers in Glasgow's Easter-house area would testify to.

He would be the first star I would meet – he would not be the last.

*

Thinking back to my earliest days, I recall meeting two members of the then popular comedy team "*The Goodies*" (it may have been *Graeme Garden* and *Tim Brook Taylor*). I also recall the stylish stage and film actress *Claire Bloom* (once married to *Rod Steiger* and a great passion of *Richard Burton's* during his pre-*Elizabeth Taylor* days) appearing at reception resplendent in a long fur coat, looking every inch the patrician star.

However, perhaps the most memorable visit (in more ways than one) from Hollywood royalty occurred sometime in the early 1980s with the visit of *James Mason*. In fact I can tell you the exact date in which he came into the building.

It was the 7th of September 1982. How do I know this? Well when he gave me his autograph, he also signed that day's date just alongside his signature.

James Mason was one of Britain's finest screen actors, who left the UK shores in the late forties and embarked on a long and successful career in Hollywood, starring in a string of outstanding classic films. He also possessed one of the richest and most distinctive voices in movie history. So it was a terrific kick for me when this distinguished movie star stepped out of his chauffeur-driven car and then walked through the front doors of 5 Queen Street.

I remember this occasion more vividly than most, as I can still visualise him arriving immaculately dressed in what looked like a very expensive overcoat, and a stylish well-cut suit and hat. The impression he gave was that of a real aristocrat, a gentleman with impeccable manners, one of the elder statesmen of cinema that only added to his admired status as one of the finest film actors of his era.

Mac was on duty again at Reception, and like myself, recognised him immediately.

"Good morning, my name is *James Mason* and I'm here for an interview," he softly said with a voice that I had heard a hundred times before in many a movie.

But would you believe it, there was absolutely no mention of him coming in, or any information about what programme he was participating with. Nothing, absolutely nothing.

Mac felt slightly embarrassed for the well-dressed gentleman and actor, as he had to admit to him that he had no note or information as regards to his arrival.

"If you excuse me, Mr Mason, I will check with the Studio Bookings Manager as to what studio you are going into." The great man seemed unconcerned and stood quietly by the desk, to await his instructions.

Mac then phoned Jean, the Studio Bookings Manager, to gain more information. "Hello Jean, I have *Mr James Mason* here at reception – and he's here for an interview."

Jean (you could say was a blunt and somewhat loud woman) replied, "James who?"

You could also easily say that Jean wasn't the kind of woman you would prefer to face on a Friday night with a pound short in your pay packet!

Mac was shaken at her ignorance as to the status of the man standing at the front desk. "*James Mason*, the famous film star, he's standing right here in front of me."

Jean replied even more bluntly, "What is he wanting??" As if the famous screen star was some scruffy old vagrant who had just staggered through the front door reeking of rum.

"He's here for an interview!" Mac answered, as he was now beginning to feel slightly embarrassed as well as extremely angered at Jean's obvious incapacity to grasp the importance of the situation.

"Oh, I don't know anything about it!" she replied. "Tell him to go for a cup of tea to the canteen, until I find out what the hell is going on."

Mac just shook his head and apologised profusely to Mr Mason, who just shrugged his shoulders and sat down at the chair near reception.

By this time, word quickly spread that we had within the building one of the great stars of Hollywood. In fact two of the older canteen staff seemed thrilled at the prospect of perhaps seeing and meeting him, with one of the ladies suddenly bursting into laughter as she claimed that she always loved him in that film *"Fanny By Gaslight"*.

It then took several minutes for Jean to find out what the programme was and what studio Mr Mason was due to appear in. Finally, once verification was achieved as to the programme, the time, and the studio, I escorted him through to the studio itself. Unfortunately, he still had a few moments before going on air, and so he sat down, rather sadly in the one lone chair that stood outside.

It was certainly an unusual sight to see this great man of the screen, sitting rather lost and forlorn, as if he had been coldly forgotten, with a BBC paper cup full of hot tea in his hand.

Once his interview was concluded, I walked him back to the reception area (where he kindly gave me his autograph – something I treasured and still have to this day). He then said thanks, made his farewells and walked out of the front door to his awaiting limo.

Mr Mason made no fuss, or furore, and was a perfect gentleman from start to finish. Despite the initial confusion surrounding his visit.

Following his departure there was much argument and debate raging as to his somewhat shoddy treatment. Mac and myself both agreed that this was no way to treat a major star of his fame and reputation. He really should have been given the full and proper red carpet VIP treatment, such as being taken to the Manager's Boardroom for some refreshments.

Bob, not surprisingly, soon appeared once he had heard of what had happened, and then said in his own inimitable way, "What a f*****g disgrace, to treat the man like that! This is *James Mason*, a big international star. He's not some f*****g piss-pot!!"

I guess that I couldn't have put it more eloquently.

*

Other great luminaries from stage and screen would pop through the doors over the years including *Lord Richard Attenborough, Sir John Mills, Sir Peter Ustinov, Dame Anna Neagle, Michael Denison, Dulcie Gray* and *Cliff Robertson*.

Sir John Mills appeared within the building on two separate occasions. The first time was when he was publicising his autobiography and so he popped in for an interview. I recall just managing to get his autograph, as he was running out the building to his awaiting car. He was wearing what I can only describe as cowboy boots, with a very large Cuban heel (maybe he was attempting more of a *John Wayne* walk that day than a *John Mills* walk?) and accompanied by a very tall, slim, blonde lady, whom I assume was his publicist?

The second time was a good few years later and he arrived this time with his wife Mary. At least on this occasion, both *Sir John* and *Lady Mills* were treated in the right and correct manner and taken to the Boardroom for refreshments and a spot of relaxation. Something that was severely lacking when poor *James Mason* visited the building!

Lord Attenborough in particular was a lovely man and a true gentleman; exactly measuring up to everything that you thought he might be in reality.

I was given the enormous privilege in doing a bit of public relations by looking after him for the day, when he visited 5 Queen Street for a radio interview in connection with one of the many charities he was involved with. I welcomed him and his assistant when they first arrived, and then took him up to the Manager's office prior to him going on air.

He was a total delight, and told me that he had recently finished editing the screen version of the hit Broadway musical *A Chorus Line* that had been filming in New York and starred *Michael Douglas*.

I accompanied him down to the studio, and sat in with him for the duration of the interview.

Once he had finished, I then escorted him back upstairs to the Manager's Boardroom where we all had tea, coffee and biscuits and chatted for a while.

When leaving the building, he turned to me warmly, smiled and shook my hand saying, "Thanks very much Lawrence, for all your help today."

I felt incredibly happy, not just in meeting a great actor and filmmaker of whom I had much admired over the years, but just to spend some time in his company and experience just how kind, thoughtful and gracious he was as a person.

In fact, several years later, I had the pleasure of meeting him again, when he was in Edinburgh promoting his much-acclaimed 1993 film *Shadowlands*.

I was invited along to the Odeon cinema, with the Newsroom film crew who were about to conduct an interview with him after the films press screening. After the film ended we were ushered through to the main cinema bar to meet *Lord Attenborough.*

I said to him how great it was to see him again, although I thought that he probably didn't remember me from the last time. "Of course I remember you, Lawrence," he replied with unforced sincerity.

And then he told me that he was flying out to New York the following day to begin work on his latest film – the remake of the old Christmas classic *Miracle on 34th Street*, in which he would be playing the character of Kris Kringle, otherwise known as Santa Claus. A perfect piece of casting I thought at the time, as I'm sure that everyone who saw and enjoyed the film would agree.

After he died I thought back to the time I spent in his company and I treasure the chats that we shared. Whatever his triumphs and successes as a filmmaker and actor, for me, I believe that his greatest triumph, was that of one of the finest examples of a true humanitarian that this country and the world has ever known.

*

Another famous movie actor popped into 5 Queen Street during the 80s by the name of *Eli Wallach.* This New York born actor is perhaps best known amongst film fans for playing treacherous and garrulous bandits and outlaws in a string of classic westerns such as *The Magnificent Seven, How The West Was Won,* and *The Good, The Bad And The Ugly.*

I had a brief chat with him on the front steps as he was awaiting his appearance in Studio 1 for an interview. He was a charming and extremely pleasant man who told me that he was enjoying his visit to the Edinburgh Festival, where he was appearing in a play with his actress wife *Anne Jackson.* I mentioned to him that my younger brother had spoken to him the day previous.

He looked at me for a second and then smiled. "Oh yes, I

remember this young man came over to me and spoke while I was standing outside Marks & Spencer's. My wife was inside buying me a pullover."

I suppose you don't expect to see the man who had starred alongside *Clark Gable* and *Marilyn Monroe*, as well as exchanging gunfire on screen opposite the likes of *Yul Brynner, Steve McQueen*, and *Clint Eastwood* standing in the middle of Princes Street waiting on his wife coming out of a shop with a jumper in an M&S bag!

We chatted for a few minutes and in my mind I half expected to hear him come out with a line from one of his famous movies, such as: "There are two kinds of people in the world my friend. Those who shop at Marks & Spencer's, and those who don't…"

Talking of *Clint Eastwood*, I would meet the great man during one of his visits to the Edinburgh Festival back in 1990.

This happened – not at 5 Queen Street (couldn't exactly visualise him queuing up in the canteen for a coffee and a bacon role. Then again, it might have made his day!) – but at the old Caledonian Hotel near the West End of Edinburgh. Again, I went along with the film crew who were going to capture his press conference following the screening of his film *"White Hunter, Black Heart"*.

He appeared calm, confident and relaxed as the assembled audience looked on with appreciation and rapt attention as this Hollywood giant talked at length about his latest film, as well as his career in general. However, once the talk was over, I noticed that one or two went over to say hello and to shake his hand.

He didn't appear to be in any hurry to depart the hall, and looked very happy to stay for that extra bit longer to sign autographs and have his picture taken.

This was too good an opportunity to let pass, so with my

black and white photo in hand, I lined up alongside the others, asked him for his autograph, mumbled an enquiry as to his next film, shook his hand and said something along the lines of, "It's been great to meet you Mr Eastwood."

He looked at me with his steely green eyes (the very same ones that usually narrowed when he was about to inquire if you felt lucky) then smiled and said, "It's a pleasure."

One thing that I did notice about him was the size of his Rolex watch. That was no doubt the genuine expensive article, and not one usually bought at some tatty old flea market for under a tenner!

When writing the passage above, it just occurred to me, that I might well be one of the very few people who has met and conversed with, both *The Good* and *The Ugly*. Unfortunately, I never experienced the opportunity of meeting *The Bad – Lee Van Cleef,* which would have been an experience in itself.

*

When I was speaking recently with a friend about my time at the BBC, and the various stars and celebrities that I met, he laughed as he said, "And did you ever meet *Jimmy Savile* or *Rolf Harris*??"

I gulped and looked at him straight in the eye and replied, "Well yes, as a matter of fact I did meet Savile."

He looked at me a bit strangely at first, as if I was about to divulge something seedy and sordid. "Funnily enough, it wasn't at the BBC, but at Meadowbank Stadium," I replied. This was when I, and a group of work colleagues took part in one of the sponsored charity walks Savile was involved with back in the late 1970s.

I even had to own up and confess that I shook his hand. But then again, I'm sure I wasn't the only one. If only you knew then, what you know now...

As a postscript to this tale, I recently received an official letter from my former BBC employers, who were mounting a major internal investigation into the scandals that had erupted all over the media and press concerning the disgraced former cigar-smoking DJ. They were asking if I had been aware of, or had heard of anything salacious connected with him. But they also added to enquire if I had witnessed "any inappropriate behaviour on BBC premises" I thought to myself, *Where do I start??*

As for *Rolf Harris*, well I didn't actually meet him, but I am led to believe that he did turn up late one evening in Queen Street (as far as I know without his didgeridoo!!) during one Festival. In fact I was told recently that after he had concluded his radio interview, he took a particular shine to the young fresh-faced female production assistant who was assisting in the studio at the time. To the extent that he attempted (unsuccessfully, I hasten to add) to "persuade" her to get into his awaiting taxi and accompany him back to his hotel! Talk about a narrow escape!

But I digress.

*

Apart from famous Hollywood stars, BBC Edinburgh also played host to many of the most distinguished Scottish theatrical figures of the day. Many a celebrated radio drama and radio education production was blessed with several talented homebred actors and actresses, who added their not inconsiderable acting skills, for the benefit of the Scottish radio audiences. Here are just a few of the names you might recognise:

Rikki Fulton, Bryden Murdoch, Eileen McCallum, Mary Riggans, John Sheddon, Finlay Welsh, Maureen Carr, Iain Agnew, John Young, Paul Young, Gerry Slevin, Tom Fleming, Bill Paterson, David Rintoul, Ron Bain, Gwynneth Guthrie.

Michael Elder, Sheila Donald, Alex Norton, Tony Roper, Ricky Callan, Phyllis Logan, Tom Watson, Robbie Coltrane, Crawford Logan, Juliet Cadzow, John Bett, Bill Torrance, Moultrie Kelsall,

Leonard Maguire, Patrick Malahide, Russell Hunter, Una McLean, Gregor Fisher, Brian Cox.

Sincere apologies, if I have accidentally left anyone out.

*

We also had a number of famous Scottish entertainers step into 5 Queen Street, including the likes of *Billy Connelly, Alastair McDonald, Tam White, Tam "Toto" MacNaughton, Tommy Smith, Carol Laula, Archie Fisher, Aly Bain* and *Phil Cunningham, Fish from Marillion, Sheena Easton* (in the days before she hooked up with a certain guy called *Prince*), *The Proclaimers* and not forgetting the unique – *Chic Murray.*

His memorable appearance during a live Studio 1 broadcast was preceded when the "tall droll" had to be physically removed from the bar of the Beau Brummell, with only minutes to spare before the live broadcast was due to start!

By all accounts, he wasn't best pleased at being forced to leave the pub, as well as leaving his glass of whisky behind, and then taken back round to the studio, where a packed audience were all seated and awaiting his presence. I suppose that's show business!

*

Around the time of the late 70s, 5 Queen Street invited a new celebrity figure within its doors. Only a few years earlier he was a relative unknown to the general public. But he would soon become famous nationwide.

His name was *Quentin Crisp.*

I had already watched the controversial, but marvellously entertaining television film that had been broadcast detailing his colourful life called *"The Naked Civil Servant"*, that featured an award-winning performance by *John Hurt* in the role of Crisp, and is rightly regarded today as a television classic.

And now, wouldn't you know it, here was the man himself in full view as he sauntered into reception.

His hair colour was faintly reminiscent to my late grandmother's favourite blue rinse, and I think his fingernails were painted a bright colour to match as well. And to top it, some rouge on his cheeks, as well as a bit of mascara to finish it and complete the overall effect. There was certainly no mistaking him, he was certainly one of a kind, and made an immediate impression from his very first appearance.

Bob was on hand when Mr Crisp nimbly climbed the stairs towards the canteen. Not quite with hand on hip, but making sure that his unique presence was there for all to see.

Bob was momentarily speechless, as he looked upon him as if an alien from another planet had landed, and he was in a state of shock as to this visitor's very camp and aesthetic appearance. Maybe the gentleman's obvious rouged cheeks and blue rinsed hair might have had something to do with it?

"Who the f**k is that?" he asked.

"That's *Quentin Crisp*, Bob. Did you not see that TV film recently with *John Hurt* playing his part?"

"No I f*****g didn't!" he exclaimed. "Well, if he's not a f*****g queer, I'm a f*****g Russian cosmonaut!" Bob was now stating the fairly obvious.

"Well, there's no answer to that one," I replied.

"I hate poofs!" Bob further added. Then looking furtively around him, he stared intensely back at me and said, "And there's quite a few working in here that I'm no too sure about as well…"

*

A few years later, the main reception area was agog with excitement, as word soon spread that the British King of Rock and Roll was coming in for an interview. Yes, it could only be the one and only *Sir Cliff Richard*.

Of course, during that time he was just good old plain Cliff, but the mere mention of his name (for some totally bizarre reason) sent a number of the female staff to go all fluffy, fluttery and funny!!

It was a very odd sight and amusing to watch.

Chief amongst them was a young, attractive blonde lady who would soon go on to wider fame as the nation's favourite weather girl – *Carol Kirkwood*. I must confess that I had quite a crush on her during her brief time in Edinburgh. I wonder if she ever knew that. Although I had absolutely no idea as to how famous (and greatly desired) she would become a few years down the line. She was working for a brief time in the religious department, and if memory serves me correct, she was always a lovely girl, forever smiling, with a happy-go-lucky spring in her step! Something that came in mighty handy, when she tripped the light fantastic on the dance-floor, during saturday night's *Strictly Come Dancing*. She has certainly found a large and appreciative audience, far removed from the narrow confines of 5 Queen Street. I wonder if she ever thinks back to those far-off days, while she is studying cloud formations and sudden outbursts of hailstones and thunderous rain. Well, for a brief moment in time – she certainly raised my temperature!!

Although on that day of Sir Cliff's visit, even she was outshone from a little lady called Eileen Philips.

Eileen (also affectionately known as "little miss dynamite") occasionally worked part time on the switchboard, and would later become part of the reception team a few years later.

It was the very same Eileen who coyly admitted that not only did she enjoy playing "footsie under the table", but also liked her morning cup of tea with the tea bag (and I quote) dipped in and out! Eileen was a lovely woman with genuine warmth and a cheeky sense of humour that endeared her to all.

It was also fairly safe to say that Eileen was totally obsessed with Cliff. She used to regale us with stories of the various concerts and shows that she travelled miles and miles all over the country, in order to see him sing!!

She even used to pay to watch him play tennis?? Yes tennis, not singing, or guitar strumming, just battering a ball back and forth over a fence! Well I suppose it takes all sorts.

She turned up at reception (complete with baby buggy) waiting the great man's deeply tanned appearance, alongside about a dozen others, all anxious to see if he really measured up to his nickname of the "Peter Pan of Pop".

On that day he was doing a whistle-stop tour of the capital's radio stations, promoting a new single, when his records were still being played over the airwaves. Something that I am led to believe doesn't happen very much these days.

So Cliff eventually turned up, all smiles, deeply tanned, wearing shaded glasses and looking trim, no doubt due to all that tennis playing. However, his manager was anything but sunny.

He glowered at everyone, not looking too happy about something or other. In fact he would quite easily have given the likes of *Lee Van Cleef* an object lesson in the art of how to produce a menacing glower!

Cliff was ushered into the remote radio studio to do his interview, as the reception crowd grew larger, awaiting his return.

About twenty minutes later he emerged from the studio, all smiles again, but his manager still looked very gloomy, with nary a hint of a smile or pleasantry upon his stern features. He certainly wasn't too pleased about the impromptu photo session that occurred around the front desk, with Eileen figuring prominently, wishing that she could push the singer into the back of a taxi, and take him all the way home! No doubt much to the annoyance of her husband Tam.

With photos taken, autographs signed and smiles exchanged, Cliff soon headed for the exit, as his manager still continued to look for the entire world, as if he had just won the lottery, yet had forgotten where he had put his ticket.

*

Another massive star (although of slightly smaller physical stature) would one day walk through the doors of BBC Edinburgh. He was one of the most popular stars of Hollywood's golden era – the legendary *Mickey Rooney*.

I believe he was visiting Scotland on a two-fold mission: to read extracts from his biography during a studio recording, and perhaps more importantly for him, he was going through to Glasgow to trace his family history. For those unfamiliar with his background, his real name was *Joe Yule Jnr* and his father was a Glaswegian, by the name of, well, *Joe Yule Snr*.

He arrived to do his stint in the studio, and I remember asking the producer at the time what he was like. He hesitated for a moment and then replied, "Well, he's a bit strange?" and that was all he said.

That didn't sound too promising. Although you tend to forget that this once massive movie child star who worked alongside such eminent figures as *Judy Garland, Spencer Tracy, Bob Hope,* and was also once married to *Ava Gardner*, was getting that wee bit older.

But alongside that, he was perceived as a bit cantankerous, tetchy and slightly moody.

Well, following the conclusion of the recording, he came down to reception, to wait upon his taxi. I then decided to have a few words with the man. But from what I could figure out he seemed very disorientated, very uncomfortable, and didn't even look me straight in the eye, or the face, as he continued to glance around, and mumble away to himself.

Maybe he had just drunk too much caffeine that morning, but whatever the reason, he seemed a bit disturbed by something.

I then tried to engage him in some form of straightforward conversation regarding his past, as well as some of the great stars he had worked with in Hollywood.

Under the circumstances, I may just as well have addressed my conversation towards one of the reception chairs, or his crumpled hat that he was painfully squeezing tightly with his hands.

I didn't get any form of sensible reply from him, or maybe he was just anxious to quickly leave to further his journey. But what I do remember from our very brief "conversation" was that he was determined to grab a bag of "some goddam' fish and chips!!" as he simply put it.

I said my goodbyes to him (I don't think he even returned the greeting) as he got into his taxi and drove off. No doubt in search of the nearest chip shop!

*

A near catastrophe almost awaited another famous star when visiting the building.

Adam Faith, singer, actor, pop entrepreneur, and star of the popular 70s show *"Budgie"*, was being interviewed about a play he was acting in at the Kings Theatre. A taxi had been ordered to collect him near 5pm to take him back to the theatre where he had a performance that very same night.

The interview was running a bit late and the taxi was patiently sitting outside the door. He then emerged, aware that the clock was ticking and started to run down the stairs.

However in his haste, his foot caught one of the large mail sacks that was lying by the front door, and this nearly hurtled him head first through the panes of the front glass doors!!

Luckily within a split second, he managed to avoid this potential accident and got out of the building relatively unscathed. I'm sure the newspaper headlines would have had a field day if a serious and damaging incident had occurred.

I can see it now: *"Famous British Actor & Pop Star Thrown Headway Through BBC Edinburgh Glass Doors Due To A Protrusive Mail Sack!!"*

*

One of the most memorable and intriguing occasions when a famous celebrity turned up at BBC Edinburgh happened around the mid-1980s.

The star in question was one of the most popular and distinguished British film actors whose work encompassed everything from romantic comedies at Pinewood studios, to austere and complex dramas, that were often European produced. His name was *Sir Dirk Bogarde.*

Little did he realise that his brief visit to 5 Queen Street would offer him up the rare and unusual experience of recreating one of his finest film performances amidst the ordinary and modest surroundings of a Scottish radio studio.

I must confess that unfortunately I wasn't around at that time (I think I must have been on holiday?) when he arrived to discuss and read extracts from one of his published memoirs. However, I later learnt of the amusing events during my return to work.

When Sir Dirk first arrived and was getting himself all prepared for his interview, he was informed (by Stan at reception, no less) that an old friend, a very dignified lady (who apparently during his younger days, he had been well acquainted with) had turned up unexpected and was now looking forward to meeting up with him again.

When Stan told him who she was, Sir Dirk then burst out with the bold statement – "Oh my god! She was my first f**k!!"

Although I was disappointed at not having the chance to meet him (maybe just as well as it later turned out!) I also missed out on a fairly amusing incident. It appeared that his interest on the day was greatly aroused when he spotted a young, boyish audio engineer who would be assisting in the studio for the duration of the interview. By all accounts, Sir Dirk became increasingly disturbed and then entranced and even enchanted, as he watched with growing curiosity as to the movements around the sound desk of this "darling boy" (as he put it) and just how was he going to get to know him better.

As to the exact identity of the "young audio boy" in question, it turned out to be my young friend Richard, now an integral part of the audio unit.

However, his audio colleagues assisting him on this particular recording soon found enormous amusement as to how one of their own could so easily, and with so little effort, heat up the ardour of a famous movie star!

So the scene was set for Sir Dirk to recreate his acclaimed performance in the 1971 film *Death in Venice*, in which he was cast as a doomed and haunted classical composer who becomes obsessed and transfixed by the lingering image of sheer physical male beauty!

Here he was again, in a faintly similar situation, as he battled his natural urges at the soulful sight of this young man who had captured his heart – not forgetting much deep stirring in his loins!

However, Venice would not provide the backdrop for this tragic unconsummated homoerotic romance, but rather the more technical surroundings of a radio studio, complete with a clumsy assortment of sound dials, voice faders, tape reels, microphones and a multitude of jack-plugs!!

All that was missing was the melancholic and emotional strains of *Mahler's 5th Symphony* to add that extra bit of passionate atmosphere to the scene, as the young engineer managed to nimbly keep his distance from the yearnings and desires of this former Rank studios pin-up idol.

At the finish of his interview, Sir Dirk left the building professionally satisfied – if unfortunately for him on the day, not physically. Sadly, he then retreated back to his comfortable farmhouse, somewhere in the South of France.

Friends and colleagues would continually rib young Richard over the course of many years, as to just how he missed out on a rare golden opportunity.

He often laughed at the memory, but concluded that he didn't quite fancy being either his "Servant" or "Victim", despite the allure of potentially living in more luxurious surroundings.

*

On a cheerier note, we often had regular visits from one half of the "Two Fat Ladies" – *Clarissa Dickson Wright*. I believed that she lived in Edinburgh, and in fact owned a cook shop down by the Grassmarket.

She was always a cheery and welcoming soul, who would pop in to do an interview, usually within the remote studio, and once that was finished, she would make a point in having a lively chat with the reception staff. She always came across as a friendly and highly intelligent woman, who was always game for a good blether, and she was always a pleasure to see.

*

Another friendly woman who popped into 5 Queen Street one day was none other than *Eastenders* actress *June Brown* (a.k.a. *Dot Cotton*).

She planted herself down on the lounge seats at reception, while awaiting her call to be interviewed, and then calmly lit up one of her cigarettes (just like her popular screen character) and chatted amiably and humorously with everyone who was there. A fine actress, a delightful lady, and a bit of a character was *June Brown*.

*

One bright morning I walked into 5 Queen Street to start work as usual. I first stopped off at reception to say hi and good morning as normal. However, I was aware of an unusual presence sitting in one of the seats behind me.

I turned around and looked down to see a wizened faced woman scowling back at me, and giving anybody else within her vicinity, the evil eye! *Oh dear*, I thought to myself. She looked like one very unhappy lady and someone who was giving off a definite vibe that she didn't want to be there.

Yet there was something about her that looked faintly familiar. I had seen her somewhere before – but where? Then the penny finally dropped. Here was the woman once described by *Orson Welles* no less, as the "the most exciting woman in the world!" It was *Eartha Kitt*. Although on that particular morning, she looked anything but exciting, exhausted perhaps, but far from what you would describe as exciting.

I remember my late grandfather recoiling in almost horror at the sheer mention of her name. "She's bloody awful!" was one of his more gentle and tempered descriptions. Quickly followed by the likes of, "You would have to pay *me* to go and see her!"

Anyway, for those not too sure who she was, in her day she was a highly successful singer, dancer, and actress, and even for a time a prominent civil rights activist. But that morning, in 5 Queen Street, she was playing the part of a right old misery guts!!

She had on her head a brightly coloured headscarf, but was looking like someone who had just been roughly dragged out of her bed at an ungodly hour, and parked down on a seat beside reception.

Maybe this "old fashioned girl" had just been dumped by her "old fashioned millionaire", and was none too happy about it.

I tell you, if looks could kill, she would have annihilated everyone that morning that crossed her path.

Someone whispered in my ear, "She's got a face that would curdle milk!" I couldn't argue with that assessment. In fact she most closely resembled the Gorgon, just as she was about to turn any unsuspecting victim into cold hard stone!!

After a while, she was taken through to the remote studio to do her link-up interview. Once that was over, she left the building, not on a broomstick, but in the back of a black taxicab, uttering not a word as she departed.

*

One day whilst working in the print room I received a phone call from my friend Martin, who was one of the audio engineers. "Hi Lawrence, pop up to Studio 2 if you get the chance, there's an old Hollywood actor here." My mind immediately went into overdrive with excitement as to whom he might be referring to.

"Who is it?" I asked.

Martin then replied, "It's an old geezer called *Alexander Knox.*"

Not too many people may recognise the name straight away but *Alexander Knox* was one of those familiar faces that crops up in supporting roles in a lot of movies from the forties through to the seventies. I knew exactly who he was, but I immediately thought to myself, *I thought he was long dead?* And then on the back of that, I also thought, *What is he doing here??*

Anyhow, I said to Martin, I would be right up, and within a few minutes I popped into the studio to see this Hollywood actor.

"Where is he?" I asked Martin at first.

"That's him over there." Martin pointed to an elderly gentleman wearing a long scruffy coat, as well as what looked like a hand-knitted tartan bonnet on his head.

Martin introduced me to the actor who turned out to be very polite, friendly and gracious.

Alexander Knox was a Canadian-born stage and screen

actor (as well as an accomplished writer) who had arrived in Hollywood around the early forties, and had gone on to make a number of well-regarded films. In fact he would even win an Oscar nomination as Best Actor in 1944 for his portrayal of the American President *Woodrow Wilson* in the 20th Century Fox film *Wilson*. During his long career he had worked alongside legendary movie stars such as *Edward G Robinson, Humphrey Bogart, Robert Mitchum, Kirk Douglas, Randolph Scott,* and *Charlton Heston*, but now here he was in a small radio studio in Edinburgh.

I discovered that he was living down in the Borders around Berwick and had travelled up to Edinburgh with some rare recordings of a relative that he had asked our operations manager if they could be transferred onto tape for posterity.

I sat alongside him and began to chat about his career and the many films he had worked on. I felt he was slightly amazed at first at how someone so young (I was, particularly at that time) would know so much about him, as well as the many films and actors that he had starred alongside.

It began to dawn on me during our conversation (I think I generously treated him to a cup of BBC tea) that his acting career had come to a halt in America when he fell foul of the *House of Un-American Activities Committee.*

This organisation had been established during the late 1940s to root out political subversives and potential Communist sympathisers within the Hollywood community.

In fact one of its most ardent supporters and activists, was none other than *John Wayne*. Mr Knox was very disparaging about "the Duke" during our talk, as well as the then current US President *Ronald Reagan*, who he felt was largely responsible for him being exiled from Hollywood.

Mr Knox would arrive in the UK and further his career by appearing in a number of popular British films that included the likes of *"Reach For The Sky"* and *"The Night My Number*

Came Up", as well as the acclaimed BBC drama series *"Tinker, Tailor, Soldier, Spy"*.

I found him a fascinating and most engaging character that despite his age (he must have been heading towards eighty) had tremendous recollection about a number of the films he was involved with and the actors he had worked with.

After his studio time had completed he shook my hand and made his farewells as he departed for his train that would take him back to Berwick upon Tweed.

Later, I spoke with Martin about the conversation I had just had with the elderly actor, and felt that this would be a terrific opportunity to invite him back at a later date to do a proper taped interview, in which he could look back over his long career.

Martin felt it would be a good idea, and so I managed to gain Mr Knox's address and wrote to him to see how he felt about it. Not long after, he kindly wrote back, and was very agreeable to return. However, he explained that he was (even at his age) a pretty busy man and would try to fit an interview within his schedule.

Unfortunately, the interview never happened. Looking back, I think I approached a couple of producers as to doing the interview, but somehow it fell through. A rare missed opportunity.

I felt here was someone, living virtually on our very doorsteps, that possessed a vast fund of stories and anecdotes that would have been pure radio gold. Not just about working in Hollywood and the British film industry, but a man who had endured and experienced that recent historical era when fear, suspicion and mistrust had ruined so many artistic lives due to a scandalous political witch-hunt.

*

During the time of the Edinburgh Film Festival, 5 Queen Street played host to two well renowned Hollywood film directors who had practiced their trade during its golden era: *Samuel Fuller* and *Andre de Toth*.

Both names may be a trifle unfamiliar to modern film audiences, but they both had acquired cult status amongst serious film aficionados and now they were in Edinburgh (on different separate occasions) as the film festival was celebrating their back catalogues with major retrospectives.

Sam Fuller was due to give a talk in Studio 1 after being introduced to his audience by *Kirsty Wark*. Fuller had made such films as *Pick Up On South Street, House Of Bamboo, Hell And High Water,* the western *Run Of The Arrow,* and the gritty war film *The Big Red One* with *Lee Marvin* and was one of the most praised writers and directors in Hollywood during the 1950s.

The studio lounge was pretty well packed prior to his appearance, as they eagerly awaited the arrival of the great man.

Then he appeared, somewhat small in stature, grizzled of features, with almost white wiry hair, whilst smoking a very large cigar (one that would give *Lord Michael Grade* some competition), as he wandered around the lounge area just prior to the recording.

Mac, who was fairly unimpressed with some of those "stars & celebrities" who stepped through the front doors, looked at the great director with some scepticism and suspicion.

"Who the f**k is that scruffy old git over there puffing on the cigar?" Mac inquired.

"That's *Sam Fuller,* legendary Hollywood writer and director," I replied with a hint of hushed awe in my voice.

Mac then said with very little awe in his voice, "What a scruffy old bastard. He looks like he's just wandered in off the street!"

Looking back, he did appear to be a bit wandered and unconnected with the occasion, even if he had just wandered in off the street, from his chauffeur-driven car.

When his talk started (it was being filmed on camera for a Film Festival special) he began to discuss an un-filmed screenplay that he was hoping to get before the cameras at some future date.

Unfortunately, maybe he was just having a bit of an off day in the studio, as he began to ramble, and ramble and ramble, and ramble. The audience were now beginning to get a little restless as they looked at their watches, hoping that the talk would soon end, as no doubt the thought of a few beers in the pub began to dominate their thought processes. The talk finally came to an end, and then after mumbling a faint goodbye, Mr Fuller soon left the building, gone in a puff of smoke that was still very much emanating from his very large cigar.

*

Andre de Toth turned up in Edinburgh a few years later, and like *Sam Fuller*, was probably close to eighty when he walked through the front doors to participate in a radio interview. *Andre de Toth* was a Hungarian-born filmmaker who settled in Hollywood, turning out a number of popular westerns with the likes of *Randolph Scott* and *Joel McCrea*. He also was a master second unit director who worked on the likes of *Lawrence Of Arabia* and *Superman*. However, perhaps his greatest and most successful Hollywood film was the 1953 horror classic *House Of Wax*, with *Vincent Price*. What made this particularly significant was the fact that it was one of the first major films shot in 3D, and that the director (*Andre De Toth*) only had one eye!

It does seem strange that a number of famous Hollywood directors from that era, such as *John Ford* and *Raoul Walsh* wore eyepatches, giving them that faintly maverick quality to their iconic image. I suppose you could also add the name of *Andre de Toth* alongside them.

I volunteered to look after him on the day and accompany

him in the studio. He duly arrived wearing his signature eyepatch, alongside a young woman who, I assume was his assistant. What immediately struck me was the fact that she too was wearing an eyepatch – but one ornately designed and studded with sparkling glass (or maybe it was diamonds?). I then introduced myself and took them both into the remote studio to set up their interview. I must confess that I liked *Mr De Toth* straight away.

He was an engaging, raffish and colourful character with a good sense of humour, and gave off the impression that he didn't take himself all that seriously. After his interview was completed we chatted away as he told me of his time in Hollywood and some of the films he had worked on.

He and his assistant thanked me for my help and then said their goodbyes as they climbed into their taxi to take them back to their hotel.

*

Another famous actor would make a welcome appearance at 5 Queen Street. He was a much-loved gentleman by the name of *John Le Mesurier.*

The star of *"Dad's Army"* and countless films and television shows, had been hired to take a prominent part in a radio play that was being recorded in Studio. I remember that he came across just as you would imagine.

He was a very polite, modest, mild mannered and quietly spoken gent who seemed to enjoy the opportunity in visiting Edinburgh, and lending his distinctive voice to this drama production.

During a break from recording, Bob decided he was going to say hello and have a bit of a chat with him. And then Bob related to me later how the conversation progressed:

Mr Le Mesurier was relaxing with a cup of tea, on one of the large red leather sofas that were situated in the lounge, just outside the studio.

Bob went over to him to say hello, when he noticed that the actor was looking somewhat morose and a little down in the mouth. Bob told me that he looked very unhappy, as if he had just been told some very painful and tragic news.

"How are you Mr Le Mesurier? You seem a bit upset. Is everything alright with you?" Bob asked.

Le Mesurier faintly smiled and seemed appreciative at Bob's friendly enquiry. "Oh thank you so very much. You are most kind. I'm alright, but I have just received some absolutely awful news."

Bob could see straightaway that the gentleman actor was upset about something and offered a sympathetic ear. "What's wrong, Mr Le Mesurier? Is there anything I can do to help you?" Bob further enquired, as he was genuinely worried about him.

"I have just received a call from my agent. Oh it's awful, terrible, I simply don't know what to do." The Dad's Army star was almost ashen-faced at being told something that had obviously upset him, and caused a slight trembling in his demeanour.

"Oh dear, oh dear, it's the worst possible news," he continued. By this time Bob was ready to call for help, as he was concerned the veteran actor was about to pass out and collapse on the floor.

"Do you know that I have to go to Paris next week?" He then glanced over towards Bob whilst saying this with a look of sheer abject terror on his face. "To make another film... with *Peter Sellers!*"

He then solemnly shook his head, drank the remainder of his tea, and slowly walked back into the studio, as if he were walking towards the electric chair.

Bob and I both mulled over his conversation with the actor, and both came to the obvious conclusion that since Mr Le Mesurier had worked on a number of films with *Peter*

Sellers before, the experience had left him both emotionally and professionally scarred.

This was an experience that he had no great desire to repeat. Unfortunately, he could not escape fate, and in a few days' time, he would be boarding a plane for the French capital. What horrors awaited him, one could only imagine…

*

I too encountered another famous figure as he was sitting relaxed in the lounge just outside Studio 1. This was during the Television Festival sometime in the 1980s, and as I walked towards the lounge, I soon became aware of a thick fog of smoke coming from the area.

I recall feeling like one of Custer's 7th Cavalry must have felt as they were journeying through the Black Hills of Dakota, for there were smoke signals everywhere! Then I recognised the guilty party immediately.

In fact the sight of his loud, colourful, bright braces gave him away.

It was *Michael Grade* (before he became *Sir Michael Grade*) who I think at the time was running Channel 4. Although on that day, he looked like a combination of *Gordon Gekko* and *Del Boy!*

He sat there on one of the long red couches, puffing away on the biggest cigar I had ever seen in my life and surveying the building as if he owned the place. Which I suppose you could say that a few years down the line, that's more or less, what would happen.

*

One morning, two famous ladies well known for their appearances both on stage and screen walked into the reception, as they had been invited in for an interview.

They turned out to be *Liz Fraser* and *Dora Bryan*. Both actresses had enjoyed considerable success in film (appearing in a few of the early Carry On series, as well as a number of classic TV comedies) and were now touring the country in a stage play that had recently set up camp at the Kings Theatre. It was a great privilege to see them both within the building, but unfortunately, on this particular day – they didn't arrive alone.

For accompanying them were two small, yappy, snappy dogs that yelped and barked their way indoors, as they trotted into the main reception area. You may be thinking to yourself, what was so wrong with that?

Well, the main thing was, no dogs were allowed within the building. It was a ruling of sorts, and I suppose ostensibly in case the loud barking upset or interfered with recordings that were taking place. So on this occasion, it didn't take long for Miss Wilson to become acutely aware of the situation, as she briskly appeared at reception to deal with it. Normally she would have had the dogs immediately removed from the premises, but much pleading from the two actresses (who stated that the interview was off unless they could keep the dogs alongside them) made Miss Wilson reluctantly relent on this one occasion. So following the interview, Ms Fraser and Ms Bryan said their goodbyes and with the still-yelping dogs on their leashes, they walked out the building to their awaiting taxi.

Miss Wilson did look a bit flustered at this alteration and bending of the rules, but she would have been even more flustered if she ever became aware that Bob used to regularly sneak his dog Hannibal into the building through one of the basement windows!

*

One of the most personally enjoyable encounters I had with a famous television personality was the two separate occasions I met and conversed with the then BBC film guru – *Barry Norman.*

For those a little unfamiliar to who *Barry Norman* is, well for over three decades, he was the BBC's main film critic and reviewer, who each week fronted the film programme, reviewing the new releases, and on the odd occasion interviewing various famous stars and directors. Not forgetting that he was also an extremely talented writer of some wit and intelligence.

Long before the likes of *Jonathan Ross, Mark Kermode* settled into the chair (both at least gave the impression that they possessed a firm grasp of film culture and history, unlike one or two others, who equally gave the impression that because they had watched the odd "chick-flick" with a bag of popcorn – that would make them instant "movie experts") *Barry Norman* was "The Man". The main man in fact, when it came to discussing all things relating to movies and the cinema.

He had been presenting the show since the early seventies, and during his time at the BBC, he was deemed famous enough to make a guest appearance on one of the *Morecambe & Wise* Christmas specials, as well as to be cleverly taken off by impersonator *Rory Bremner*.

Remember the off the cuff phrase – "And why not…" It was originally attributed to *Barry Norman*, but in fact it was *Rory Bremner* who coined the phrase, and it sort of stuck with him for all time.

It was sometime in the mid-80s that I received word that he was popping into 5 Queen Street to do an interview. I automatically volunteered to look after him for the duration and to make sure that his brief visit to our humble station would be a pleasant one.

He duly arrived, introduced himself at reception, and then sat down at the couch until his interview was due to take place.

I immediately struck up a conversation with him, and found him a fascinating storyteller, very pleasant and engaging as he told me of some of the various stars he had encountered during his time as a reviewer and a journalist.

I was particularly enthralled when he told me in great detail about the time he met *John Wayne*. He had gone over to the USA to meet the big man during the press launch of *"True Grit"*. I got the impression that Barry wasn't entirely enamoured of Wayne the man, although he admired him as a screen star.

During the press junket, Wayne had been downing a few large whiskies that were keeping him well oiled as he fenced off various questions from all comers.

Barry then started to question and probe him about his political leanings. Not a very wise move perhaps, but he was attempting to elicit some form of response from him nonetheless. Big Duke was now beginning to get somewhat irked at this "goddamm limey's" line of questioning.

He got up and then began to lurch towards Barry, no doubt with the intention of taking a swing at him! Luckily, some of Wayne's entourage stepped into the breach and managed to calm him down before any real damage was done.

I think they also eased the potential punch-up by giving him another large glass of booze, which seemed to do the trick.

When I asked Barry what he really was like after meeting and talking with him, he answered without hesitation, "He was an absolute idiot!" I think he was mainly referring to the time during the height of the Vietnam War, when Duke's solution to ending hostilities in South East Asia involved threatening to bomb Moscow!

We chatted agreeably both before, and after his interview, and he also told me how much he had enjoyed doing his series on the *"Hollywood Greats"*.

He told me that of all the stars he profiled, *Errol Flynn* was the one that most fascinated him, as well as the one individual he wished he had met in real life.

During the course of his Hollywood Greats series he also

enjoyed the experience of meeting *Steve McQueen's* first wife *Neile Adams*, explaining to me that he found her a lovely woman, warm, humorous and friendly. This greatly helped with his research, as during the course of his interviews, she furnished him with a fund of fascinating and interesting stories to tell him of her late ex-husband.

It was soon time for *Barry Norman* to leave and we shook hands and said our goodbyes, as he walked towards his taxi that was waiting to take him to his next destination.

But this would not be the last time that our paths would cross as he would reappear in Edinburgh about seven years later.

Barry Norman once again appeared at 5 Queen Street around 1992, this time accompanied by an assistant PR, and he was in Edinburgh to publicise his latest book, as well as make a personal appearance at the Book Festival.

The book in question was entitled: *100 Best Films of the Century* in which he selected a top 100 films that he personally felt represented the highest achievements in the art of the cinema.

Of course this was only his opinion, yet when browsing through the book I found myself generally agreeing with the majority of his assessment.

I managed to have a few words with him before he was due to do his interview, and informed him that I would be seeing him later at his talk at the Book Festival.

This would give him the opportunity to discuss his film selection, no doubt raising the subject with the audience as to why certain films were missing.

During his stay at the BBC he was now going to be interviewed by one of the Arts programmes most prominent presenters. This was a man who had achieved success as a singer in the pop charts, as well as someone renowned (at least I think that's what he was described as?) for having his finger on the pulse of the Scottish arts scene – *Mr Pat Kane*.

I had been given permission by the programme's producer to sit in the recording booth to watch and listen to the interview and was looking forward to *Barry Norman* discuss at length about the films he had profiled in his new book.

Yet the interview didn't get off to a sparkling start as young Mr Kane started to pontificate about what he felt constituted a good film. This brought about a look of confusion and bewilderment upon the face of *Barry Norman*, who must have been wondering as to what direction the interview was heading.

The author then began to discuss at length *John Ford's* classic western *The Searchers*.

Despite his earlier embarrassing run-in with *John Wayne* a few years back, *Barry Norman* was of the opinion that Big Duke gave his greatest performance in the film, as well as the fact that he regarded it as possibly the best western ever made.

This prompted young *Pat Kane* to utter the following words that I can still recall all these years later: "I don't like westerns. Because of the way they portrayed the Native Americans."

I just shook my head at the awful pretentious piffle now coming out of his mouth, and I'm sure that *Barry Norman* was of a similar mind.

I don't think the veteran film critic was prepared for the pseudo-intellectual hogwash that was being presented to him in the shape of an interview.

For my money, there is one thing to discuss and debate the artistic and entertainment credentials of a film in detail, but another when you attempt to enforce your own viewpoints during the course of an interview.

For someone who had been brought up on a steady diet of westerns on both the cinema screen and the television (many starring *Wayne* and directed by *John Ford*) Mr Kane's earlier statement was a little bit jarring. After all, the interview was not intended as a revisionist treatise on 19th-century American history. Maybe he had got his guests mixed up?

Barry Norman did look slightly baffled at Mr Kane's questioning technique, although I suppose at the end of the day, they were never going to entirely agree on everything.

I sat there thinking to myself that I could have done a far superior job than the politically active, west coast musician with the university degree had done.

At least my film knowledge and movie-going background would have been on a fairly similar wavelength to *Barry Norman*. At least that's what I thought at the time, and I'm sticking to my guns!

I went along to see *Barry Norman* again later that evening at the Book Festival event (the place was packed out with no spare seats visible) and enjoyed his talk as well as the good-humoured way he took the various questions thrown at him from the audience. No doubt he was glad that the thorny subject of "Native Americans" failed to crop up during his time there.

*

One day whilst enjoying my lunch in the canteen, I was introduced to an actor who was performing in a radio drama production that week. The gentleman in question was called *Laurence Payne*. Now his name may not be overly familiar to many these days, but for me and for those of my generation, he was best known as the TV detective *Sexton Blake*, a part he played with distinction during the 1960s. He also enjoyed a thriving career on stage and screen (working with *Laurence Olivier*, no less), with numerous films and TV work to his credit.

Next time you watch *Ben Hur*, watch out for *Laurence Payne* playing the role of Joseph at the beginning of the great epic.

He also appeared in a *Hammer* classic called *Vampire Circus*, a screen version of the *Edgar Allen Poe* story *The Tell Tale Heart*, and a number of TV productions including an episode of *The Saint* with *Roger Moore*.

Laurence Payne was indeed a lovely charming man, who I greatly enjoyed chatting with that week, as he reminisced about his career and the many parts he had played. I later found out that he was an accomplished author as well, with several books to his credit.

When one of my colleagues asked, "Who was that old guy you were chatting with in the canteen?" I told them it was a famous actor of stage and screen, as well as describing some of the roles he had played.

Unfortunately I was met with a blank mystifying look and a reply of, "Never heard of him?"

One fascinating and unknown fact concerning *Laurence Payne* was that he participated in one of the most famous screen tests in film history.

A screen test that has over the decades intrigued many film scholars, yet has rarely – if ever – been seen.

This was back in the early 1960s, when director *David Lean* and producer *Sam Spiegel* were casting around for their upcoming epic – *Lawrence of Arabia*.

The filmmakers were looking for the ideal man for the leading role, so they approached a young, talented English actor by the name of *Albert Finney*.

An elaborate and expensive screen test soon was set-up and filmed in a studio in London, with the young *Finney* taking on the role of *TE Lawrence*. One scene had the young actor sitting alongside *Laurence Payne* (dressed in Arab robes) as they shared a pivotal scene in the interior of a desert tent.

The film of course went on to be eventually filmed in 1962, among the deserts of Jordan, Morocco, and Spain. Featuring another young actor by the name of *Peter O'Toole* in the starring role.

History relates that neither *Mr Finney*, nor *Mr Payne* figured anywhere in the finished production – just a small interesting footnote in movie lore.

*

In 1992 actor, writer, comedian, and popular world traveller *Michael Palin* was due in Edinburgh to publicise his new film that was being screened at the old Odeon cinema. Usually the arts department would have sent one of their "young gun experts" to review the film, as well as complete an interview for a later broadcast. However, on that day (for whatever reason) no one was available, and so I was asked if I could step into the breach.

There was no need to ask me twice, as I headed up to the cinema to watch the press screening of the film and later to talk to the man himself. After the film (which was called *American Friends*, and based on the diaries of *Michael Palin's* great-grandfather) I was ushered into the manager's office to meet the star.

For the next hour we sat and chatted amiably as *Michael Palin* discussed the film, his great-grandfather's story, as well as other aspects of his career.

The whole experience was greatly enjoyable, as we sat, talked, drank tea and munched our way through some chocolate biscuits provided by the cinema manager's assistant.

So it's safe to say that *Michael Palin* was another famous celebrity who I found in the flesh and in person to be friendly, unaffected, intelligently engrossing and amusing company.

*

One great star that I was due to meet when he was visiting Edinburgh in 1991 was none other than *Sir Michael Caine*.

I had been a fan ever since I first saw him on screen way

back in 1964 battling Zulus in that classic film. So the opportunity to meet him, as well as sit in the studio while he was being interviewed, was going to be an experience to savour.

One day the programme's producer asked me if I could collate some background research, so that the interviewer (the late *Neville Garden*) would have sufficient material to help him with his interview. This I did without hesitation, and then eagerly awaited the London-born film star's arrival. Then disaster struck! Well, disaster for me anyway. I was struck down with a nasty flu virus!!

Talk about bloody bad luck! So instead of spending quality time with one of the world's most famous movie stars – I was stuck in bed, sweating, coughing and sneezing and feeling bloody miserable.

However, after the great man had done his interview, departed the building and was long gone to his next film location, I returned to work, feeling worse than usual.

One bright spot though, throughout my misery, was that I was later given a signed copy of *Sir Michael Caine's* biography. I suppose it was a small, if appreciative compensation for missing out on meeting the man himself.

*

Jessye Norman is generally renowned as one of the world's greatest opera singers. So it wouldn't be beyond the realms of probability that she would turn up at the front doors of 5 Queen Street, during the Edinburgh Festival. Indeed, the front doors would play a large part in her grand entrance to the building as for several seconds she found it extremely difficult to get through them!

At that time Queen Street had large glass doors that could prove to be just a little problematic and awkward in negotiating.

This was a common occurrence, particularly when some

individuals might be under the influence of drink (which as you can imagine happened on several occasions) and if the person attempting to negotiate the glass doors was of, well let's say, large stature. *Jessye Norman* certainly (at least at that time) was a lady of considerable large stature. So it took a little time for her, and her extravagantly proportioned physique, to eventually master the intricacies of the door and then finally step into the awaiting reception area.

A little later she was due to appear in one of the studios above reception, and so she wandered through the corridor towards the lift, hoping that this would take her to her destination.

Unfortunately, to her horror, she discovered that what awaited her was not a normal lift for human passengers, but the goods lift that was mainly used for transporting boxes of frozen fish, slabs of meat, tins of assorted foods and bulky technical equipment. She wasn't best amused and made, if not exactly a song and dance about it, at least an aggrieved aria of dissatisfaction at the lack of a proper lift. Now she would have to climb the stairs one slow step at a time, towards the awaiting studio.

*

Rudolf Nureyev, now there is a name that dances on the tongue… so to speak.

He was undoubtedly the most famous and talented classical dancer of his day (a man who was probably responsible for making ballet more popular amongst the mainstream audiences of the 1960s and 1970s), and he would arrive in Edinburgh to participate in a televised interview.

I think this special event coincided with the Edinburgh International Arts Festival, in which artists from all over the globe would congregate and perform to rapturous applause amongst cultured audiences.

However, the great man who had performed all over the

world from London to Paris, and from New York to Moscow, would get his eyes well and truly opened when he appeared at 5 Queen Street.

Nureyev emerged from his chauffeur-driven limousine and introduced himself to Mac (who often had a tendency to be on duty whenever someone of international stature and world fame would came a calling) who then welcomed him into BBC Edinburgh.

Unfortunately, Mr Nureyev was about to be given a very rude awakening.

He stated that he had been asked to do the interview (which would take place in the small television studio), but at first, after a long journey, he now wished to freshen up with a hot shower, and a change of clothing.

So he naturally assumed he would be escorted to the "Star Dressing Room".

Yes, you heard me correctly – the "Star Dressing Room". Knowing what BBC Edinburgh was like back in the 1970s, the very notion of a "Star Dressing Room" (just love that phrase) is enough to make you end yourself in tears of laughter.

For the reason is – we didn't have a "Star Dressing Room". In fact, until a few later years down the line, I don't think we had anything that closely resembled that description.

Mr Nureyev was indeed in for a shock.

"But I must have a dressing room!" he implored. "I cannot go in front of cameras unless I have washed, freshened up and changed my clothing." Mac at this point wasn't entirely sure how he was going to placate this male prima donna with the dancing feet.

His brain was racing to see if he could come up with a solution to the problem.

"I am so sorry Mr Nureyev, but as this is just a small radio centre, we simply do not have the same kind of plush changing facilities that they would have through at the BBC in Queen Margaret Drive, Glasgow."

This didn't exactly go down too well with the dancer and his PR assistant who was now huffing and puffing in exasperation.

"Isn't there anywhere in the building in which the maestro can change and have a brief wash before he does his interview?" his assistant asked.

All this time Mac was racking his brains for a solution. Then, all of a sudden, he came up with one. It might not be ideal, and far from what the great man had no doubt been used to during his illustrious career, but there was no other option, it would have to do in an emergency.

Mac locked the front door and said, "Mr Nureyev, would you kindly follow me down the stairs? I think I know somewhere that might do for now."

The dancer and his assistant followed him down the winding stairwell, which led from reception and along the long corridor, until they came to – "The Howff".

"The Howff" as previously described, was the rest room for the house staff, but not the first place that you would automatically think of taking an internationally famed ballet superstar into.

The light was on, the door was open and the room empty, so ideal for the great Rudolf to change into his onscreen attire.

Yet what he must have thought, when he finally walked into the room? God only knows.

The room had an unusual aroma that could only be best described as a mixture of stale tobacco smoke, smelly wet dog, and half eaten, leftover greasy bacon rolls.

Scattered over the table were copies of *The Sun* and *The*

Daily Record newspapers, as well as several grubby, soiled, well-thumbed pornographic magazines. Three or four large mugs were in evidence with half gulped tea and coffee now lying cold and forgotten. One mug in particular had a strange, unusual substance lying at the bottom that may well have given *Sir Alexander Fleming* palpitations if he had ever witnessed it.

"Will this do for now, Mr Nureyev?" Mac cagily asked the dancer.

Nureyev was at a bit of a loss for words at what lay before him, but as they say, beggars can't be choosers, and he mumbled a grudging, "Yes," before laying down his suitcase and taking off his coat.

Before Mac left him to get ready, Nureyev then asked him, "I must wash my hair, is there any shower facilities?"

Again Mac had to apologise on the BBC's behalf (this entire scenario must have been utterly embarrassing at the time) and explained that Edinburgh was severely lacking in such luxuries.

Yet then again, he had another brainwave. "Mr Nureyev, will you follow me for a second?"

Mac then took him across the corridor to the basement gents' toilet and said to him, "I'm very sorry, but this is probably the best we can offer you under the circumstances."

Nureyev looked around the bare, bleak, white-tiled toilet that was complete with cubicles, urinals, and sinks that now stared back at him.

"I wash in this??" he asked with his thickened Russian accent, and a look of sheer horror on his face.

"Again I am very sorry, but it's the best we can do at the moment," Mac replied.

He then pointed towards the largest sink that was deep enough to wash his hair. Unfortunately clogging it up was a dirty, stinking mop head that Bob had earlier been using for washing the front steps. Mac carefully removed it and ran some hot water to clear the unappealing mess in the sink.

Nureyev just stood there shaking his head and wondering what more horrendous sights awaited him.

"Do you have jug, so I can wash my hair?" he then asked Mac in his thick accent.

"I'm not sure," Mac answered. "I'll go and check if I can find something that will help."

Mac went back into the howff and the only item that looked big enough to do the job was one of the old tea mugs.

He ran back through to the gents and washed out the "Penicillin" that was lodged at the bottom, handed it over to the dancer and asked, "Will this do?"

Rudolf Nureyev now stood with the shirt off his back, clutching an old tea mug that just had been washed out with boiling water and began to wash his hair in the large sink.

Mac decided to leave him to it for a while, and walked back up the stairs.

The interview went ahead as scheduled, and it passed off fairly successfully.

Rudolf Nureyev said his thanks to Mac as he left, and walked out the building towards his awaiting car.

Not sure if the experience he endured at 5 Queen Street that evening would later come back to haunt him, but it's funny that the tea mug he used to wash his hair with, was never seen again…

*

Many other famous figures stepped into the building over the years including the likes of: *Britt Ekland* (standing on the outside front steps, puffing on a cigarette before her interview), *Ben Elton, Terry Wogan, Michael Bentine, Cannon &*

Ball, Willie Rushton, Barry Cryer, Ned Sherrin, Rory Bremner, Norman Rossington, Brian Cox, Sandi Toksvig, Josie Lawrence, Rula Lenska, Richard Stilgoe, Rich Hall, Brian Blessed, Belinda Carlisle, Greg Proops, Susannah York, Jane Asher, Mark Kermode, Frederick Jaeger, Julian Glover, John Challis (Boycie from *Only Fools & Horses) Alan Bates, Sir Derek Jacobi, Sir Douglas Bader, Alan Price & Georgie Fame, BA Robertson, Eric (son of Kirk) Douglas,* some famous writers by the names of *JK Rowling, Ian Rankin, Val MacDermid, Liz Lochead, George MacDonald Fraser* and one prominent member of the *Bay City Rollers, Stuart Wood.*

*

We also had a visit from the celebrated husband and wife team of *Ludovic Kennedy* and *Moira Shearer.*

I particularly remember the image of the gracious and flame-haired actress and classical dancer *Ms Shearer* (the star of the much loved *Powell & Pressburger* classic *The Red Shoes*) all alone in the vast Studio 1 arena, sitting down and playing the piano. Out of curiosity, I briefly popped my head around the door while she was playing, and noticed that she turned and gently smiled in my direction, while she continued to delicately caress the ivory keys with a sure touch of class. She was a real lady of discernable style.

*

Oh, how could I forget, we also had a brief visit by none other than the Canadian actor *James Doohan* – otherwise known as *Scotty* from *Star Trek.* He arrived one day and then he was very boldly beamed into the old remote studio to do an interview.

Although it must have seemed a little strange for the guy that day, being surrounded by what you could only describe as 100% genuine Scottish accents!

*

One evening during a lavish Hogmanay bash at 5 Queen Street, we even had a visitation from one of the most photographed celebrity couples in show business – *Catherine Zeta Jones* and… no, not *Michael Douglas* but *John Leslie*.

This was still quite a few years before *Ms Zeta Jones* headed for Hollywood, hit the big time, married movie royalty and fully embraced Oscar-winning stardom.

As for *John Leslie*, well, his path took him down an entirely different road. In fact (just like myself) he would turn up as a volunteer broadcaster with a local radio station *Castle FM* (more of this later).

This unfortunately turned out to be the wrong move for the guy, as unknowingly, he stepped right into a radio outfit (that had earlier evolved from the much missed *Leith FM*) that would soon become enmeshed in all kinds of problems and attracting all kinds of negative publicity, as it soon began to find itself mired in deep controversy. Leading to it becoming badly tarnished as a consequence.

Which included (alleged) fraud, embezzlement and the misappropriation of funds.

This was a fact that has necessitated some intense interest and scrutiny by the radio and advertising authorities – as well as the police.

I think that like dozens of others (again including myself), *Mr Leslie* quickly, and wisely, moved on from the mess. An announcement soon followed – "*John Leslie* has left the building."

*

Another day we had a visit from the popular TV and Carry On comedian *Terry Scott*, who was appearing in a play at the Kings Theatre and duly arrived for an interview.

I saw him walk along the corridor towards the remote studio and mentioned to one of the guys on the desk: "Is that *Terry Scott*, I just saw?"

The reply came back thus: "Aye that's him right enough –

and he's f*****g reeking of drink!" What a Carry-On!! Show business eh?

*

The string of show business luminaries visiting BBC Edinburgh didn't just stop when due to the refurbishment, we temporarily moved out of Queen Street.

I recall during our time in the Thistle Street building looking on as the likes of *Barbara Windsor, Dave Allen* and *Sir Lenny Henry*, wandered in to do the odd interview during the latter half of the 1980s.

I particularly recall the wonderfully diminutive *Ms Windsor* with her distinctive blonde hair tottering through the department, as she gaily clip-clopped in high heels towards the front door!

Not forgetting (how could I?), that we also had many famous politicians of all shapes, sizes and political affiliations step inside Queen Street and Thistle Street.

According to my memory, we had at one time, or another: *Gordon Brown, Donald Dewar, Menzies Campbell, Robin Cook, Alasdair Darling, Malcolm Rifkin, Alex Salmond, John Swinney, Nicola Sturgeon, John Smith, Michael Forsyth, Tam Dalyell, Malcolm Chisholm, Mark Lazsarowiz, Charles Kennedy, Denis Healy, Ron Brown, Margo McDonald, Jim Sillers etc., etc.*

You name them – we had them.

*

Many of the politicians usually arrived alone, or accompanied by a lone assistant for either a radio or a TV slot, and for the most part, they were generally friendly, chatty and made time to appear approachable and attentive to the staff on reception.

However, there was always the odd one or two (no names mentioned) who stormed in looking none at all happy, grunting an almost inaudible gruff good morning, and then as soon as their coats were off, the demands began.

They wanted coffee, they wanted newspapers, they wanted a telephone and they wanted taxis etc., etc., etc. And they wanted it all now!

Well, I suppose you could put it all down to the pressing pressures of political power.

Around the time of devolution and the eventual arrival of the Scottish Parliament we would receive visitations from any number of BBC London's political big hitters. Including the main figurehead of Question Time himself – *David Dimbleby*, no less.

Unlike a few of his contemporaries, he turned out to be a charming gentleman, who I recall seeing chatting amiably and with some humour with some of the reception staff, while he was waiting on his taxi.

There was another gent, not quite so charming, around the same period (he was a very high profile political correspondent from TV Centre in London) that allegedly spent a great deal of his time (in between probing camera interviews) attempting to verbally (and hopefully for him) physically seduce one, or two of the female staff!

Unfortunately, despite his gallant efforts with the smooth London chat, he failed to achieve any success with his very own personal "swingometer"!

"What a filthy, sleazy, pervert!" was one of the milder descriptions of him, as he soon departed for his return flight back to London, with his desires unfulfilled!

Thinking about it, and from what I saw, quite a few of the news journalists who came and went over the years at 5 Queen Street, gave one the impression that they were (especially in their own vivid imaginations) devastating lady-killers.

Perhaps their journalistic status and expanding egos became too tightly meshed as they sauntered around the building (and nearby public bars) thinking that they were a cross between *Errol Flynn* and *George Clooney.*

*

Two other regular visitors, whose towering expertise in their respective areas made them automatic authorities when intellectual analysis was required on radio, or TV, they were *Professor John Curtice* and *Owen Dudley Edwards.*

Although at first glance they both gave the benign impression of being slightly bumbling, eccentric academics, it soon became obvious when speaking with them, that their combined intellects were pretty well awesome.

Professor Curtice's role as a political analyst with a speciality on electoral issues made him an indispensable commentator on the political arena in Scotland, and how that touched upon and affected Scotland's position at Westminster.

Suffice to say he was very much in demand during the recent Scottish Referendum, as well as during any national or local elections.

Owen Dudley Edwards too made frequent visits in his role of historian. He did come across as looking like the perfectly clichéd absent-minded professor!

Once again, here was a gentleman whose knowledge when it came to Scottish and Irish literature was simply mind-boggling. I even remember him turning up one night on Reporting Scotland, dressed in the guise of his hero *Sherlock Holmes* (complete with cape and deerstalker hat) while doing a piece on *Sir Arthur Conan Doyle.*

*

We also had another figure who was never off the television, or out of the Scottish press during the 1980s; and who would make frequent, and often annoying visits to both Queen Street and Thistle Street.

This was none other than the late *Wallace Mercer,* the former chairman of *Heart of Midlothian Football Club,* who, you could say, during this period, was quite a controversial and divisive figure in the capital city.

Like one or two of the politicians, he would barge his way through the front door, briskly walk towards the reception desk, and then the demands would begin all over again. He demanded newspapers, he demanded coffee, and he demanded, well you get the picture.

He bristled with indignation one morning when – without as much as a mere please, or a thank you – he snapped at Mac (who was on duty that morning on the thistle street desk) by saying, not "Could I possibly please have a cup of coffee?" but, "Get me a cup of coffee!"

Mac, then calmly informed Mr Mercer, by pointing to the stairs that led upwards from reception, that there happened to be a vending machine on the first floor that served both tea and coffee, and that this would only cost him a mere 20p!! To add further insult to injury, Mac then informed him that if he was stuck for change, he might have some spare silver in his pocket.

Mr Mercer bristled once more, and then grumpily walked up the stairs towards the vending machine to buy his own coffee. Not a happy man that day, but then again, he rarely ever was.

One day (when his profile, fame and notoriety was approaching its absolute peak) he walked into the building at Thistle Street, obviously expecting automatic subservient treatment from the staff.

By this time his frequent visits, allied with his growing dependency on the media, must have given him the warped impression that he could treat the BBC (and its staff) in any way that he wanted. Notice of his impending arrival usually prompted the odd expression such as: "For f**k sake, Wallace Mercer's coming in at 11."

On that particular day, Suzette was on the desk and was

not for taking any of his smug, superior attitudes. "Yes sir, what can I do for you?" she calmly asked him. He was a little taken aback at her display of, what he considered, a sufficient lack of respect as to his status.

"Don't you know? I'm here for an interview!" He angrily snapped back at her.

"And can I have your name please, sir?" she further enquired. Mr Mercer was now almost apoplectic, with his face turning a deep shade of scarlet (or should that be maroon?).

He then came out with the line that usually accompanies an individual celebrity, who feels that he (or she) is not receiving a proper level of deference: *"Don't you know who I am?"* To add some weight to this outrageous display of arrogance and egomania, he produced a crumpled copy of the *Daily Record* and thrust it in front of her face.

She could now see that a large picture featuring his exact image, with accompanying headlines, was indeed clogging the majority of the front and back pages of the said tabloid.

Suzette was as cool as you like, glanced at the newspaper and then looked back at the now fuming Mr Mercer standing in front of her, and replied, "And what is your full name sir?" He was now speechless, and began to resemble one of those wacky *Warner Brothers* cartoon characters, red of face, eyes all bulging, and with steam emanating from both his ears!

Suffice to say that Suzette wasn't a lady to particularly annoy, as witnessed by an over amorous news reporter, who received an entire pint of beer poured all over his head. Soaking his expensive shirt and flashy tie into the bargain!

*

A far more pleasant and welcoming visitor to BBC Edinburgh was the voice of rugby himself – the late *Bill McLaren*. I first met Bill sometime in the 1970s and liked him instantly.

Although I must confess that I do not in any way regard

myself a rugby fan (you could say that I prefer the ball at my feet, instead of in my hands), Bill was, without a shadow of doubt, a perfect gentleman in every way. Everyone who encountered him in 5 Queen Street liked and admired him for his innate professionalism, his gentle good humour and air of calm good-natured dignity.

I often managed to have a brief chat with him – and his good lady wife – when he occasionally popped into the canteen for lunch, or a coffee, and look back on this time with fondness. If any one individual epitomised the best and the purest example of broadcasting integrity and everything that was good about the BBC in Scotland, you needn't look any further than the late great *Bill McLaren*.

*

As an addendum to this chapter, it wasn't just while working within the hallowed corridors of BBC Scotland that led me in encountering famous celebrities.

Not that long ago, while doing a spot of Festival Fringe reviewing, I found myself sitting next to the actor *Ian Lavender*. This is the very same actor perhaps best known for playing *Private Frank Pike* in *"Dad's Army"*.

We were both in the audience about to watch a one-man performance by another popular comedy actor from the same era – *Jeffrey Holland,* probably best known for playing the character Spike from *Hi Di Hi*.

Mr Holland was brilliantly portraying *Stan Laurel* in a gently moving and humorous Fringe show about *Stan Laurel's* final farewell to an ailing *Oliver Hardy*.

As luck would have it, I managed to have an enjoyable chat with both actors after the show.

Two fine actors and lovely guys as well.

*

On another occasion, a few years back, and whilst I was

returning home from a far-flung holiday, I had the misfortune in setting off the metal detector at the airport.

Straight away I was frisked by one of the security personnel, as they began to frantically search for whatever particular item I had on my person that had set off the alarm (it turned out to be a ballpoint pen by the way!)

Feeling a little bit embarrassed at holding up the queue, I immediately turned round to meekly smile while offering some form of a limp apology to those standing patiently behind me, only to be met by a glaring and rather unpleasant look by the gentleman standing just at my back. I turned back around and then for a brief millisecond I though to myself, *I know that guy!* I then turned back around again, only for a second time to meet the glowering, unhappy stare of the gentleman in question, who turned out to be none other than – *Bryan Ferry*!

It seems that the British pop legend and *Roxy Music* front man was desperate to get to the Executive Lounge prior to his return flight home, and I (even for only a few fleeting minutes) was keeping him back.

No doubt he was anxious to sample the free coffee and newspapers while enjoying the exclusive company of the young dark-haired girl on his arms! I got the impression she wasn't his wife, although I could be wrong?

Finally he was ushered away (with his accompanying lady friend) just before I summoned up the nerve to ask for his autograph. Although I am sure if I had asked, the reception I may well have received from the "old singing smoothie" would no doubt have left me with *"Both Ends Burning"*!

CHAPTER 5

*Holy F**K!!!*

If there is one shining example that sticks long in my memory for summing up just how chaotic, calamitous and downright funny BBC Edinburgh could be, happened one day during the 1980s, that involved the ostensibly simple transportation and removal of a photocopying machine from the basement, to the ground floor. This routine operation involved four participants, and one supervisor to navigate proceedings.

But then again, didn't the supposedly simple transportation of a piano up a long flight of stairs with two gentlemen by the names of *Mr Laurel* and *Mr Hardy*, turn into one of the most hilarious events ever put on screen?

*

So let's start at the beginning. During this period, I found myself running the BBC's Printing and Duplicating room, deep within the bowels of 5 Queen Street.

We had two copier machines based in this room. One was a large bulky monster of a unit, ideally suited to churning out hundreds and hundreds of pages of drama scripts, features programmes, and endless pages of schools broadcasting publicity.

Then, there was the smaller copier. It was a mere fraction of the other's size, and ideally suited to be used for minor copying jobs.

One day, I received an instruction from my Administration supervisor who, shall we say, was called Bella – or "Hurricane Bella" in certain quarters. I cannot fully recall her official title at this precise moment, but that more or less conveys her position and reputation. So she told me that we were going to be getting a new photocopier, and so the old one would have to be empted and removed.

Bella wanted the copier to be totally drained of toner, prior to it being transported from the basement to the ground floor.

For those not too familiar with what toner is, well a good description could be that it resembles thick black oil. Not the sort of substance you want splattered on your hands, or clothes – but more of that later...

So, I was given the responsibility to drain the copier. This I did, reasonably successfully I thought, as I watched with fascination (not enough excitement in my working day, I hear you say) as the thick black mess was slowly and ever so carefully piped into a large container for it to be later disposed of.

However, there was always going to be the possibility of some small residue amount remaining within the copier. But if the equipment's removal went smoothly with no real upheaval or damage, it should remain within the machine. At least that was the theory?

To remove the machine, demanded the physical efforts of not one, but four individuals, to negotiate its slow and steady journey up the narrow winding stairwell.

For this very special occasion, I was going to be joined by Bob, Harry, and my young colleague Fraser. But not only that, the House Supervisor, the splendidly bearded and ramrod straight (he was always ramrod straight, something that occasionally caused a lot of feverish consternation – but that's another story...) Mac.

As it turned out, he would be supervising the operation in his own inimitable fashion.

At first, we all gathered together to see how we were going to remove it carefully out of the room and up the stairs. There were, I remember, four small handles situated both at the back, and at the front of the copier, which would make its transportation that little bit easier. Or so we thought?

Bob (who was in a particularly aggressive mood that day – what a surprise!) and Fraser lifted the copier from the front, whilst Harry (a man who was never known to acknowledge papal authority in his time, and who also enjoyed a "right good swally") and myself manoeuvred it from the back.

All during this time, Mac was standing alongside, making sure that all was going according to plan.

We got out of the door of the print room and along the small corridor ok, but then came the tricky part – the stairs.

All was initially going fine, as we eased our way up the narrow stairs, one small step at a time. But Bob seemed to be in a bit of a rush, as he then tended to thump and bump the machine (accidentally, or otherwise) with much fury, against the side of the wall.

"Take it easy, Bob," Harry was heard to say, as he watched with growing trepidation at Bob's cavalier attempt at getting the copier up the stairs as quickly as possible.

"Watch it Bob, yer taking big chunks oot the wa'!'" Harry cried again.

Bob seemed to be oblivious to both of Harry's warnings, as well as the permanent damage he might be doing to part of the building. Paint and crumbling plaster then began to fall upon on the stairs, as it was gradually heaved up yet another step.

Both Fraser and I looked at each other with growing unease, no doubt wishing we were somewhere else. Like being far away and in a different part of the building. Having a cup of tea in the canteen, for instance, sounded much more preferable.

"Bob, try and keep it away from the wall," Mac instructed. All the time as he was standing nearby and supervising – or something resembling that.

Bob was now getting into a more agitated state as he pushed and banged the copier, as we were slowly approaching the top of the stairwell.

Then, our worst fears materialised.

Bob thumped the edge of the copier with such brutish ferocity, it was no great surprise that the front lid flew wide open!

Right at the same time, a large splurge of black, messy goo splattered across the wall, closely resembling the map of Africa, and running down in long black streaks against the bright paintwork.

"For f**k's sake Bob!!" Harry shouted out. "Whit are ye dain??"

Then, simultaneously and completely unannounced, as copier carnage was full upon on us, around the corner suddenly appeared Bella.

"HOLY F***K!!!" she screamed at the top of her voice, whilst simultaneously slapping her hand hard against her forehead. Her loud banshee-like scream emanating from both of her lungs caused great commotion, and much opening of office doors in the above floors.

This led to a number of production staff becoming rudely alerted to the racket and din coming from the area, as well as to the rabble of raised voices and somewhat fruity language that was being banded around in unison.

"What the bloody hell's going on down there? We're trying to conduct an important meeting!!" rang one angered voice, not exactly crying from the wilderness, but from outside one of the offices in the floors above.

Bob coldly looked up towards the furious producer, who was now venting his anger towards the floor below.

"Who the f*****g hell is that bastard shouting at?" he asked, just as he was helping to move the copier to the ground floor level. "Let him come down here and try and move this f****r of a machine!" Bob added, as everyone now attempted to ease up, calm down and assess the catastrophic situation.

Bella now surveyed the shambles and the hodgepodge of machine and mess that lay in front of her, with increasing frustration. How could so simple and straightforward an operation, descend into such disorganised chaos?

At the same time, a voice was heard to quietly mutter on the sidelines, "Look at ma suit. Look at ma f*****g good suit!!" Mac could only look down in horror at what was once his immaculate, well-pressed, dark grey suit, that was now speckled with thick black ink. He looked dazed, and at a loss for words, as to exactly how this had all happened, as the gooey mess formed a surrealistic Daliesque pattern of sorts all over his jacket, shirt, tie and trousers.

"It was that bastard Lawrence – it's all his fault!!" Bob shouted out, as he pointed the finger of blame squarely in my direction. "He never emptied it properly, otherwise it wouldn't have made all this f*****g mess." Bob was anxious to lay the finger of blame at my door, and to deflect any responsibility as far away from himself as possible.

"Look at the state of ma good suit," Mac again muttered as he shook his head and no doubt wished that he had remained behind at reception.

Fraser and I couldn't look at each other without bursting into laughter. Although Bella was far from amused, as she pondered (once she had eventually calmed down) about how she was going to rectify the damaged and toner-decorated wall.

"What a state ma suit's in!" Mac could be heard muttering again, as he disappeared into his office to reflect on the day's events.

"I'm going to make a cup of f*****g tea," Harry uttered once we had finally moved the copier to the front of the building, as it awaited being uplifted to its future destination.

Later, as things quietened down a bit, Fraser and I popped into Mac's office to see how he was. We walked in as he was sitting in deep and reflective contemplation behind his desk. He looked up at us both as we stood there before him, the two of us desperately trying not to laugh out loud.

Mac just sighed and sadly shook his head and then said, "Look at the state of ma f*****g suit!!"

*

I almost forgot, there was yet another occasion a couple of years earlier, when a number of us found ourselves roped into moving another large item, up many more stairs!

The canteen had been delivered of a very large and very heavy piece of catering equipment that was required to replace the older one.

The only problem being that the canteen was almost up three flights of stairs, right near the very top of the building. I would have thought at the time, that the company, who were providing the equipment, would have had sufficient hardy and experienced employees to deliver it from their van to its final destination.

But no, it was left to a number of the house staff and assorted volunteers (unfortunately including myself) to sweat and strain profusely, in order to heave it up the stairs.

I think it took about eight of us (including Frank the house electrician and the general handyman Tom, who were both long in years and should never have been involved in so physically arduous a task) to slowly and carefully move it up towards the top of the building.

I now have a slight feeling of how the slaves of ancient Egypt must have felt when building the pyramids all those centuries ago, as the task began to resemble a scene from *Land Of The Pharaohs*.

Anyway, between us we struggled manfully with the horrendous weight of this awkward piece of equipment whilst the Engineering Managers at the time (Jim Spankie & Alex Mclean, Queen Street's answer to Prof Jimmy Edwards & Prof Severus Snape) looked on, never once offering to help us, or share the load. Although during the journey, one of them did ask us to be careful and not damage the walls, like some whip-yielding overseer. This misjudged concern made one or two of "the slaves" mutter the odd swear word under their breaths. In fact, all that was missing, while we struggled with the weight of the damned thing was a few lines from the song *Ol' Man River* – "*Tote that barge lift that bale…*" You get the picture?

After much heaving and hoeing, as well as what felt like an interminable struggle involving strained muscles (not forgetting much blood, sweat, and tears), we reached the summit of our eventual destination.

We all gave out a collective sigh of relief at completing the task. Bob wiped some sweat from his forehead and said, "That was a f*****g disgrace asking us to move that monstrosity up these f*****g stairs!" Then referring to the two Head Engineering Managers who roped us all in, he further added, "If it was up to those two bastards, they would have you working like a f*****g black man!!" Not perhaps the most subtle, or in today's parlance, the most politically correct thing to say, but I guess he was just voicing what a number of us felt at the time. "I thought that slavery had been f*****g outlawed years ago!!" Bob further added.

As for Frank and Tom, it's a wonder the two older guys didn't collapse with a heart seizure at having to do the kind of job that was better suited to much younger men! Looking back with the benefit of hindsight – it was simply outrageous.

At the same time, Harry (after working up quite a considerable thirst during the job) kept dropping equally unsubtle hints to one of the engineering bosses about opening up his expansive drinks cabinet and giving the workers a little liquid refreshment, as a small reward for their collective efforts.

Suffice to say, his pleas fell on deaf ears, as Harry's reputation as an Olympian imbiber had no doubt preceded him!

This didn't stop him from muttering and growling audibly, while glancing in the direction of the two senior figures. "Not as much as Harry, ken ye drink, nor f**k all!" Quickly followed by, "They two bastards, they wouldn't gie' a bairn a kiss!" as he wearily and thirstily trundled his way back down the stairs.

CHAPTER 6

Coming To A Green Room Near You!
The Midnight Movie Shows

The First Aid Room wasn't the only part of the building that some members of staff could use for a spot of rest and relaxation. There was also the Green Room.

The use of the Green Room was I recall, primarily for production staff to view television programmes, and then much later, it was relocated in another part of the building and used to entertain visiting VIPs, as well as many radio and television programme contributors.

The first Green Room in 5 Queen Street had a very large television set and a number of comfortable chairs ideally positioned to gain a good view of the screen. The room was small, cosy, and tended to be kept dark to add to the atmosphere.

However, at the beginning of the 1980s a new entertainment phenomenon appeared that took its rightful place alongside the TV – the video recorder.

It's a little hard for youngsters today, amidst all the different kinds of technologically advanced gadgets that are available, to fully understand and appreciate what the presence of a video recorder would mean for millions of homes.

With this being the case, I suppose the BBC would be one of the very first establishments to have a recorder within its walls.

So, the video recorder would arrive with trumpets blaring and find its allotted place in the Green Room.

*

For movie fans (including myself) this would open up a wide new world in which you could watch over and over again, all of your favourite films, in the comfort of your very own home.

Yet, it also opened up the opportunity for the instant availability of let's say, "other types of films" to also sneak their way in. This was going to be the advantage of having a Green Room complete with a TV and a video, and it would turn out to be very handy indeed.

Around the same time, BBC Edinburgh had recently begun operating a 24-hour security service, in which the building would be manned by a selection of individuals on a rotating shift pattern.

So it was the midnight shifts that would eventually prove to be the most popular, for reasons soon to become apparent.

I began to hear the odd story filtering through about the Green Room, the midnight shift, and the local Edinburgh constabulary that began to intrigue me.

During one of those night shifts, the security man on duty at the time, would often have the occasional visit from a couple of passing policeman who were patrolling the area. They would be maintaining the peace and quiet, as well as making sure that all was safe and well in the city centre.

Friendships were quickly formed, with much tea and coffee drunk, and I'm led to believe the occasional chocolate biscuit thrown in for good measure.

This would soon manifest itself into regular visitations, with a number of the law officers on night duty knowing that they could always pop into the BBC for a chat and a cup of tea, whilst doing their normal duty of keeping crime and disorder off the streets.

At first glance, this appears to be all very normal and innocent, as well as an opportunity in maintaining good relations with the law.

However, things began to perk up a bit when, on one occasion, a couple of officers on a short tour of the building, came across the Green Room.

Lying in front of them was a large television set, but perhaps more importantly – a video recorder.

I can well imagine the looks on their collective faces during this time. I'm sure it would have been not too far removed from the looks of someone coming across some fabled hidden treasure.

I can only guess at how their imaginations must have been working overtime at this momentous discovery. A video recorder, yes, a video recorder, a piece of equipment that can play – videos!

You might be asking yourselves, where we are heading with this, but for now we abruptly shift time and locations.

*

The time is an early afternoon, and the location, a shop in Leith Walk. Not a butcher or a baker, or one selling fruit and vegetables, but a shop whose front is somewhat mysterious, as well as hinting at great mystique and curiosity about what lies behind its darkened doors.

But our local constabulary knew, and knew only too well what lay behind its facade – and it turned out to be not apples, and pears!

The shop in question had, what you would call, a bit of a "dodgy reputation".

In fact, its main purpose was providing all forms of "adult entertainment" that could range from, well I'll let you figure that out for yourselves!

The law officers confiscated dozens and dozens of unusual items, but in particular, they confiscated – videos, lots and lots of videos.

They removed the said items into the local police station, to keep them out of harm's way. But there was also an ulterior motive. Since they couldn't play these particular films at the station (now that would have been something!!) and it was highly unlikely that they could take them home, where else could they be viewed?

"Eureka!" No doubt one of the young officers suddenly experienced an almost religious revelation, at what seemed to be the perfect answer. They could be taken along, under the cover of night, to the BBC building at 5 Queen Street, where they had a television and a video.

It made perfect sense; they could be watched in the twilight hours in peace and harmony, with tea, coffee, and biscuits provided.

Like the later activities surrounding the First Aid Room, the post-midnight gatherings in the Green Room soon became common knowledge amongst a very select few. Even my own good self decided to pop along one night just to see exactly what all the fuss was about.

It may have been a late Friday night, when I decided to see for myself, just as the witching hour was growing nearer. I slowly approached the building and then rang the front door bell. The security man on duty (I can't exactly recall which one of the team was on call that evening) opened the door and invited me in.

"The first film has already started, but there are a few others still to be played," he told me. He then offered to make me a cup of coffee, passed me an already opened packet of chocolate digestive biscuits, and then with hot mugs in hand, we proceeded to the "cinema", where a packed house awaited us.

He quietly opened the door, and I could already hear several grunting noises coming from the television screen that could only be described as animalistic. As I looked in, there sitting before me, were one or two of my colleagues, as well as several custodians of law and order, who appeared to be very much at ease and relaxed, with their helmets off and jackets unbuttoned While all the time, their eyes were permanently glued to the energetic physical images now performing on the TV.

To be honest, and at first glance, I thought that I had inadvertently come across a furtive meeting of "the secret policeman's ball".

However, on that particular night, I'm sure that patrolling the dark mean streets of "old reekie" in search of all types of criminal activities must have been far from their collective thoughts. For at that moment, they were much more fascinated and gripped by what was unfolding before their attentive eyes upon the large television screen in front of them.

The titles of some of the films turned out to be bizarrely humorous. One in particular that proved a much-loved favourite was *"Debbie Does Dallas"*. I don't think it had anything to do with a certain JR, or featured ten gallon hats in the plot, but that production always brought forth gasps of appreciation from the uniformed officers, as they gulped their milky coffees, and munched on chocolate Jaffa Cakes. While the girl in question was, ahem, entertaining them, I always wondered why the filmmakers never embarked upon a sequel, such as "Debbie Does Dumbarton". No doubt it would have found just as appreciative an audience, as the original had for staff and police back then in the BBC's Green Room.

Other titles that found their way onto the Green Room TV screen included such delectable goodies (and believe you me we were not talking about Disney versions here!) as *"Goldilocks & The 3 Bare Bottoms"*, *"Snow White & the 7 Stiff*

Soldiers" and *"Rumplebareskin"*. One particular favourite among the crowd was I believe a feature entitled – *"Caroline & The Amazing Cucumber!"*

I am quite convinced that version did not originate from the pen of *Roald Dahl*. So no wonder it was usually standing room only in the Green Room on certain evenings.

I suppose like all good things, the late night movie entertainments screened at 5 Queen Street would eventually come to a sad and abrupt end. I think that it may well have coincided when the police station superiors finally got wind of what confiscated items were regularly disappearing from their building. So the film festival premiere presentations came to a not unexpected halt.

However, the police maintained their regular visitations to the building – both during the day and into the evening. On one occasion, an altercation erupted between two officers of the law! Now there's a thing. How could that happen?

So what we had, were two police visitors (one of them was a regular guest known simply to all as Ally) deciding to have a bout of fisticuffs at the main reception area. Was it over a woman, was it over money, was it over a porn video, or perhaps it was all down to who was getting the last chocolate biscuit??

Whatever provoked them, blood was soon spilt, fists raised and angry voices raged far into the night. The two "coppers" now began to wrestle on the floor and hit out furiously at one another, as they both tried to gain the upper hand.

It began to resemble an old *John Wayne* saloon brawl!

If Miss Wilson had walked in on them – there and then – no doubt she would have been horrified at such goings on in the main reception area. Not surprisingly followed by a loud cry of – you guessed it – *"You Can't Do That Here, This Is The BBC!!"*

Once the grappling had eventually all calmed down, one of

the officers glanced at the sight of lots of blood that was now splattered all over his shirt. "I can't continue on duty with all this on me!" he said, pointing to the red mess decorating what was once his crisp, clean white shirt. But, no fear, the security man on duty that evening decided to come to his rescue. "You can borrow one of the spare shirts we have. It will probably fit you, as I think that you are roughly about the right size." The policeman smiled contently at the thought of going back on duty with a brand new shirt following his bloodied punch-up. Yet what was presented to him was not quite what he was expecting. "I can't wear that, look at the f*****g state of it!" he said. The shirt was hardly Persil white, in fact it looked almost worse than the bloodied shirt he was already wearing.

It was a murky grey colour, slightly frayed at the collar and cuffs, un-ironed, slightly crushed, and looked as if it had been a very long time since it had seen the inside of a washing machine. The policeman shook his head in disbelief, but then shrugged, and said "Oh, what the f**k, I suppose I'll just have to wear it." He removed the bloodstained item, threw it into the bin, and then proceeded to put on the other shirt. He lifted the arms and said, "Phew, it's got a f*****g funny smell!"

Yet I suppose under the circumstances, he had little choice in the matter. He didn't want to return to Gayfield Square and face the wrath of his superiors, looking like an extra from a Hammer horror film. So he just shrugged his shoulders, put his jacket back on, said his goodnights and walked out into the cold night air. Although going by the state of the shirt he was now wearing, it could very well have walked out on its very own!

*

I always wondered, and pondered, as to what the reaction might have been if the BBC Scotland management at the time had ever discovered what was going on within the darkened confines of their own premises, very late at night?

Then again, maybe they already knew, or half guessed what was happening. Yet perhaps it may have been a small price to pay to keep the law in close proximity? I suppose that it is something that we will never know.

CHAPTER 7

The Good, The Bad, And The Utterly Certifiable

I suppose that working within an organisation over 25 years brings you into contact with a wide variety of individuals and personalities. Some good, some bad, some dull, some amusing, and a few that can best be described as defying both logic and believability! I met all of the above with variable results, during my time as an employee at BBC Edinburgh.

I remember having a conversation, not so long ago, with a former colleague who looked me straight in the eye (and with the slight hint of a sly smile) said, "BBC Edinburgh was full of eccentrics!" I'm still a little unsure whether she was including me amongst that assessment, but I suppose it was a fairly accurate description nonetheless.

*

One particular individual I remember during my very earliest of days at Queen Street, made, what you could say was, a most unusual impression. I believe he was a fairly high-profile Gaelic TV producer who regularly visited the building from the west. What made his appearance especially striking, was the fact that he wore a very obvious copper-toned toupee and puffed away on his pipe, while walking up and down the reception corridor. However, what made his presence slightly unsettling (particularly for a 16-year-old like myself) was the fact that he tended to look up and down at you most oddly! Almost as if he was closely inspecting a prime slab of rich Italian ham that had been hanging from a delicatessen's ceiling! At one point, I half expected him to ask me if my preference was for Snails or Oysters! It was then passed on to me by a concerned, if slightly amused colleague that the gentleman in question always tended to look that way towards any young teenage boy who came within his close vicinity. I quickly made it my point to stray out of his viewing range whenever his hairpiece and pipe re-emerged on the scene!

*

In 1978 a seismic change happened to BBC Scotland that shook up the calm and twee complacency of 5 Queen Street. This was the arrival of Radio Scotland.

Massive changes in the production and presentation of programmes, giving them a more decidedly Scottish slant, were now upon us.

For Edinburgh, this mainly involved the arrival of Good Morning Scotland, as well as the massed staff of News & Current Affairs, along with Radio Drama.

As one individual sarcastically observed: "I see that we're getting a right shower coming through from the west."

Nevertheless, this really shook the place up, and it probably needed it as well. They were now adding a bit of much-needed energetic life into the old place. Although I got the impression that a number of the older staff were a bit put out at this radical change in the building's atmosphere. That aside, there was now a vibrancy evident, which necessitated the building operating a 24-hour, 7 day a week opening policy.

With that about to happen, it really now felt like a proper broadcasting centre, and not like some comfy old gentleman's club!

*

When I first started working for "Auntie Beeb", my

YOU CAN'T DO THAT HERE! THIS IS THE BBC!

immediate boss was a lady called Miss Jean Wilson. In fact it was this lady in question who, on a number of occasions, uttered the immortal line "This Is The BBC!!" – particularly when some embarrassing catastrophe happened on the premises, involving one (or more) of her staff.

She was prim, quite proper, almost stately and patrician in her appearance, and extremely well organised. Speaking from a personal viewpoint, I always found her a fair, straight, honest individual and someone I respected both as a person, as well as respecting her position as an administrator.

Unfortunately, many found her a little bit too prim and proper (she was often jokily referred to as either "Miss Jean Brodie" or the "Mother Superior") and her stern manner tended to make a few uncomfortable. Yet for me, she was fine, although she would often, without thinking, say or do things that made you laugh – at least not in her presence, but very soon afterwards.

One such occasion occurred when it was reported to her that someone had been defacing the walls of the gents' toilets near reception. She consulted with Mac (who by this time had been elevated to the lofty position of House Foreman) in order for both of them to investigate the scrawled vandalism.

They then delicately entered the toilets (obviously when unoccupied) to examine the artwork! By all accounts, she wasn't best amused by what confronted her, and demanded that the defacement be removed immediately. Although, from what I later learned, she was slightly confused as to the subject of the drawings in question. Perhaps she thought the images confronting her were some form of surrealistic abstraction?

While all this time, the mysterious artist (perhaps inspired by the works of *Dali* and *Picasso*) had decided to bring his own individual vision of art for the staff's amusement. When surveying the work, in all innocence, she mentioned to Mac that it did seem a bit strange to draw "birds in flight" on a toilet wall – as she put it.

Well soon afterwards, the avian artistry was quickly removed, and the walls scrubbed clean and more or less, put back to normal.

Mac told a number of us exactly what had transpired during their joint investigation. "She thought that some sordid bastard had drawn birds in flight on the walls," he said. "I couldn't tell her there and then, that they were no more birds in flight, than flying through the air!" After much laughter, we enquired as to exactly what kind of drawings they actually were.

Mac then laughed again and said, "I'm surprised that she didn't work it out. It was a couple of huge cocks with big hairy balls!" What more could you say. But the burning question remains: was it art?

*

One of my first Christmases spent at 5 Queen Street coincided with an all-out strike! I hadn't long joined the union when there were distant rumblings in the air about the possibility of some form of industrial action by the staff centring on a proposed pay rise. It's incredible to think of it now, but looking back then, almost forty years ago, the BBC union members were looking for something in the region of a 20% pay rise!! If memory serves me correct, the eventual outcome of the dispute didn't fall too far short of that figure.

Anyway, it was a couple of weeks before Christmas and the mood (just like Scrooge's offices) was a little gloomy, as the union members were all geared up to flex their industrial muscles and cause a bit of calculated disruption.

In those days, any strike threat in the run up towards Christmas would have maximum impact, as it would potentially and effectively damage the BBC's Christmas TV schedule. Just think of it, no *Eric & Ernie,* no *Two Ronnies,* and heaven forbid – no Queen's Message! Just a blank screen, and no radio output as well, as the nation were about to sit down to tuck into their turkey, sprouts, stuffing and pudding!

To put this into perspective, these were the days that existed long before the advent of digital and satellite television, with their multitude of channels.

There were only three TV channels then – with two of them belonging to the BBC!

Well, I remember the day when strike action was officially announced, with almost the entire staff prepared to walk out, leaving a very skeleton presence to man the reception. In fact Miss Wilson took up residence behind the desk, all on her own, just as everyone was putting on his, or her coats, to walk out the front door.

She looked somewhat harassed as she began to take call after call, from many a disgruntled licence fee payer. Just as I, and others were about to leave, her face looked startled and shocked as she put down the receiver following one obviously unpleasant call. Then she called out in her finest cut glass Morningside voice, "Someone just called me a shit!"

Not long after, the dispute was eventually resolved successfully, everyone returned to work, and the Christmas TV schedules reached the screens and the airwaves unimpaired. Although I gather that following her experience on the front desk, Miss Wilson's nerves must have taken that little bit longer to recover.

*

I remember another event that tested Miss Wilson's patience to the limit, and concerned a freelance news journalist by the name of *Mike Russell*. I got the impression that freelancers in general, were not quite her cup of *Earl Grey tea*, and that she viewed their presence (journalistic mercenaries, with no great loyalty towards the Corporation) with grave suspicion.

As far as she was concerned, they were not proper BBC

staff, and I suppose, a bit of a necessary evil. However, they existed well out of her realm of authority, and so if they misbehaved or caused any ructions, she couldn't do much about it – more's the pity. Yet, on this particular occasion, she didn't hold back. The story began when Mr Russell approached the two young girls in the mailroom (no, not in that way!), Jane and Suzette.

He asked them if they would do him a favour and venture out to the local off licence and purchase a half bottle of whisky for him. He was feeling a little parched, you could say, and fulfilling that well-established image of the hard-drinking news hack.

After he left, Suzette in particular, mulled this request over in her mind and came to the obvious conclusion that this task simply wasn't in her job description. And to be fair, she was perfectly correct.

A rich vein of Leith-style bolshie bullishness ran through her, as she proceeded to get official clarification by informing Miss Wilson about this unusual request from the thirsty journalist. "He asked you to do what?? How dare he!!" How very dare he, I hear you say, as Miss Wilson shouted out in outraged anger as Suzette informed her what was said.

Once the initial shock had abated, Miss Wilson then swiftly marched down to the newsroom to confront Mr Russell, face to face.

She walked in and then gave him her answer with full, undiluted ferocity. She told him – in no uncertain terms (in her best *Jean Brodie* voice) – that "Her Girls" are not employed by the BBC to run after the backsides of freelance reporters, by supplying them with strong alcohol.

Mr Russell mumbled a half-hearted apology and from then on purchased his whisky by himself. Hilarious.

As an addendum to this story, I much later learnt that very same *Mike Russell* had been a former drummer with *The*

156

Rolling Stones, no less.

Unfortunately, on that particular day, you could say that he received "No Satisfaction" from the unleashed wrath of Miss Wilson!

*

I always wondered what it was that made quite a few of the newsroom journalists such, well, almighty boozers and totally unapologetic pissheads! Their acknowledged skill fingering the keys of a typewriter, was only equalled by their skill fingering the top of a vodka, or whiskey bottle.

The unfortunate casualty list included quite a few of those talented scribes, whose sublime gift with words, went almost hand in hand with their gift for self destructive, monumental, alcoholic guzzling.

Several of the news guys were giving a pretty good impression that they were attempting to audition for the title role in *Jeffrey Barnard Is Unwell*. With one or two of them displaying a well-practised skill for spectacularly falling off bar stools!

Of course, they weren't the only ones working in the place who possessed lethal breath that could strip paint at ten yards! There was some almighty competition going the rounds (no pun intended) that involved the odd producer, presenter, and (no, not candlestick maker) cleaner!

So was it the intoxicating atmosphere in the place, or was it something that was being placed in the tea, or the coffee? It certainly wasn't bromide, that's for sure! Or was it something enforced and underlined in their contracts? Emphasising that not only would they report the news accurately, dispassionately and with professional integrity, but simultaneously get smashed out of their heads in the process!

Yet at the same time, a few of them were hiding bottles in secret locations, furtively swallowing spirits during breakfast and arriving for work looking like they'd just slept overnight in a dog kennel – along with the dog.

One journalist in fact, kept his secret stash of whiskey hidden behind the cistern in one of the gents' toilets. Perhaps he was the very same mysterious artist who was guilty of drawing "birds in flight" on the toilet walls, whilst imbibing out of his half bottle of Grouse?

Not sure if the noble profession of journalism still resembles the kind of tacky image it once had, but certainly from my vantage point, many of the news hacks gave off the impression that they could well attempt to drink *Oliver Reed* under the table!

With some of them eager to give that possibility a right good bash.

On the other hand, I sincerely hope that I haven't given everyone the impression that all of the news journalists were overly fond of cradling a bottle in their arms.

The vast majority of them were top professionals, exceptional writers, and many of them also exceptional human beings, who were pleasant to share good conversation and convivial company with.

Chief among them was the wonderful *George Hume*.

George was, in my own humble opinion (for what it's worth), one of the finest writers and broadcasters that BBC Scotland had under contract during the bulk of the 1980s.

A larger-than-life figure that often found himself butting heads with stubborn BBC bureaucracy, and normally got the better of them through a mixture of guile, wit, intelligence, and determination.

As an incisive investigative journalist, George fronted his own programme called *Hume At Large* in which he tackled in his own inimitable fashion, many of the pressing and important issues that were affecting Scotland during that decade.

George was also a marvellously entertaining character to converse with. Complete with a great sense of humour and a fund of wonderful stories that made him always an engrossing figure to talk to.

One particularly cutting observation regarding a certain member of staff that he had little time for, made me chuckle away for hours on end. If only she knew.

One story I recently heard about *George Hume*, concerned one particular day in the newsroom, in which he was beginning to become a little exasperated with something or other. Maybe it was the traffic wardens, or perhaps more likely the beaurocratic excesses of the BBC internal system?

Yet that day, George simply had enough. So, seemingly infused with the manic spirit of *Keith Moon*, George picked up his typewriter (remember them?) and casually chucked it through the window! They don't make them like that anymore!

Alongside Bob, George would also find himself immersed in a daily war of attrition with the marauding and dreaded traffic wardens. George equally took great delight in making their lives a misery, but he utilised slightly different methods to Bob in dealing with them.

During this time, hundreds of official letters would regularly arrive at Queen Street, sent from Edinburgh's District Council, and all addressed to George.

I got the impression (and I don't think I was too far off the mark) that they were all to do with unpaid parking fines.

When George arrived I passed them on to him and with a smile he said, "Thanks Lawrence, I know what I'll be doing with them!" He then placed them in his briefcase and walked towards the newsroom.

I am convinced that like all the others he accumulated, they resolutely remained unpaid. Until he was finally summoned to court and paid whatever fine he was charged with.

Also like Bob, George had his own faithful four-legged friend – his dog Monty.

George was probably hoping that Monty's growling and menacing presence would frighten off his sworn enemies – the traffic wardens. Which did happen frequently.

George sadly passed away around 1992, while battling ill health in his final years. Yet he remains one of the finest examples of what a BBC Scotland broadcasting journalist can achieve, with his legacy, an intelligently enduring one.

*

Apart from a variety of jocular and eccentric journalists, the newsroom had in its midst a real gentleman of the old school. He possessed what could only be described as "a pure BBC voice" and whose authoritative vocal delivery made him instantly recognisable – it could only be the wonderful *Bill Jack*.

I don't think I can ever recall seeing anyone walk into 5 Queen Street with such an impressively straight-back officer-like swagger as Bill.

He strode through the reception and corridors like a brigadier inspecting his troops on a parade ground.

All that was missing was the sound of a massed-band striking up the opening chords of "Col Bogey," as he marched in.

And he spoke with the kind of calm, solid voice of authority that you would only find in old British war films that usually starred *John Mills* and *Jack Hawkins*.

I could also easily visualise Bill knocking them back in the officer's mess, or ordering up another gin sling at *Raffles Hotel in Singapore!*

Resplendent in his dark blue blazer and striped officer's tie, Bill had that kind of empirical image.

Bill's good lady wife Muriel was also an occasional and

YOU CAN'T DO THAT HERE! THIS IS THE BBC!

welcome visitor. Usually when waiting around at reception for Bill to finish for the day.

Unfortunately, Muriel was also sadly afflicted by an unstoppable taste for the bevvy, and like so many countless others, would often find herself being literally "poured into a taxi" at the end of the night. This would invariably happen after a long, wild, boozy evening spent in Henderson's bar – a jovial hostelry that was situated in Thistle Street. She was a pleasant woman, was Muriel. However, she had what was commonly known as a parched throat and a drouthy mouth. Something she shared with so many during this period.

In fact for the three-year duration that we worked in Thistle Street, Henderson's Bar fought for supremacy with the old Beau Brummell, for the much sought-after title of "Unofficial BBC Edinburgh Club"!

So it's no exaggeration to state that Henderson's bar profits must have hit an all-time high during the three years the BBC was camped virtually right next door!

Oh how their accountants must have wept genuine tears of grief and sadness, when we all moved back to Queen Street!

At first glance, Bill appeared like a bit of an old fashioned anachronism amidst the hurly-burly of a more modern newsroom. You could easily imagine him doing some form of wartime commentary, or narrating a Royal, or official state occasion.

But what shouldn't be forgotten was that apart from his immaculate professionalism as a newsreader, he was, to everyone he encountered, a good natured, kind, and lovely man to boot.

Bill was like a living relic from a bygone past.

A man from an era that was calmer, more refined and more reflective.

At all times, amidst all the surrounding madness, he wisely

kept his appearance attentive, his humour intact, his trousers well pressed and his upper lip stiff.

*

One thing that constantly tested Miss Wilson's patience (whilst also causing much amusement to many on the sidelines) was attempting to deal with the house staff whenever they were required to work during a Studio 1 concert.

This, more often than not, would happen during an evening, and usually on a Saturday, when they were expected to be having a rest day off.

The guys directly concerned with this were of course, Bob, Harry, and during this time the third part of the triumvirate, a chap called Al (more of him later).

The three amigos were duly informed that their services were required for covering the concert, when an audience was in attendance – and on a Saturday night. Harry was all for it, for this meant to him that glittering and exalted word – overtime!

This would give him more money in his pocket, and thus, more money to spend in the pub on drink. A chance, so to speak, to get right blitzed at the BBC's expense!

Unfortunately, Bob took an all too different view. He hated doing overtime, particularly at weekends, and would make any excuse to get out of it.

On this occasion, Bob point blankly refused to do any overtime. His unbending intransigence in this matter necessitated bringing over the Personnel Officer from Glasgow, as well as the Edinburgh union representative, to arbitrate, and to, well, make sure that all was done fairly and squarely, for the benefit of everyone concerned.

"I'm no' doin' any f*****g overtime!" Bob fiercely announced to all who would listen. "They can f*****g shove it as far as I'm concerned." He then added, "My weekends are sacred, I like to go out on a Saturday night with my wife!" Bob was simply not going to be budged on this point of principal.

Anyway, a meeting was called for, and all were then duly sat in the office to discuss the matter at great length.

There was Bob, Harry, Al, Mac (in his official position as house foreman), and another chap called Bob Hooker, who was the union rep. Batting on the side of the BBC (and hoping to talk round the troublesome trio) was Miss Wilson, and the personnel officer from Glasgow.

The conversation ebbed and flowed, with each participant putting forward his, or her, point of view.

Harry got his priorities right, straight away. "I want to know how we're going to score out of this financially?" he asked.

"What do you mean, Harry?" Miss Wilson replied.

"Well, if you want us to work on the Saturday night, it better be worth our while – like treble time for instance!"

While all this high-powered negotiations were ongoing, Mac was staring out of the window, taking deep breaths and wishing that he were somewhere else. Staring out the window was what Mac usually did, whenever he was participating in a meeting that he didn't particularly want to be involved with. "Now c'mon Harry," added the personnel officer. "You have to come and go a wee bit. How about time and a half?"

Harry mulled this over in his mind, although he was not entirely convinced. Yet I suppose it might be better than nothing.

Just then, Bob, who was shaking his head with anguish, decided to put in his two-penny's worth.

"Look, I'm not doing any overtime at the weekend. For one thing, I don't need the money, and anyway, I'm taking my wife out on Saturday night!"

"What about you, Al?" asked Miss Wilson to the younger member of the team.

Al (who had not that long started with the BBC) began to mumble and stumble, by getting his words all in a tangle, all at the same time.

Yet he confirmed that he would only do the overtime, if the others all agreed.

By this time, the debate was beginning to get a little heated, with voices raised, and tempers threatening to boil to the surface.

In order to make his point truly heard, Bob then slammed his fist hard on the table, looked straight at the direction of Miss Wilson and the personnel officer, and then came out with the following statement – "Look, if I have to work at the weekend on overtime, I want to know who is going to take my wife out on the Saturday night."

They now both looked at each other with grave puzzlement and murmured back to him some lame excuse.

Bob then turned his full attention to the personnel officer and loudly repeated (after he had slammed his fist once more upon the table), "I want to know who's going to take my wife out on the Saturday night. Are you going to take her out?"

The personnel officer was slightly at a loss about what to say, and tried to make light of the situation by answering, "Well, eh, eh, Bob, I can't take your wife out, because I'm going out myself on Saturday night."

For Bob, this was not what he wanted to hear. "So it's ok for you to go out and enjoy yourself on a Saturday night. But I'm stuck in here doing overtime, when my wife is looking forward to me taking her out!"

This entire ludicrous charade lasted almost a full hour, as the arguments appeared to be going absolutely nowhere.

After much deliberation, Bob finally relented and admitted

defeat (once he had cooled down, and refrained from banging his fist on the table any more) and eventually agreed to do the weekend overtime. Who eventually did volunteer to take Bob's wife out that Saturday night, remains a mystery to this very day.

Harry rubbed his hands with glee at the prospect of more drink money heading in his direction, while Miss Wilson was close to being a nervous wreck, having had to preside over such an unnecessary and fruitless debacle.

Mac stood up and just slowly and sadly shook his head, and turned to look in the direction of both Bob H the union rep and the personnel officer, as if to say, "Look who I have to work with on a daily basis," as well as, "What an embarrassing shambles of a meeting that was."

*

Al, who I mentioned earlier, became part of the triumvirate along with Bob and Harry around early 1975. He was a much younger guy; in fact he was probably roughly about a dozen years older than myself. He used to arrive for work carrying what I can only describe as a soft leather "man-bag".

Now I had never seen a man-bag before, or a man carrying such an item, apart from pictures and portraits of wrinkled Pony Express riders of the old west.

So apart from that example, I had – up until that point – not been aware of the image of a man carrying one. Neither it seems had his two new work colleagues. This immediately drew suspicious comments from Bob right away, as he was going to have to work alongside someone who carried "a f*****g handbag!" as he delicately put it, in a manner far removed from the likes of *Lady Bracknell*.

Al possessed what you can only describe as a dreamy faraway attitude to life and equally a dreamy faraway look in his eyes, as if his mind and imagination was not entirely on his work, but constantly somewhere else.

While chatting one day, I asked Bob if he had ever seen that old Hollywood horror movie *I Walked With A Zombie*.

Bob looked over towards the chair where Al was sitting. He then looked straight back at me and said, "No, but we f*****g work with one!" Al was totally oblivious to the nature of the conversation as he slowly puffed on his cigarette, while simultaneously blowing numerous smoke rings into the air!

Al could often be found wandering around the corridors (usually with a brush firmly gripped within his hand) and muttering to anyone who might be interested: "I'm bored, I'm bored, I'm f*****g bored!"

On other occasions, usually when he was in a lighter, more frivolous frame of mind, he would equally be found standing with one hand on his sweeping brush, and the other perched upon his hip. Then with a voice borrowed from some outrageous Pantomime Dame, he would cry out for all to hear: "Cinders – you shall go to the ball!!" Suffice to say that from then on, I always watched out if he was behind me!

One of my abiding, and slightly disturbing memories of Al, is one of him sitting in his chair during a tea break, smoking away and gazing into space as if he was deeply communicating on a celestial level with some distant deity.

In fact, that day I popped into the rest room and there he was, relaxing in his chair with his trousers unbuckled, gazing lovingly down at his prize possession, which he was now stroking with much tender care!

He was unaware that for a few seconds I was standing at the door, but he then slowly looked up at me and dreamily said, "What do you think?" I stood there for a brief moment not sure what to think, apart from getting out of there pronto, as well as being far enough away in case the potentially startling image of Miss Wilson suddenly walking in, unexpected. Which she was often prone to do. No doubt if she had, she would have screamed out aloud in his direction, saying, *"Al, you can't do that here! This is the BBC!!"*

Anyway, with that in mind and trying to alter the conversation into another area, I said, "Aye, that's very good Al," as I then attempted to get out of the room pretty sharp. "I'm off to the canteen for a cup of tea," and with those words, I left Al to his physical ponderings, as I ran up the stairs as fast as I could.

I once overheard Bob and Harry discussing Al one morning, with the conversation going something along the lines of this: "What's the matter with that bastard Al?" Harry pondered. "One minute he's gabbing away and he's all talk and the next minute he say's f**k all, and he just stares into space!"

As quick as a flash, Bob gave his immediate opinion on Al's apparent mood swings – "Constant masturbation!"

"Aye, you're probably right there," replied Harry, as he picked up his copy of the *Daily Record* and carried on reading.

When Commissionaire Bob L was hosting one of his regular Saturday evening social gatherings, Al (accompanied by two lady friends) decided for a laugh to gatecrash. Bob L was completely unaware that his gala evening of sophisticated wit and expensive wine, was soon about to be disturbed by the presence of a drunken Al and his two floozy pals!

On the following Monday morning I asked Bob L how his party had gone. "That f*****g bastard Al turned up *uninvited* with a couple of f*****g lesbians, drunk out of their mind."

By this time I could see the anger mounting in Bob L's face as he was describing the events that previous Saturday.

"I had to endure him and those two dirty whores in my house!! They made a right f*****g mess and broke one of my good vases – the bastards!"

Al loved his music, particularly soul music and one day while I was passing the Studio 1 lounge area, I became aware of someone singing. I peeked through one of the entrance doors, and there was Al, in the middle of the floor using his sweeping brush like a concert microphone.

He was swaying, strutting and sashaying, with what I can only describe as total gay abandonment, as if performing at Wembley arena, imagining himself as a combination of *Diana Ross, Aretha Franklin,* and *Tina Turner!*

He was a one-man *Pointer Sister!!*

"It should have been me… waaaaaaa, it should have been me… waaaaaaaa…" he sang, totally unconcerned if anyone was watching. I'm sure that Al wouldn't have looked too out of place taking the lead in a touring production of *Call Me Madam!*

If only he had been around today, I can imagine him auditioning for *The Voice*, or even *The X Factor*!

Well at least he was happy in his work.

About a year later, Al took his man-bag (although not his sweeping brush/microphone) and finally left the building!

*

Often Bob would question the judgement (as well as the eyesight) of Miss Wilson and the personnel officer over their selection process when it came to choosing new additions to the House Services team.

His usual summing up was swift, straight and very direct – "Well you pay rubbish wages – and you get rubbish staff!"

There was also one guy (his name momentarily escapes me) who for several weeks in the late 1970s would find himself working alongside Bob and Harry.

However, with him being not long into the job, he would find himself placed under suspicion from the police, and stuck deep into a major murder inquiry! Suffice to say his BBC career was over before it had even begun, and unsurprisingly, he wouldn't return.

It does make you seriously ponder on what kind of selection process HR/Personnel were conducting in unearthing some of these "characters" during this period.

Two particular individuals who came under Bob's careful scrutiny were called Chris and Barry.

Bob delicately described them thus: "Two big f*****g lazy English bastards!" Then pointedly adding for Miss Wilson's benefit: "Has she got some prejudice about starting a f*****g Scotsman in the job?"

*

Chris first arrived and then once he slowly (very slowly) left for pastures new, Barry soon stepped into the breach. Despite their towering height and deceptive image of latent strength, both gave the immediate impression that they couldn't summon up the sufficient energy to unwrap a chocolate biscuit!

Chris, for example, wandered slovenly and sloth-like around the building with a rolled up fag stuck in the corner of his mouth, while carrying a black plastic bin bag that was protruding out of his back pocket, trailing indecorously on the floor. Hardly a glowing advertisement for BBC Scotland!

His pretence at doing some work was fooling nobody – particularly Bob.

While during Barry's time he had to take regular intakes of his inhaler whenever any arduous physical work was called for.

Big Barry was a Scouser (or as Bob described him – "a shit-stirrring Scouser") who also became known in certain quarters as "fookin' Barry".

So it was generally perceived that those two gentlemen who originally hailed from south of the River Tweed were not highly regarded as striking examples of two supposedly fit and agile men ready for a full day's hard work.

Perhaps Bob indeed had a valid point in questioning management's selection process (not forgetting their eyesight?) in fulfilling that role.

When I began working at the BBC in 1974, there were about a dozen cleaners responsible for predominately cleaning the offices, the canteen, and the main reception area. A little sad, if I suppose a sign of the times, when the time came for me to eventually leave in 2002, there were only three cleaners left.

During the course of their work, which of course took place very early in the morning, a few of the cleaners were known to inadvertently interrupt the odd producer and his female assistant in, what you would best describe as a compromising position and situation! So it wasn't quite *"What the Butler Saw"*, but more along the lines of *"What The Cleaner Saw"*.

I always found it a bit baffling that three could manage to effectively clean a large building that once was cleaned by twelve. Was that some form of progress – or more likely exploitation? I guess the jury is still out on that one…

During the cleaners' heyday (for want of a better phrase) there was an office created specifically for the senior Television News Manager.

We never had one when I first started – just the TV News Editor – but all of a sudden this gentleman soon appeared from Glasgow. The rumour mills soon went into overdrive as to this hurried development, along with his sudden and unexpected appearance.

Perhaps as news and current affairs coverage in Edinburgh was increasing, it was looked upon that we needed someone of that status to oversee things at a senior managerial level.

However, the main rumour concerning the gentleman in question, was that he had upset the then Controller in Glasgow (not only criticising his editorial judgement, but also alluding to some form of sexual politics as well) who instead of terminating his contract, decided to have him punted and exiled through to Edinburgh.

So he was, in a sense, put out the road, and far enough away to avoid any more unpleasantness for him. At least that's what the bulk of the rumours maintained.

He was given a new office, complete with brand new furniture, a large expensive television set and (wait for it) a large and well-stocked drinks cabinet.

I don't think that the drinks cabinet was ever locked (rather foolish considering all the thirsty individuals who resided in the building during this time!) and the manager only utilised it when entertaining senior news colleagues or visiting VIPs.

However, he soon began to notice that some of his spirit bottles were becoming a little less spirited in volume.

He had whiskey, gin, and vodka resting on the shelves, along with some port and brandy. So a very tempting target for someone in need of a libation – regardless of what time of the day it was.

With his stocks diminishing rapidly, he then decided that enough was enough, and reported the case of the missing alcohol to Mac, who no doubt had his own suspicions. With this being the case, he was now ready and determined to catch the mystery drinker red handed.

This would soon happen.

In fact, the guilty party turned out to be one of the cleaners. From what I learned, she had no complaints and no one to blame but herself for eventually being caught.

This was due to the fact that she could often be found swaying from side to side when operating a hoover, as well as slurring her words very early in the morning when handling a tin of polish and a duster. A very obvious giveaway, you might think.

Mac then caught her in action, as he walked into the office in order to confirm his suspicions, and discovered her not only polishing the table, but polishing off the confines of the drinks cabinet – with the alarming image of a large bottle of vodka wrapped around her lips!

She was then summoned to explain her actions – which she could now hardly deny – and sacked on the spot.

Her parting shot as she staggered out the front door was shouting out towards Mac's direction while he stood at reception "Ya big bearded-faced bastard!!"

Suffice to say, she never returned.

*

Mac would also find himself in a similar position to Bob one night when BBC 2 decided to ditch an old Hollywood movie, for the glories of cricket!

It always amazed me the BBC's constant obsession with this specific game, regardless of how unpopular it was north of the border, but the powers that be decreed otherwise. We would get cricket, lots of it – whether we liked it or not.

On this specific night, Mac had taken over the reception during the early part of the evening. This all happened around the time we decamped out of 5 Queen Street for the tiny offices at Thistle Street.

This would be for a period of roughly three years, whilst the bigger building was being refurbished, something that came about due to the collapse of the "Greenside Project". But that's another story…

Wouldn't you know it, just as Mac sat down at the front desk, the phone started to ring incessantly. Once again, a cricket match had overrun, and the film that was originally scheduled to appear on BBC2 had been cancelled. *Big Duke Wayne* it seems had been rudely bumped for big *Beefy Botham!*

The vast majority of the Scottish viewers were furious and

outraged at this, and so they decided to – yet again – voice their displeasure by telephone, towards the BBC. Although what a small radio station, and a temporary one at that, could do under the circumstances, is anybody's guess.

Call, after call, after call, came through, as Mac had to cough up with the same old information and excuses.

This was to no avail, for the way that all the callers saw that it was simply not good enough, it was his responsibility, and he was entirely at fault. And to top it all, they wanted him to resolve this issue ASAP!

"It's bloody outrageous! I don't pay my BBC licence fee to watch f*****g English cricket! Get it off now and put the film back on immediately!"

This, as I imagined, would be just one glowing example of what some of the angered viewers were now venting towards poor besieged Mac.

I'm not sure just exactly how many calls he received during that evening, but it must have been considerable.

The following day, he had the look of a man who was drained of life. "That f*****g phone never stopped ringing all night. All about the f*****g cricket being on!" he told us. "I tried to explain to them, that it had nothing to do with us, but nobody was interested," he further explained.

"Did you not tell them that we had no control over the TV schedules?" I bravely asked.

"Of course I did, but one bastard who called up wouldn't take no for an answer, and demanded to speak to someone in charge! I gave him the number for BBC Glasgow, and then I slammed the phone down! What a f*****g night I had," he concluded.

Funnily enough, about a day or so later, an article appeared in the *Daily Record* newspaper.

A certain "Mr Angry from East Lothian" had contacted

one of the newspaper's journalists, and was venting his fury towards the BBC in Edinburgh.

As the story went, the man in question stated that he had phoned the local BBC telephone number, and was brusquely spoken to by someone on reception duty, who told him simply: "Please don't phone me – phone Glasgow!"

The newspaper would have been rubbing their hands with glee at the implications, as well as this blunt announcement by an unnamed "BBC Edinburgh spokesperson".

No doubt vainly attempting to divert responsibility, as well as pushing all the loud and abusive calls from Edinburgh, straight through to Glasgow.

The article in the *Daily Record* caused several of us to laugh and giggle, as the "BBC spokesperson" named in the piece, could only have been Mac, as he was the only man on reception at the time.

Although, when the tabloid article was showed to him, he denied all knowledge and offered up this answer: "That wasn't me. I don't know anything about it." This caused us to laugh even more, which he didn't like.

He totally dismissed the newspaper's claim that he had told the annoyed gentleman in question, that he would have been far better off calling BBC Glasgow, than wasting his time calling BBC Edinburgh!

As a footnote to this story, it has always caused me great amusement whenever I used to read in any of the newspapers this constant reference to "a BBC spokesperson". Often this description would be offered up whenever a scandal, or calamity, or controversy threatened to engulf or embarrass the corporation.

I always wondered if there was indeed an office say down at Television Centre in London (sadly now no more) that had these bold words emblazoned on the door: "Office of the BBC Spokesperson".

I always wondered how you could apply for such an exalted position. What were the criteria? What specialised skills or knowledge was required before you could describe yourself as – "a BBC spokesperson"?

Maybe I'm being just a little facetious, but it often puzzled me as to what they (male, female – or both?) looked like, and why you rarely saw their faces revealed on screen, or in print?

I often imagined that "a BBC spokesperson" looked not unlike a stern headmaster, with a long grey beard and thick glasses, standing imperious and autocratic, while making sure that BBC policy was rigidly adhered to in all circumstances.

Yet for one night only, Mac embodied (whether he was aware of it or not?) the Scottish public's personification of "a BBC spokesperson".

A great pity that on that occasion, he didn't appear to embrace or revel in that privileged position.

*

During my time at Queen Street, we often had a number of individuals who would eventually go onto bigger and better things. Certain people, who I suppose, used their brief time working in Edinburgh, as a temporary sojourn. This would probably turn out to be a small, but very important step towards a potentially towering career at the very highest levels of television broadcasting.

A number of illustrious names would step into the entrance of 5 Queen Street, usually arriving fresh from university, with numerous letters after their names, and unbridled ambition coursing through their veins during the 1970s and 1980s, while spending a short period working in Edinburgh, honing their craft.

I often got the feeling that a few of them never exactly embraced Edinburgh with any degree of warmth, and looked upon it purely as a brief stepping stone for much greater things that would lie ahead. But maybe I'm doing them a disservice.

Some of the most high-profile names that began their careers within the narrow confines of 5 Queen Street, before climbing the lustrous ladder upwards, were the likes of *Kirsty Wark, Billy Kay* and *Lesley Riddoch*.

Roughly around the same time we also had an elegantly dressed and slightly pompous gent by the name of *Michael Buerk* who appeared from, well, somewhere important, and turned up at 5 Queen Street as the new Energy Correspondent. Once again, we never had one of those before. Yet I guess what with the startling discovery of oil and gas in the North Sea, we sure needed one now.

So an office was decked out with brand new (expensive) furniture for the smooth gent (who would later go on to make his name and reputation on the television news down in London) to feel quite at home in.

I don't remember if he also had a fully stocked drinks cabinet installed. Perhaps on this occasion, he didn't require one? Maybe just as well, considering the momentous thirsty activities of some of the house staff (don't forget the cleaners!) that were working there at the same time!

So he was presented with this all-new office in order for him to do his work. Even though, for a great deal of the time, he was rarely there. I suppose all that reporting about oil, gas, and drilling in the cold North Sea, meant that he would be more out, than in.

The few occasions he was around, he came across to many as a somewhat aloof individual, who gave off the impression that he was just a bit too good for this tiny, remote parochial, radio station. In fact his stay at 5 Queen Street barely elicited a mention in his biography, which I suppose says something.

Maybe I am doing him a bit of a disservice, and apologies are forthcoming if I am. Although I'm sure that he always felt that he was destined for a brighter and more high profile future, presumably down south at Television Centre. This indeed is what would eventually happen for him.

Yet my abiding memory of him (as well as many of my colleagues at the same time) was that he would on the odd occasion, venture over to reception, smile in the direction of whoever was on duty, and ask the burning question (burning question!!): "Do any of you guys have any cigarettes on you?"

A little strange, I thought, considering what his salary may have consisted of at the time, and what many of us were earning in meagre comparison.

But, such is life! He obviously needed his smokes. Even internationally famous newsreaders, can sometimes find themselves caught short without any cigarettes to hand. I recently noticed that he is presenting a weekly programme on Radio 4 called *"The Moral Maze"*.

Funny, that all those years ago, he used to be seen wandering around the old Edinburgh building in a bit of a "smoky haze". Coincidence or what?

Years later, whenever I used to catch him reading the BBC 6 O'clock News, I always pondered if he had managed to eventually relinquish his need for the dirty weed, or whether he was still scrounging the odd fag from some of the news team, or reception staff at TV Centre?

He has also recently broadened and lightened his appeal (in a manner of speaking) by turning up and slumming it with the "celebs" on *"I'm A Celebrity, Get Me Out Of Here!"*

Not quite sure what that was all about, but he still managed to give off that privileged air of stuffy superiority. The one I first witnessed in 5 Queen Street, all those years earlier.

*

Frank and Tom, now there are two names to conjure with!

Frank was the House Electrician, and often gave the impression that he had been with BBC Edinburgh almost from its very inception.

He was "an old soldier" who refused to fade way, as it were, and had fought in Burma with the 14th Army. Yes, the very same "forgotten army" that was so beloved, and dear to *Dame Vera Lynn's* heart.

You had to have instant respect for someone like Frank, who had served his country with bravery and devotion, throughout the far-flung corners of the British Empire.

He was also a proud member of the *Burma Star Association*, a group of men who stood stoutly and defiantly against "the wee yellow men", as Frank often described them.

Bob however, was of the opinion that all those years spent deep within the steaming, treacherous Burmese jungle had done something irreparable to Frank's psyche.

I guess anyone having to endure such horrific dangers and privations, thousands of miles away from home and your loved ones, would alter anyone's perception of life.

Frank was known to mutter away to himself, and also apart from his electrician duties, possessed what you could only describe as a massed library of assorted literature.

Yet Frank did not keep the combined works of *Tolstoy, Dickens, Proust, James Joyce, Jane Austen* or *Thomas Hardy* enclosed within the walls of his workshop, it was something much more in demand, and to some, much more desirable.

Alongside his pliers, screwdrivers, copper wiring and electrical tools, Frank kept a well-stocked library of pornographic magazines that would have made the *Emperor Tiberius* green with envy!

With this being the case, he could quite easily be the most popular individual in the building, as well as his workshop being the most frequently visited.

One regular visitor (in fact he was hardly ever out of the place) was Donald Monro the Television News Editor.

Donald was the man responsible each and every night

during the week, for making sure that the capital city's news managed to make it onto the Reporting Scotland screens. Yet, the importance of the news was hardly the most crucial thing on his mind at this point, going by the regular frequency of his visits to Frank's workshop.

Usually you would see him disappear into the basement, and then about ten minutes later, he would quickly emerge from Frank's workshop, clutching a large A3 BBC internal envelope that was literally bulging at the seams with literary material, of a sort.

So it was safe to say that the contents of what lay within the envelope, was of much more pressing urgency, than what crucial news items were about to be revealed on BBC Scotland at teatime!

One other amusing story concerning Donald happened when I encountered him one morning down in the basement area just outside the print-room.

I began to be aware of the echo of some loud banging noises, allied with a few choice swear words. I opened the door and there stood Donald looking none too pleased, with a look of angered frustration spread across his features. "This f*****g bastard of a machine won't f*****g work! Something's f*****g wrong with it!" Donald spouted as he was now seriously physically assaulting the printer with both fists. I looked on, just as he was getting more and more angry, as he was vainly trying to copy some urgent press releases.

"Let me have a look at it, Donald, and I'll see if I can sort it," I said to the flustered news editor, thinking that it may require a call-out for an engineer, or even some form of medical help, owing to the severity of Donald's blows upon its structure.

I looked closer and then noticed something that made me almost laugh out loud. The stupid bugger hadn't even turned the printer on!! No wonder it wasn't working. And this was the man responsible for editing Edinburgh's TV news items for Reporting Scotland!

From my perspective (and most likely a few others), Donald appeared to lead a reasonably charmed life as Edinburgh's TV news editor.

The job of getting news items on screen for that evening's Edinburgh Reporting Scotland slot seemingly ran a close second to the many freebie lunches he enjoyed and was regularly invited to.

You would always catch a glimpse of him either climbing into a taxi – or climbing out of a taxi, following a rather long and leisurely lunch. Paid by someone else of course! Everyone recognised that Donald was the undisputed king of the free lunch – usually with lots of free wine thrown into the bargain!!

Yet, for all that, I found Donald a likeable guy in some ways, and I felt a little sorry for him, as it appeared he was being finally hustled out of the door, as his time as the TV news editor was coming to an end, with the general consensus being that he was no longer up to the job, which left his limitations somewhat exposed.

This was not helped by the arrival of the News & Current Affairs team from Glasgow, which made the newsroom a much more boisterous and busier office as a consequence.

Donald would eventually retire, but about a couple of months following his final departure, the newsroom received a mysterious phone call.

Apparently Mrs Monro had called to speak with her husband? Well, what can you say? But it looks as if good old Donald had accidentally, or deliberately, omitted to tell his lady wife that he had actually left the BBC and was now officially retired! Which beggared the question: what was he telling his wife? And where was he going first thing in the morning??

Some details like that are best left undiscovered.

Yet prior to this discovery by his wife, Donald (just like The Terminator) would be back!

Well, at least he was back, first thing early in the morning.

This mystifying reappearance, involved Donald emerging from the back of a black taxi, walking into the building, and then without a care in the world, helping himself to the newsroom's newspapers.

He would then say his cheery farewells to whoever was on the reception desk, and with a very large bundle of the morning's papers gripped under his arms, he would then climb back into the taxi and head for... wherever he was heading, with evidence possibly pointing towards the press club at the West End?

This would happen for several mornings on the trot. Yet, at the same time, when he reappeared in the morning, he would bring back the previous day's papers and dump them into one of the waste bins near reception!

Then he would head off back into his awaiting taxi with all those early morning editions.

The regular disappearance of the morning's papers (including *The Scotsman, The Herald, The Telegraph, Daily Express, Daily Record, The Sun, Daily Mail* etc., etc.) caused a lot of scratched heads in the newsroom (with the blame unfairly pointed towards the suppliers), until the penny finally dropped.

When Donald's successor (it may well have been the very quiet and gentle-natured *Bob Dickson!!*) discovered where his papers were vanishing to each morning, he wasn't best amused, to put it mildly.

So the time finally arrived for Donald to purchase his own morning newspapers, instead of helping himself to a large bundle of freebies

One postscript to this story came to light later when it was discovered that not only was Donald (who was officially retired at this time, in case we forget) helping himself to the newspapers, he was also ordering the taxis each morning – on the newsroom account!!

What a guy!

When Donald finally left (and had no doubt eventually smoothed things over with his wife) he promised to take both Mac and myself out for lunch – his treat – so this was something to look forward to.

He booked a table in the upstairs Abbotsford Restaurant in Rose Street and both Mac and myself walked along to the pub to meet up with him.

The lunch was superb as we enjoyed a couple of bottles of wine, while reminiscing about hilarious past days at the Beeb. However, Donald soon gravitated the conversation towards his favourite subject – sex!

Flushed with red wine, and with his eyes bulging with unbridled lust, he then began to laugh and chortle loudly about all the young girls he loved drooling over while on holiday abroad. For a moment he began to resemble *Les Dawson's* comic character *Cosmo Smallpiece*, who used to get all hot and bothered when describing buxom females.

I could sense Mac feeling a little uneasy at Donald's full-on descriptions of bikini-clad blondes on the beach. Particularly when emphasising the sight of "golden nipples, glistening in the sun!" I found it greatly amusing, but Donald's voice began to get louder and louder, and I could also sense some of the other diners in the room looking at him while not hiding their embarrassment.

Donald was now in full flow, and enjoying himself with the combination of expensive red wine and a feverish imagination, working overtime. Finally, after a couple of hours, both Mac and I thanked him for our lunch, as we made our excuses to leave and said farewell. "We must do this again sometime?" Donald said as we waved him goodbye and headed back down the road.

"That was the most f*****g embarrassing lunch I have ever experienced," Mac stated.

"Do you not fancy meeting up with Donald again then?" I asked him with my tongue pressed slightly within my cheek.

"That will be f*****g right! Never again!"

When we got back round to Queen Street, Fraser was waiting for us and asked us both how the lunch went. "Great food and Donald was in typical roaring form," I told him.

However, Mac saw it very differently. "A right f*****g embarrassment!" he said, and then he stormed through to his office.

Once I told Fraser the details of what had happened, like myself, he just couldn't stop laughing!

Frank was the electrician responsible for seeing that the building ran effectively, and that the power was always functioning. When I first arrived Frank looked as if he was due to retire there and then, and I had the impression that his retiral date, couldn't have been that far off.

The problem was, that Frank – and Frank alone – was the only man who appeared to have intricate knowledge of all the internal wiring of this vast building.

He was extremely reluctant to pass on his knowledge to anyone else, which made him quite a unique figure during those days.

Yet it soon became apparent that Frank could not last forever, and that the BBC management would have to take matters in hand and eventually employ a replacement.

However, before that happened, Frank was gifted with a number of yearly contract extensions, that kept him working well past his official retirement age.

This suited both parties at the time, as Frank could

continue working, and the management would put off, for yet another year, the prospect of bringing in someone new who would have to start virtually from scratch, in learning about the vast network of complex wiring in the building.

One day during the Edinburgh Festival, Frank was asked to work extra hours on a Sunday, as the Manager at the time (known affectionately to many as "Old Jock") was laying on a lavish function in Studio 1 – not for the staff I hasten to add – but for a number of the fringe performers and assorted "artists" who were in the capital during that month.

Although, from what happened during that function, "piss artists" would have been a far more accurate description, as the majority took full advantage of the BBC's fathomless generosity.

So lots and lots of wine and nibbles were ordered and then duly set up within Studio 1 for the hungry and thirsty artistic mob to descend upon it with avaricious glee that Sunday afternoon.

Frank mumbled and grumbled about having to come out on a Sunday, but orders from his boss meant he was required to do the lighting, and he was the only one capable, or responsible at that time to do it.

The following day, Frank couldn't wait to tell us what had gone on (or come off!) during the party. From the way he described it, the Manager's Festival Fringe Function degenerated into a mass drunken orgy of almost Romanesque proportions. Going by Frank's vivid description, if the *Emperor Caligula* had walked into the proceedings, he would have felt right at home.

With the easy availability of so much free booze, this inevitably and very quickly, led to the mass loosening of inhibitions, morals, and countless zips and buttons, as the guests took up the gesture of the BBC's relaxed, free-flowing hospitality with energetic and lustful gusto.

Frank related how a number of "the artists" had awkwardly stumbled and clambered onto the stage – with full wine bottles in hand – and then proceeded to remove their clothes and indulge in all manner of outrageous lasciviousness.

This all happened behind the vast, heavy, swaying curtains, which now began to bend and sway with rampant physical movements. And to think that on this very same stage many years earlier, once stood the immortal *Charles Dickens*, no less, giving one of his treasured readings. Although going by Frank's feverish descriptions of what happened that day in the studio, it was anything but a *"Bleak House"* with many anticipating some *"Great Expectations"*, that generally accompanied some ultimate *"Hard Times!"*

"They were all f*****g at it!" Frank firmly asserted. "And that dirty old git (referring to the elderly senior manager who had organised the event) had one hand on a big bottle of wine, and his other hand on some young blonde's arse!! The randy old goat!! You should have seen the f*****g mess the bastards made as well."

Harry then put his money's worth in. "Aye, you're right there Frank, as we had to clean up the f*****g mess those bastards made earlier this morning!"

Not to be outdone, Bob then entered, stage left. "You know I found several packets of f*****g condoms at the back of the stage! The dirty bastards!"

After their animated recollections of what happened during the party, Frank with a weary shake of his head, then slowly walked up the stairs for his regular cup of coffee.

When the day finally arrived for Frank to leave, it was left to Debbie (who was the newsroom secretary at the time and like many of us, had become quite fond of Frank) to take him out for a farewell drink and a spot of lunch.

This was due to the fact that his superiors, by all accounts, couldn't be bothered to show their appreciation for all his hard work and years of steady service, by treating him themselves.

After the lunch, Debbie marched straight up to the Operations Manager's office and let him have it with both barrels! She later told me what had transpired: "Did you enjoy your lunch?" she cheekily enquired. The manager was at a loss for words as to her line of questioning.

"Well, since you couldn't be bothered to take old Frank out on his last day – I took him out and we had a bloody good lunch and a bloody good drink – and he thoroughly enjoyed himself!"

With that parting shot and angry words, Debbie stormed out the office, leaving the Operations Manager speechless, and alone with his thoughts.

I suppose if Frank had been given the straight choice of having lunch and a couple of drinks with his two bosses, or alternatively with an attractive young blonde news secretary – there was simply no contest.

During his time with the BBC, I became very fond of Frank, and when he did eventually retire, he and his wife Margaret would make periodic return visits to the building to partake in a coffee in the canteen and have a catch up with myself and some of the staff.

When he passed away, I was the only employee who attended his funeral, which I thought at the time pretty shabby and somewhat shameful, considering the long service he had given BBC Scotland.

I remember vividly on the day his coffin being escorted into the funeral chapel, carried by a group of Burma Star veterans. He deserved no less.

*

Tom arrived sometime in the late 1970s and took up residence as the House general handyman. Like Frank, he was getting on in years, and also like Frank, he was a very personable and likeable guy. At first glance, he looked like a slightly frayed at the edge and roguish *David Niven* type, with a mischievous moustache and a glint in his eye for the young ladies.

Tom had also served his country with distinction during the war. For example, when someone once asked him if he had ever been in Germany, he smiled and then said, "No. But I've been over it many times…" Suffice to say that he had a very honourable background with the RAF.

It was always very amusing, particularly early in the morning when you visited the canteen, for just there around 9:30, both sat Frank and Tom at the very top table near the window, having their morning cup of coffee.

One of the Audio Crew cracked that in his mind the two old guys resembled *"Statler & Waldorf"* from the *Muppet Show!* I could see the resemblance, as the two of them chatted and laughed together whilst eyeing up some of the young girls with a devilish twinkle in their eyes.

One day during the Edinburgh Festival (or as someone observed, the time of the year when the building was inundated with the wild, the weird and the wacky!) Frank and Tom were enjoying a wee break and a coffee at the couch near reception.

There was a show of sorts happening in Studio 1, with the public coming and going, alongside various colourfully costumed fringe performers, who were all looking to get their shows promoted.

Frank and Tom's attention was suddenly alerted to a tall, statuesque lady with very long hair, very long legs and a never ending split in her skirt. The two old gents looked on with all eyes bulging, as they couldn't quite believe what lay before them.

Their tongues were soon hitting the floor as they foamed

at the mouth with their eyes rolling in their sockets, as they followed the glam lady as she was walking up and down the corridor. Frank and Tom kept looking at her, and then at each other, chuckling away with saucy glee.

But then, their combined looks of unbridled lust, soon instantly turned to shock, as "the lady" in question calmly walked into the gents' toilet that stood alongside the reception.

Unbeknownst to Frank and Tom, I think that on that particular day, we had been visited by one of the lady boys from Bangkok. If the old guys had been shocked, I shudder to think what the reaction might have been if someone also had been standing in the gents' at the same time!

Tom could be often found patrolling the building with his large screwdriver firmly gripped within the palm of his hand. He may not have done much work – but he was all ready to go whenever the occasion arose.

One day he wandered over to the reception desk for a chat, whilst carrying the aforementioned screwdriver.

"Working hard today, Tom?" asked Mac. Tom smiled straight back and showed Mac his erect screwdriver. "Yes, I've been doing a lot of screwing today!!" You couldn't help but laugh at this curious observation, as Tom giggled away to himself.

Then as a couple of lady visitors stepped up to the reception desk, Tom's face reddened slightly, as he walked away, with his screwdriver still erect in his hand.

Maybe Tom had managed to get one over Doctor Who no less, and was the first man to possess a sonic screwdriver?

As I said, Tom was a very likeable guy, but he harboured a secret. He led a double-life, and one that, his wife knew absolutely nothing about.

From what I could gather at the time, Tom made periodic visits down to the borders – particularly at weekends. To his unsuspecting wife, he was doing OBs, better known as outside broadcasts.

However, it soon becoming common knowledge that Tom appeared to be doing more outside broadcasts than your average OB engineer!

One day Mac asked him (with a hint of a smile), "Are you back down the borders again this weekend, Tom?"

Tom replied with his usual roguish Terry Thomas style smile (hinting that he was up to no good), "Aye, that's me off back down there on Friday."

Apparently, Tom's dark secret was that he had a mistress – and a younger one at that – a lady who resided down in the borders. However, that was not all.

He also had a young family to this woman. So Tom's life (from us looking on the outside) appeared just a little precarious and risky for a man of his age. Talk about living dangerously, but I suppose, stranger things have happened.

On one occasion (while he was safely settled down in his alternative home) his wife phoned up the reception at Queen Street to find out exactly where he was "working" that weekend. There had been a sudden family emergency, and it was naturally imperative that she got a hold of him – as soon as possible.

Although if she was to discover the truth she would get a hold of him alright, with potential homicide being a strong possibility.

So with Mac on duty that particular Sunday, he faced a potentially awkward situation when Tom's wife demanded to know where he was, and how she could get in touch with him as it was extremely imperative!

Mac calmly explained to her that to his knowledge, there were no outside broadcasts happening over that weekend. Although in reality, he knew exactly where he was. He had to think quickly on his feet before he inadvertently dropped

Tom right in it.

Tom's wife was no doubt slightly puzzled and confused as to his whereabouts, and no doubt she would be demanding some serious answers when she eventually got to speak with her errant husband.

Then a little while later, Tom appeared at the BBC's front door. He had just arrived back at St Andrews Square bus station following his borders bus journey, and just by luck popped into the building before heading home.

Only to be then told by Mac that his wife had been frantically calling to get in touch with him.

Tom was ashen faced. Was the game finally up for him?

He thanked Mac for not giving the game away, picked up his overnight bag and headed out the front door as quick as he could.

I later believe that Tom had come up with some form of believable and logical excuse explaining his absence over the weekend, while at the same time managing to convince his wife that all was fine and above board.

But it was a close run thing that weekend for Tom – the randy old rascal. I always wondered if he ever packed his sonic screwdriver in amongst his pyjamas during those trips.

The BBC Scotland Controllers of the time were picked up and driven from point to point and venue to venue in a black chauffeur-driven BBC car.

Their drivers were two amiable guys called *John MacLean* and *Jim Macbeth*.

John and Jim were frequent and welcome visitors to Queen Street, whenever they were transporting the Controller to whatever function in Edinburgh he was due to attend on that day.

John was a cheery chap, with an impish sense of cheeky humour, who during his visits, usually passed on a few snippets of news and gossip from the west. Which might well have had some ongoing interest to us in Edinburgh.

I suppose that possibly sitting in front of the Controller driving him around everywhere, undoubtedly gave him certain access to information that most of us were ignorant of.

In fact the story going the rounds at the time was that our very own beloved Controller, had another side to him. Apart from being the top BBC man in Scotland, apparently, he was also a part-time pig farmer! Not sure if this porky tale had any real basis in fact, but I must confess that it made for some amusement amongst the staff.

Come to think about it, maybe that was the primary reason that bacon and sausages were always plentiful in the canteen around this time?

Jim, on the other hand, looked not unlike a Victorian undertaker. He was tall and slow moving, carrying with him an equally dark and mordant sense of humour.

Both John and Jim usually sat around for a few hours (usually enjoying a blether, a few cups of tea and a few smokes on the outside front steps) while waiting on their inevitable call to pick up the Controller.

One day, Jim was sitting with Mac, Fraser and myself having a break and chatting away, as you do. Fraser was explaining that he had experienced a little accident regarding his front teeth that now required a potentially painful visit to a dentist. To say that he wasn't looking forward to it, was putting it mildly! "Dentists!" began Jim. "Don't talk to me about f*****g dentists. I could tell you a few horror stories about f****** dentists!"

And then Jim proceeded to tell us one particular gruesome tale about one of his past visits to a dentist that left him, not surprisingly, with very painful memories.

The gory story that Jim now revealed to us was like something out of the Spanish Inquisition! "I was in f*****g agony for days!!" Jim told us, with a genuinely pained look that meant the memory had still not entirely left him.

On listening to this, poor Fraser now looked like a guy about to endure several agonising hours on the rack!

His face went from pure white to almost sickly green, and he visibly shook at the terrifying prospect that now possibly awaited him on the dentist's chair.

"Aye it was pure f*****g murder!" Jim calmly added, as he puffed on his cigarette and then gulped another swig of tea.

*

Then we had The Security Men. This, I suppose was a collective term for a very eclectic group of gentlemen (for want of a better phrase) who arrived around the late 1970s in order to, well, keep the building secure.

Although one or two of the staff muttered at the time that they should have been kept secure from their often vulgar and intrusive presence.

The comfy, gentile (if outdated) days of the traditional BBC Commissionaire (at least in Edinburgh) were coming to a close, to make way for, well a very different style. This, you could say, would bring almost as much unintentional hilarity over the next few years.

It was fairly common knowledge at the time, that in order to become a BBC security man, or indeed a BBC Commissionaire, you had to have had some form of past military service, or time employed within either the Police or the Fire Brigade.

Looking back on those days, it was deemed more likely that you would be well suited to the position, if you had unflinchingly carried out orders, while possessing a form of disciplined background in the various services. At least that was the theory?

Although, I have a feeling (whether correct, or not) that

with today's employment laws, that form of selective and restrictive practice would no longer be allowed. Maybe I am way off the mark with this, but who knows?

Anyway, I suppose the new security men's arrival coincided with the feeling that what with the building now housing the Good Morning Scotland and News and Current Affairs teams, it was probably wise to have it manned 24 hours a day – 7 days a week.

So over the next decade, we saw a real mixed bunch of guys donning the dark uniform and manning the front desk, as well as patrolling the vast building during the twilight zone.

And it's fair to say, that the overall general opinion regarding one or two of them, came to the conclusion that they themselves perhaps belonged in the twilight zone – permanently!

We had Stan, Dougie (incidentally, they are the only two still working within the Corporation, although not strictly for the corporation, but in slightly different roles), Archie, Bill, Ellis, Bernard, Peter, Pat, and last but not least – Hector and Sandy.

*

Archie was a large, lumbering, slow-moving character, who would arrive to do his shift, settle down behind the front desk, make himself a cup of tea, and then slowly and carefully put on his slippers, as if relaxing for a night in front of the telly. How he would have summoned up the thrusting energy to tackle any potentially threatening intruder, while moving at a snail's pace wearing well-worn slippers, was beyond me.

*

Then we had Ellis. He was, as I recall, an ex-fireman and a jolly, good-humoured individual to boot. Although, we later discovered that the origins of that good humour invariably came out of a bottle. A bottle that would soon become empty. He would often start his night shift after an exhaustive session in the pub (or the fireman's club), and then settle down to a good night's sleep in the Green Room (the very same one that would be later used for the midnight movie shows).

Like Archie before him, Ellis also took the opportunity of coming to work to complete his shift, wearing comfy slippers. No doubt after consuming much hard liquor earlier in the day, he was overdue for a good night's kip.

The unfortunate thing in all of this was that he momentarily forgot he was being paid to patrol the building and to keep on high alert in case of any emergencies that may befall the place, prior to the morning's arrival.

One night, he was in such a sound sleep in the Green Room (no doubt dreaming of ten green bottles hanging on the wall) that the police were called out in an emergency. This was because Ellis failed to check in that all was well and in order – which he was expected to do at regular intervals.

The police scoured the building looking for the mysteriously vanished security man, as alarms were raised that he may have had an accident – or perhaps an altercation with an intruder that had left him ailing in some darkened corridor.

Eventually the officers switched on the light of the Green Room, and it was here they found Ellis, snoring for all his worth and finally woken from his drunken slumbering by the police, as if nothing was amiss.

He left the BBC shortly afterwards.

*

We then had Bernard who was with us for a short while, before his talents were recognised by BBC Glasgow and he moved over to the west.

Bernard had been a former officer in the SAS and had the correct and proper military bearing to make him an ideal man on the front desk. Certainly, in retrospect, he was far more ideal that a few of the "characters" who would replace him.

The tale of Bill was one of both great amusement, as well as a telling cautionary tale, that almost brought about almighty repercussions that would have been felt all the way from 10 Downing Street to Buckingham Palace.

Bill was another jolly individual, a man who constantly saw the funny side of life – as well as the funny side of the BBC – which wasn't difficult. He was always laughing, which made him an agreeable colleague, although it occasionally irked some others.

Someone likened him to one of those comical nautical figures you would often find at seaside resorts, such as "Jolly Jack Tar" the jovial sailor.

Well his last day as a BBC employee would prove to be more hilarious than any visit to a funfair could ever be.

As it was Bill's last day, he was cordially invited up to the manager's boardroom for a farewell drink. During that time we had two relatively new senior managerial figures that hadn't been with us all that long.

They had both recently arrived with much pomp and circumstance from England and declared it their joint mission in life in raising the broadcasting profile of Scotland's capital city, way beyond its previous regional constrictions. It all sounded very good, but perhaps it was too good to be true, as it eventually turned out.

Oh dear, they almost raised the profile alright, but not in the way they had originally promised, or envisaged.

Bill went up to the office in the early afternoon, and as we all thought, he would be back down after 30 minutes or so. But an hour passed, then another, and then another. Bill finally emerged from the room laughing his head off and ever so slightly smashed out of his mind! From those who were there and witnessed it (including myself), we got the feeling that Bill and the two managers had – between them in the space of a few hours – drank the drinks cabinet dry!

Bill would finally stagger out the front door after one final laugh, tossing his *Harry Worth* style hat high in the air, and then he could be seen swaying along the street, until he disappeared out of view, never to return. I always wonder if Bill realised the impact his last day at the BBC achieved.

Not only did he depart with the smell of strong booze on his breath – but also he managed to inadvertently take two senior managers with him!

What was originally supposed to be an innocent farewell drink, with a soon to be departing member of staff, had quickly turned into a rowdy, boozy session of almost rat-pack proportions, that later could well have had very serious political and monarchical implications.

As the staff later found out (with much gleeful amusement) the two managers were so far gone drink wise that as a jest, they called up the duty office in BBC Glasgow to make a very serious announcement. One that could very well have set in motion events that could have caused major ructions – all the way to the very corridors of power.

The tabloids would have had a field day if it had ever come to light at the time. Nevertheless, it was the "talk of the steamie" and caused much merriment amongst the staff, as to how two such senior and respectable managerial figures could have acted with such ineptness and reckless abandonment, by turning themselves into a pair of drunken buffoons.

*

It was no great surprise that throughout my time at BBC Scotland, secrets were never kept secret for very long. Controversies, scandals, abrupt removals, mysterious arrivals, all became speedily common knowledge among the staff.

And this was long before the arrival of instantaneous social media. Maybe the jungle drums (along with Bob's clarinet) were just too finely tuned in relaying the story to an all too eager staff that was greedy in lapping up salacious chitchat. Particularly when it involved certain bumptious figures of high authority that had made a complete arse of themselves!

Well, suffice to say, the two gentlemen in question, were soon "strategically removed elsewhere" with all reference to their previous incarnations in Edinburgh being swiftly erased. Ultimately, they were sent back south and homewards – no doubt to think and drink again.

Now you see them – now you don't! You could say that they vanished quicker than many of Stalin's generals, prior to the outbreak of WW2!

What they told a rather stunned Glasgow duty officer was simply that Her Majesty the Queen had suddenly and sadly passed away!

Now remember, this was almost 40 years ago, and the implications of this becoming common knowledge at the time, would have put all other scandals in the shade.

Ironically, it wasn't too long ago that a BBC journalist (not sure if he was drunk, stupid, or just in dire need of a sensationalist story?) fell into the same trap and decided to do something similar.

Only this time he tweeted the dreadful news, which then hit the public's attention within seconds! Maybe a few weeks locked up in the Tower without any access to social media would cool his eagerness to tweet and teach him a lesson?

Makes you wonder which is worse: a tweet, or a twit?

So, back to 5 Queen Street. A brand new Edinburgh Manager (who at first glance, appeared to be the very polar opposite of his predecessors), soon replaced both the individuals who had come close to initiating a nationwide scandal.

He was a quiet, solemn, austere character who, from what I could see at the time, made no attempt, or effort, to ingratiate himself or in any way communicate with the staff.

Appearing fleetingly as a mysterious ghostlike figure, he almost slipped unnoticed into the building. Ironically, spending most of his time – more out than in. A very different individual you could say to the rowdy likes of *"Frank & Dean"* style characters who preceded him!

So anonymous a managerial figurehead he was, and so minimal his overall impact appeared to be, that I couldn't for the life of me recall anything substantial he did during his time in charge.

Yet I assume that during his brief tenure, he must have made sure that the boardroom drinks cabinet would be properly padlocked up and that farewell drinks for departing staff, would now be very much a thing of the past. Maybe in hindsight that decision was probably a very wise one.

Anyway, back to the security men!

Another temporary addition to the team arrived during the late 1970s, and he was called Pat.

He was a much younger guy who had served time with the army in Northern Ireland, so I suppose at first glance looked like he would fit in well and eventually turn out to be an ideal part of the group. I liked Pat, and he had a personable, easy-going nature that made him easy to get on with.

Yet, a few were unsure about some of the stories he told about his time in Ulster. For instance he told many that he had in fact been "Chased out of Belfast by the IRA!"

Not sure if this was due to his military activities in the Ulster province at the time – or the fact that he was a died-in-the-wool blue nose who supported Rangers? Maybe it was a combination of the two?

However, there was something else about Pat that ultimately led to his dismissal – he gave the impression that he enjoyed the company of nubile young schoolgirls.

In fact, one evening (while he was ostensibly on the night shift) he was disturbed in the old cloakroom by a member of staff who found him with a girl of about 15 years of age.

From what we later learnt, he wasn't exactly helping her with her homework – at least not in the traditional sense! His time as an employee was soon up after that, and like so many others, he left under a cloud, never to return.

As a postscript to this, about two or three years later, while I was walking down Leith Walk late at night, I heard this voice cry out from the shadows: "Hiya Lawrence."

I looked around and I then I spied in a darkened shop entrance, none other than Pat, with his arms wrapped around a young girl, who looked as if she had just left school!! Maybe after all, he was just again helping her with her homework??

*

We also had Peter, who joined the security team at roughly the same time.

He was a quieter individual who had served in the submarines, but who seemed to suffer from, what I can only describe as pent up sexual frustration.

Although, I suppose in those days, he wouldn't be the only one, since the majority of the building's staff appeared to be afflicted with that malady – in one form or another!

Peter would often make lewd and naughty suggestions towards young Wendy (who was about 16 at the time and working in the mailroom) as well as openly confess to all that his wife was not indulging him in his rightful conjugal rights (at least I think that's what he was implying?).

This manifested itself one day, when due to his pent-up sense of frustrated fury, he ended up putting his right fist through one of the walls at the back of the reception desk, connected to the old mailroom.

To be honest, it was a false wall, so it didn't cause him too much physical damage, although the wall in question was another matter.

This particularly destructive act of, whatever it was, didn't go down all that well with the Operations Manager, who enquired as to what had happened, and made several tut-tut noises in Peter's direction. Peter left for pastures new not long afterwards, no doubt in search of more walls to put his fists through.

*

The two most memorable (or notorious depending on how you look at it) members of the security staff during this period were Hector and Sandy.

Hector arrived all fired up with enthusiasm and drive to make BBC Edinburgh as safe and secure a building as he could possibly make it.

He was a man with a mission in life, yet he also gave you the impression that he was destined for higher and greater things.

Being the main man security-wise (at least in his head) at 5 Queen Street wasn't enough for him, he saw himself as a latter day James Bond figure, who gave all the impression that his true vocation was ultimately to work for either MI6 or the CIA. Protecting a Prime Minister, or a President, was not beyond the realms of possibility for this guy.

His somewhat officious manner rubbed a few up the wrong way during his initial introduction to the staff. But as time wore on, he mellowed somewhat, becoming more likeable, yet still harbouring ambitions that hopefully would lead him to a position of higher authority.

At the same time, Hector also had the uncomfortably disconcerting habit of singing away to himself the song "Someday my prince will come…" Not sure exactly what to say about that, apart from, well, nobody's perfect.

Some of his colleagues often jokingly referred to him as

"daddy cool", although whether that description was meant as a compliment, or just a wind-up, the jury was still out! At the same time, it was commented by a number of the audio crew that Hector possessed "something of the night about him".

Maybe that applied to his tangible relish while patrolling the dark, silent corridors during his night shift.

One week, Hector's then wife, decided to test out her hairdressing talents by giving him a bubble-perm! The initial shock when he walked through the front door at his new appearance caused a few gasps – as well as numerous giggles.

Mac looked at him open-mouthed and announced: "What a f*****g mess!"

Hector, at first a little upset, then replied that he felt happy with his hair and that in his eyes, it looked ok.

Mac continued to give his opinion throughout the day, emphasising and slowing his words down to give them extra impact. "What... a... f*****g... mess!"

Another of his security colleagues commented that he thought he resembled a cartoon character that had just shoved his fingers into an electric socket!

Despite all those caustic comments, Hector just brushed it all off (no pun intended!), as he was more than happy with his new look. He also had it in his head (apart from a bubble perm!) that he was a bit of a "ladies man". Perhaps that's where the name "daddy cool" originally sprang? Following his somewhat acrimonious separation from his first wife, Hector now threw himself into his new "swinging bachelor" phase, as he looked around for assorted ladies to sweet talk and chat up.

He even tried his "charms" on a female union rep that was visiting one day from England. After taking her out for a relaxing drink to the Beau Brummell, following a long and fairly heated union meeting, she gave her withering assessment of his charms to those who were there at the time, "He bores the f*****g pants off me!" Following that, she then departed for her train soon afterwards, with her pants still happily attached to her person, I'm led to believe.

Hector also set his passion towards another "lady" he had encountered in the same pub (although from what I had heard from a variety of sources, describing her as a lady is a bit of a stretch of the imagination!) whose command of the English language confirmed to all that like a few others, she had not attended a Swiss finishing school for young girls! The story that was going the rounds pointed out that she had had more partners than a law firm!

Unfortunately, their "brief encounter" resulted in Hector making a swift appointment with his GP, followed by several weeks drinking nothing stronger than fresh orange juice.

A chastening experience no doubt for this nocturnal Casanova.

Hector later related a strange tale that happened when he became friendly with the famous Irish actor of stage and screen, *Patrick Magee*, who was participating in a radio drama play in Studio 1. It appears that the grand actor and the younger security man had hit it off and so they decided to go out one night for a few drinks.

So there we had the unusual spectacle of an actor famed for films such as *Zulu* and *A Clockwork Orange*, as well as tackling the complex works of *Harold Pinter* and *Samuel Beckett*, about to embark on "a night out on the piss" with good old Hector!

Nothing ominous there we generally thought, until the following day, as a few of us quizzed Hector as to just how his night turned out.

"Aye, it was ok, we went to the Beau Brummell and then tried a few more pubs, but I must have gotten really drunk," he told us. He then added with a completely straight face: "I must have blanked out at some point, for I woke up all alone in the back of a taxi, outside of my flat, with my trousers around my ankles!!" I might add that the late stage and screen actor was nowhere to be seen at this point.

We were all left a little speechless at this startling confession from Hector, but he calmly shrugged it off, and never elaborated any further about exactly what dramatic turns unfolded on that night.

Hector's initial introduction to the weird and wonderful world of the night shift occurred fairly early on in his Queen Street career.

By this time the building had attained a reputation for strange goings on, mysterious noises and things that go bump in the night! With those spooky events not just centred upon the confines of the First Aid Room!

Hector was heard to complain that during his first post-midnight experiences of patrolling the building, he had been aware of loud and unusual banging noises originating from the back of the building, along with unearthly and almost supernatural moans and groans.

This seeming evidence tended to add credence to the suspicions that the building was indeed haunted, and haunted by some form of otherworldly spectre.

Hector was at first slightly unnerved by this unsettling phenomenon and began to proceed very carefully in his investigation.

He would go on to check the rear area with stringent attention, although each time he did, the noises abruptly ceased, and there was simply no sign of anyone around when he carefully opened the back door to investigate.

Finally, one night, the banging and moaning noises became frighteningly loud, almost to the point of him calling in the police – or even in desperation, an exorcist. Hector again moved slowly and gingerly towards the back door of the building, as the noises were reaching a terrifying crescendo.

With a deep intake of breath, he quickly opened the door, only to find a young teenage couple startled at being rudely interrupted and disturbed, as they had just been utilising the very same back door as a honeymoon bed!!

Another funny story concerning Hector happened when he was off duty. One of the security staff had called in sick and so was unfit to complete his shift. The only candidate to take his place was Hector. So Mac (in his then position of House Foreman) ordered a taxi to go direct to Hector's flat to see if he was available in an emergency to come in to cover the shift.

Mac duly arrived, alighted from the taxi and pressed the flat buzzer. Hector answered, and Mac announced his arrival. He then walked into the building and just as he was about to knock on the door, it quickly opened, and there standing in front of him, was Hector.

He was completely devoid of clothing, as naked as nature intended, looking a little bit sleepy and ruffled, yet not at all that disturbed by the intrusion.

Mac stood there for a few seconds, slightly taken aback at what was standing before him, as Hector resembled a cast member of *Planet Of The Apes*. He then bellowed, "For f**k's sake Hector, get some f*****g clothes on!"

Well shortly afterwards, both Mac and Hector (this time fully clothed, I hasten to add) quickly returned to Queen Street by taxi to continue their day's work.

Later that same day, Mac appeared somewhat quiet and a little morose, giving the impression of a man who was in a worried state of arrested shock, and quite possibly in much need of a strong double brandy.

However, at that time, he would have to make do with a soothing cup of tea to calm his frayed nerves. I brought up the subject of Hector's flat to Mac and how surprised he must have been of him turning up unannounced and unexpected at the front door.

Mac looked straight back at me and shook his head, and then with a look of a man who had witnessed something surreal, strange and unnerving, simply said: "I got the shock of my life when Hector opened the door. He was absolutely bollock naked, as if he had just fell out of his bed."

He then shook his head once again and muttered, "It looked like a squashed hedgehog!!" He then shook his head once again and wandered back to his office. I suppose you could say that there was no answer to that.

Hector also had the alarming habit of flashing (no, not his squashed hedgehog this time, thank God!) but his payslip, for all to see.

This proved a particularly controversial move, as from a distance, it appeared that he was painfully rubbing it in to the likes of Bob and Harry, just exactly how much he was earning. This would prove a very sore point and built up a great deal of anger, envy, resentment and malice amongst quite a few of the house staff at the time. Hector was often caught boasting that, what with shift allowances, overtime and the likes, the security men were simply raking it in!

In fact, there was a general view that in some instances, they were making far more money than some of the senior producers.

So it came as no great surprise that he was found cheerfully telling everyone that he had recently applied for an American Express Platinum credit card!

Hector was known to take this boastful stance one step further, and he could often be found walking with a broad grin on his face, into the "unofficial BBC Edinburgh club" – the Beau Brummell pub, that was just situated along the road. He would order up his pint and then to those colleagues standing alongside him, take out his wallet, and produce his monthly payslip. Then he proceed to show it to everyone around, displaying just how much money he had made that month.

It was a gesture worthy of the *Harry Enfield* character *"Loads of money"*. However, this sort of crass, boastful behaviour would backfire spectacularly, by bringing with it a lot of bitter accusations that were soon brought abruptly bubbling to the surface.

Once he became aware, Bob in particular took great offence to this, as he was more than vocal about it to anyone who would listen. "They sit all day long on their fat f*****g arses, doing f**k all and earning all that f*****g money! There's something not f*****g right about it," he loudly complained. "We're working our f*****g pan out, and getting a mere fraction of what those lazy, f*****g bastards are earning!"

Bob was now like a dog with a bone clenched firmly between his teeth, grimly determined not to let go, and making sure that the entire building was aware about how much the security men were earning in comparison with everyone else.

"These bastard security men are earning more than the f*****g producers!" was one of Bob's favourite sayings at the time.

Harry too, was equally vocal, that is whenever he was sober enough to string the proper words together. "F*****g bastards!" he would exclaim.

"And that Hector's the f*****g worse. He was in that pub the other night showing off to everyone just how much he was getting."

Both gents now complained vociferously and bitterly to the union about how much they were earning for doing (as they put it – hard graft) in comparison to the security men's vast earning capacity for doing "f**k all!" as they delicately put it.

The arguments ran long and hard over the months and I suppose it was safe to say that a widening gulf soon emerged between the security men and the house staff, owing to the disparity in their wage scales.

With this in mind, I don't think they ever exchanged Christmas cards, or gifts? This mounting envy would eventually culminate in what would later be notoriously known as *"The Black Bin Bag Dispute"*.

*

During the early 1980s there arrived Sandy. He had successfully come through the interviewing process, with Miss Wilson announcing to all present that he was "a splendid chap and a wonderful choice". Oh how she must have regretted saying that, as once he had settled into his role, the portents of doom were soon upon her.

Speaking personally, I had no real beef about Sandy, one way or another, but as an amused observer, it was just uproarious to see him cause so much catastrophe and calamity on virtually a daily basis.

Particularly when dealing with his close working colleagues, while not forgetting the many individuals and various departments who happened to come into contact with him.

Well Sandy started out ok, but it wasn't long before he began to upset one or two individuals.

This would be a number that would increase quite rapidly, as the days, weeks and months progressed. For example, there was one occasion, when someone delivered a large bouquet of flowers to reception.

The flowers were due to be collected by a lady VIP who was due to collect them at some given point. The flowers lay there for a day or two and then, suddenly, they were gone. The lady eventually arrived at reception to collect them, only to be told that they weren't there.

An investigation soon followed, as Miss Wilson was left a little embarrassed as to their mysterious disappearance.

What had happened to them? Had they been stolen? Had they been chucked in the bin? Further investigation then soon brought to light that the culprit was none other than Sandy. He had decided to take the flowers home as a gift for his wife!! To say that Miss Wilson was not amused is an understatement – in fact she was erupting with fury. However, this was just a small taste of things to come for the poor woman.

Because of his somewhat blunt, abrasive, crude, and unnecessarily officious manner, Sandy made himself a few enemies, particularly amongst the Audio crew, as well as with one or two of the news staff.

In fact, one of the Audio guys cheekily quipped one day, "Sandy is the kind of guy who can empty a pub quicker than a bad barrel of beer!"

A trifle harsh perhaps, well to be honest maybe not, as I actually saw this very fact in action one night.

One evening, a few of us were in the old Beau Brummell pub having a beer after work and discussing the day's events, when in walked Sandy. Well, before you could say Beau Brummell, several excuses were quickly uttered.

Everything from, "I need to get home," to, "I've not had my tea yet," to, "Is that the time? I've got a bus to catch," and soon Sandy would be standing there alone at the bar, while everyone else was rushing by him to get out of the front door, just as quick as they possibly could!

Some of his own colleagues regarded him as a bit of a harmless buffoon, but he managed to wind many up – sometimes without even trying. Mac in particular had a bit of a hard time with him, as he seemed determined to make his life awkward and difficult.

Even Bob had a bit of a run-in with Sandy at reception.

Not too surprising there, as I guess it had an air of inevitability about it.

Sandy made the enormous mistake of taking a swing in Bob's direction – this would turn out to be a very bad move on his part. In fact for a brief moment, fists began to fly, and raw, loud insults were exchanged, as they had to be separated and finally Bob was hustled downstairs, before it really turned nasty.

Not so much the "rumble in the jungle" as the "rumble at reception".

Or BBC Edinburgh's very own version of *Fight Club!*

Good job there was no visiting management or members of the public visible around when that melee started.

They later shook hands and kind of made it up, but I could sense that Bob's burning resentment towards Sandy was still very much in evidence.

In fact, if I had a pound for every time I would hear Bob say, "You'll never guess what that f*****g bastard Sandy's been up to now," I would be sitting relaxing at sunset, while sipping an ice-cool cocktail in my own personal luxury yacht, while it's lying moored in the Maldives!

Sandy's gross eating habits could also be known to disturb one or two at the time. Bob in particular.

Bob came down from the canteen one afternoon shaking his head at something he had observed, and which had seriously shaken him up. "I've just seen that bastard Sandy gorging and stuffing his fat f*****g face up in that canteen! He's just scoffed two – *that's two* stuffed green peppers. The bastard just couldn't get them down his gullet quick enough!" Bob continued as he was shaking his head in sheer disbelief. "From where I was standing, the greedy bastard's face almost turned as green as the stuffed peppers!" Then Bob, carrying his clarinet case under his arm, wandered back down the stairs, muttering away to himself, "What a f*****g fat greedy bastard!"

Sandy regularly incurred the wrath of the majority of the audio engineers, who used to shudder at the mere mention of his name. There was more than one instance when he would refuse them entry into the building late at night, when they were due to be collecting technical equipment for an upcoming Outside Broadcast.

He had taken his instructions of not letting anyone into the building once he was on a night shift, literally.

Although it must have escaped his notice that the building was in fact, a broadcasting centre, and that the notion of radio broadcasting in particular, was a high priority and all told, pretty important in the grand scheme of things

So this situation would usually involve a number of the audio crew gaining access – whether day or night – either to work on recorded programmes, or just in to collect equipment for an forthcoming programme.

This very fact appeared to bypass Sandy's muddled thought processes. Many a poor audio engineer was often left fuming and furious with anger and frustration whilst banging on the front door, shouting out Sandy's name in anger, to let them in!

He also did something similar to one of the news announcers, who again would find himself standing impotent and frustrated at the front door, while trying to gain access.

The poor guy had the BBC Ten O'clock news to read that night and Sandy was nowhere to be seen. Eventually after frantically and frustratingly banging on the front door, the newsreader was finally let in by one of his news colleagues, and he quickly ventured up into the newsroom to get himself ready for the ten o'clock broadcast.

But just then, the newsroom door burst open and Sandy walked straight over to the newsreader, with a face like fury. He then berated the poor man for ringing the bell and banging on the front door, while all that time Sandy was apparently engaged in the toilet!!

"Do you shite?" he loudly and aggressively asked the newsreader. "Do you shite? Well while you were banging on the door I was having a shite!!"

The newsreader, not unexpectedly, was by now a bag of nerves, not ideal as he was soon about to read the ten o'clock news live on air.

Sandy eventually stormed out of the room, by all accounts making a bit of a vulgar spectacle of himself (nothing new there), which didn't exactly endear him to those around. Subtlety, manners and good grace, was not, you could say, his strong point.

Following such an aggressive verbal onslaught, the poor nerve-shattered newsreader soon sought solace in a bottle of Bombay Sapphire, as he was probably in dire need of a very large double gin and tonic. Who wouldn't be, after that upsetting confrontation with a post-toilet security man!

On hearing about the appalling events on that night in question, not surprisingly, it soon made the staff amused and disgusted in equal measures. I overheard Bob and Kenny MacIntyre in animated conversation about this very matter one morning.

"What a crude bastard!" Bob began. "If he had spoken to me in that way, I would have punched his f*****g lights out!!"

Bob and Kenny were of the shared opinion that Sandy was (and I quote) "An absolute shite-house of man" (unquote).

Kenny just laughed as he began to head back towards the newsroom, by adding, "Aye that Sandy, he's some f*****g man."

On one weekend shift, Sandy allowed a couple of freelance news cameramen to use the main reception area for a photography experiment that utilised some form of spray chemical. As a result, a large area of the carpet around the main reception was now badly marked and damaged and would prove very difficult in restoring.

When she witnessed the mess the following Monday morning, once again Miss Wilson was beside herself with anguished fury. A major investigation was mounted to discover the guilty party (or parties?). It didn't take long when the identities of the two freelance cameramen came to the fore.

However, what made it more of an issue (she couldn't do much about rebuking freelance staff, which made her position even more frustrating) was the discovery that Sandy was on duty that day.

What later came to light was that he was partially responsible for actively participating in the carpet disfigurement. This may have gone a long way in rushing her decision that enough was enough, and that the time for her to depart was now imminent before more disasters fell upon her.

Sandy's overall behaviour had made him a bit of a polarising figure and just about the most unpopular guy in the building – particularly amongst the journalists and the Audio unit. With his deranged activity going a long way in hastening Miss Wilson's decision to seek the relative spiritual calm of retirement, before she delved deep into the Valium bottle!

I often believe that it may have been Sandy and his various misdemeanours that eventually prompted her to say her farewells and go, as perhaps her nerves just couldn't take it anymore. Not forgetting Mac's blood pressure, which was regularly put under daily assault due to Sandy's tiresome and oafish behaviour.

*

The final push perhaps occurred when there was a growing dispute amongst the house staff and the security men, as to whose responsibility it was to put out the black bin bags for collection. Voices were raised and fingers pointed in all kinds of directions, as all the leading players stated that "It's not my f*****g job!!" In fact, that above statement was perhaps used more times by more people than any other, during my entire 28 years as a BBC Edinburgh employee. Maybe I should have used that as the book's title? But I digress.

Sandy had by this time become a union representative, somewhat strange since he vehemently refused to join the union when he first started, but life is indeed strange, as you often find. As are, I suppose, some people.

Meetings after meetings, after meetings, were arranged between the affected staff, the union reps, personnel officers and numerous representatives from senior management, to try and resolve this deepening and evolving crisis that had all the potential to cause maximum embarrassment, and equally, pages of tabloid interest.

Both parties refused to budge on a point of principal, with Sandy and (not surprisingly Bob) being the most vocal in their determination that they weren't going to be taking out the bin bags, as it wasn't their… well you get the picture.

Anyway, it got so bad and the arguments raged on and on, that it eventually accelerated way beyond the local level.

It was now heading towards the highest level possible, and that would eventually bring into play – the Director General of the BBC himself!! Hope you are all following this?

It was now, yet again, "the talk of the steamie" that the Director General, the very top man of the Corporation based down in TV Centre London, would be intervening in a dispute about which of the Edinburgh house staff was ultimately responsible in taking out the black bin bags late at night!

Well, after a fashion, the situation was resolved and eventually good sense finally prevailed and the valued time of the DG was ultimately not called upon. He was no doubt a relieved man at that, as I'm sure he had much more pressing issues to deal with at the time.

A compromise was eventually reached and (before the tabloids got a hold of the potentially hilarious story) the house staff had been offered "a financial sweetener" of sorts.

So they were now finally responsible for the onerous task of lifting the black bin bags all the way from the basement area, into the front street to await collection.

Although, both Bob and Harry were fairly outspokenly vocal that they had in fact been set up, stabbed in the back and ultimately stitched up. "They must think our f*****g heeds are zipped up the f*****g back!" Harry growled as his disappointment began to slowly sink in. Although a few extra notes that would eventually find their way into their weekly wages, helped to smooth away any further stormy arguments.

Looking back, it's the kind of story that makes you shake your head with total disbelief – you simply just couldn't make it up.

Although I could well imagine the newspaper headlines at the time coming up with something along the lines of: *"BBC Director General Intervenes In A Load Of Old Rubbish Dispute!"*

Sandy would eventually follow Hector in departing Edinburgh for (as they thought at the time) the far more lucrative and prestigious positions that awaited them in BBC Glasgow. Big Barry (one of the house staff who was also known to stir things up a bit and cause the odd fractious incident during his time), travelled west with them.

No wonder one member of the audio crew blew a large sigh of relief as he announced with a broad grin on his face at their eventual departure from Edinburgh, "Phew, thank f**k we have finally got rid of the nutters!!"

I couldn't possibly comment.

*

By the beginning of the 1980s, we had another addition to the new look BBC Edinburgh – *Phil Aikman.*

Phil was a one-man sound archivist, who had come to set up and run the sound library.

He was another immensely intelligent and knowledgeable individual, who proved virtually indispensable to so many departments within the building. And what Phil didn't know about music, wasn't worth knowing. Not surprisingly, his immeasurable worth towards the musical sound quality of many a programme was simply immense.

It was a very sad day when (with many financial and structural changes approaching on the horizon) the sound library was closing down and Phil was being forced to move on. I always thought that he was a great loss to BBC Edinburgh during this time. And he was a lovely guy as well.

On a happier note, in recent years I have often bumped into Phil and his wife and you could say that he has totally reinvented himself as – a gardener for hire.

From what they both told me, this was proving to be a job and a role among the bracing outdoors that (although hard work) has brought him enormous enjoyment and fulfilment.

Without doubt the busiest time during the year at 5 Queen Street always happened during the month of August when the Edinburgh International Festival was in our midst. This was the time when the eyes and the ears of the world focused intensely upon Scotland's capital city.

For many of us then no leave was allowed during the month, as all were required to be on hand and on duty, as the building was going to be abuzz with excitement – or so we thought.

I vividly recall my first year of the Festival, in which we had a number of staff and departments descend upon us from Glasgow, as well as London.

What they thought of this small, cosy, modest radio

station was anybody's guess at the time.

I remember being asked to deliver an important letter to *Mary Marquis* (for those unfamiliar with the lady in question, let's just say that she was the *Jackie Bird* of her day!) who was staying at the George Hotel, just around the corner.

I approached the main hotel reception desk and explained my mission. Then, I was given Ms Marquis's hotel room number, and with letter in hand, I proceeded up the stairs and along the corridor.

I knocked at the door, and it quickly opened.

There stood *Mary Marquis* in her slip (or underskirt) coyly hiding her embarrassment behind the door.

"I have a letter for you," I shakily explained. With her face all aglow, she thanked me, took the letter, and then quickly closed the door.

No doubt (unlike millions of Reporting Scotland viewers) I may have been one of the very privileged few that saw her in that particular pose.

Another famous lady who was around during that time of the Festival was *Esther Rantzen*.

I was asked to escort her (as well as taking with me a few flasks of coffee) round to the production office, which was situated in the rented office floor in Thistle Street.

I remember her being quite pleasant and friendly, and this was in the days before she really became one of the more famous faces on television.

*

There was always a mighty upheaval whenever visiting staff descended upon us during August, with many being very vocal in their demands. There was the odd one or two Festival production staff that tended to treat us Edinburgh lot with barely concealed contempt and annoyance, topped up with a dash of ill-concealed arrogance.

You often got the feeling that they really looked down upon us, that we weren't proper BBC people, who were renowned for making BBC programmes of any substance and importance.

I suppose it was just a general feeling I got, as did so many others during this time, which all went a long way in making many dread the very mention of the word Festival, as it brought with it so much hassle, upheaval, aggravation, frayed tempers, egotistical tantrums and problems of all kinds during its entire duration.

For most of the house and admin staff, working during the Edinburgh Festival was looked upon as more of an exhausting trial than a celebration of the arts.

At least it felt like that during the first couple of decades I was working there.

Bob then inevitably added his two-pence worth to the debate.

"We spend all our time cleaning up after the backsides of all those toffee-nosed ponced up f*****g bastards from Glasgow and London! I hate the f*****g Festival!"

Many of the Edinburgh staff found themselves totally divorced from any of the Festival activities. So they must have looked on with great amusement – and bemusement – at everyone else running around for an entire month like so many freaked out headless chickens!

Also, due to the many requirements of the Festival, this meant that for us (one way or another) being directly involved, the month of August became a no-go area when it came to taking leave.

Putting it bluntly – no holidays during the duration of the Festival.

To be honest, it didn't bother me that much, but there were always a few mumbles and grumbles going about from quite a few of my colleagues, that they couldn't have any time off in August.

Throughout my entire 28 years, I only found myself being absent from work only once during Festival time. This rarity was all down to me ending up in hospital, after experiencing a broken wrist while playing football at Meadowbank.

The hospital doctor thoughtfully signed me off for a full two weeks – right in the middle of the Festival!

This (as you can imagine) didn't go down too well with my boss Bella, but I had a legitimate line from the hospital, so there was little that I, or her for that matter, could do anything about.

That year, I managed to experience, and even enjoy the Festival, without the usual attached maddened hassle that it normally brought with it.

A funny thing was during the majority of the Festival's run quite a number of very high profile and important London staff would normally book into the George Hotel.

Then, once they had no doubt consumed a full and hearty breakfast, they would go on to order numerous taxis to take them all the way around to the studios at 5 Queen Street – which was a brisk two-minute walk around the corner! The taxi bills must have been astronomical!

However, around ten years before the building eventually closed, I felt that the Festival was beginning to be much more warmly appreciated by the staff than it had ever been the case before.

We now felt that the Edinburgh staff were finally viewed as an important and integral part of the proceedings, and not simply taken for granted – running after the backsides of over demanding visiting producers, researchers and production assistants.

There appeared to be a less austere and elitist attitude prevailing, greatly helped no doubt by the live broadcast shows that went out late at night – skilfully produced and presented by our very own people.

This was a free performance for the public that (it still exists to this day, although in a very different guise and venue) presented highlights of many of the fringe shows that were happening in Edinburgh during that month.

For just over an hour we witnessed singers, musicians, comedians, actors, writers, as well as a number of faces that would soon go on to far greater fame.

One such individual I remember seeing was *Paul O'Grady* in his alternate guise of *"Lily Savage"*. Although I can't for the life of me recall seeing him head for the gents' toilet in full drag!

However, the regular discovery of several condoms in the balcony on the morning after the recording went a long way in displaying just how much the audiences had obviously enjoyed the show!

*

One aspect of working during the Edinburgh Festival (that more or less directly involved me, as well as a few of my colleagues such as Dot, Lorraine, and Suzette) happened around the last weekend that coincided with the Television Festival.

The Corporation's big hitters (the good, the great, the odious, and the dissolute) all assembled in the capital to discuss, debate, argue, and analyse the combined aspects of television's merits, faults, controversies, and just exactly where it was all heading over the next few years. Wherever that may be? I wonder if they ever realised that several years down the line, the BBC would inadvertently (with the Government's ever so gentle prompting) become a part of the Benefits & Welfare System. Not quite sure how Lord Reith would have reacted to that unexpected event.

Anyway, our minor role in all this back slapping (and occasional back stabbing) junket necessitated in us all coming into the building at an extremely ungodly hour. Then around the crack of dawn, after being collected from our homes by taxi, we proceeded to go through each and every morning newspaper to check on any news item, or story, that mentioned the BBC. Whether in a flattering, or an unflattering light!

We then had to cut, copy, and collate all the relevant items into a small compact booklet that broadcasting's finest, could relax, read, and divulge while they were all simultaneously munching into their breakfast of porridge, coffee, and kippers!!

And here came the good part of it all. After our early morning efforts were complete, we were then escorted around the corner and taken to the George Hotel. This was nothing less than a little treat for us doing our bit for the TV Festival. We were then treated to an eat all you can slap-up buffet breakfast.

It's making me hungry just thinking back on it! Those were the days.

*

One of the most successful bands that would always draw an appreciative audience with their own brand of up-tempo jazzy swing music during the Festival, was an outfit known to all as *That Swing Thing*.

They would entertainingly perform regularly in Studio 1, usually to a packed and appreciative crowd. Although from time to time, the band's name would often get mispronounced and a little mangled along the way, as they would often be described as *"Swing That Thing"*.

A somewhat unfortunate description, considering that was exactly what the lead singer would (allegedly) be caught out doing live over the Internet, just before his arrest by the police! I wonder if the officers of the law told him to *"Jump To It Daddy-O!!"* as they escorted him to the station for questioning.

The canteen, no doubt from its very early incarnations, became a regular place for the staff to not only to eat lunch and drink tea, but also for the staff to congregate and chat, as they mulled over the day-to-day events at work.

It later became a place where producers could easily meet up and chat at leisure with contributors, actors, writers, etc. as programmes present and future were discussed at length, amongst the endless cups of coffee.

Funnily, I also remember from my very early days, that you could also light up a cigarette, while drinking your favoured beverages. How times have changed!

*

The various individuals who worked in the canteen were another fairly mixed bunch. But I guess that in the most part, they were an agreeable bunch.

When I first began work there in 1974, I recall the canteen ladies as being friendly, chatty and always happy go lucky (at least on the surface).

Although you would often catch (inadvertently) the odd catty and caustic comment, aimed at one or two of the staff regarding their often condescending attitude, mode and style of attire, personal hygiene, and bafflingly undefined sexuality. But I suppose that went on in most workplaces during this time. Or did it?

So, at first there was Maisie, Rose, Edith, Peggy, and the head cook around that time a lady called Marion.

Marion in fact would depart a few months after I joined, yet as a sequel to this – and showing just how life can often take you by surprise when you least expect it – I would be reacquainted with Marion some thirty-odd years later. This would happen when we found ourselves working alongside each other at Standard Life Bank.

Marion is a lovely woman, warm, funny, colourful (her hair often a startling kaleidoscope of primary shades), spirited and full of fun, and it was terrific to get to know her once again, after all those years. During this time I discovered just how much her life had been altered and shaped once she had left the BBC.

Many a time we would chat and laugh and reminisce about BBC Edinburgh, and some of the people we both remembered.

And it was Marion, more than most, who prompted and encouraged me to attempt to write all my recollections and anecdotes down in print. So, if for anyone, this book is for you Marion, for having the simple belief that I could do it.

*

Then there was Jessie (who worked there over a long period and then would return once the refurbishment was completed), and Katy, who was now the new head cook.

Katy was a large buxom girl, and I think (going by some of her chat) was a farmer's daughter no less, and for some strange reason, took a particular shine to me.

At least that's what I thought at the time, considering the extra helpings of rice pudding, bread and butter pudding with custard, and apple crumble that she regularly heaped upon on my plate! Perhaps like *Shakespeare's Cassius*, I was in possession of a "lean and hungry look".

*

Peggy was a particular favourite and another lovely woman who become a good friend over the years up until she retired in the mid-1980s. She had been widowed quite young, as her late husband (who had worked at the BBC before my arrival), had tragically passed away.

She then moved from the canteen to the duplicating/print room and provided many of us with many a laugh over the years. Her warmth, generosity, and kindness towards myself, is something that I always recall with a great deal of fondness.

Peggy would enjoy a good night out, a few drinks and lots of laughs (she always attested that brandy made her randy!) and she also enjoyed participating in some good-humoured banter with Bob.

*

On many an occasion, Bob (purely in jest – at least I think it was?) would pop down to Peggy's room and ask her if she fancied going away for a romantic weekend to a country hotel, where they would make mad passionate love on a four-poster bed!

Peggy would laugh out loud at this suggestion and then tell Bob, "Away you go you mad bugger! What about your wife?"

Bob never missed a beat and replied, "I'll just tell her that I'm doing some overtime that weekend. She'll never know I'm away."

Peggy (still chuckling away to herself) said, "Och, Bob, you are some man. Anyway, I've got plans that weekend."

Bob (who was laughing just as loud himself at his outlandish audacity) then said, "You will never know what you've missed Peggy – as my cock is full of vitamins!"

Peggy was now in convulsions of giggly laughter as Bob walked out the door and then wound his way back up the stairs.

Peggy always enjoyed the company of Edith, who had a very wry, and dry sense of humour. Edith was a widow and fancied her chances (slim at best) of being the housemistress of Bob L the Commissionaire.

Often she would sneak into the mailroom at the back of reception when Bob was changing into his working clothes, hoping to catch sight of him in his scanty undergarments!

This she would do from time to time, as she popped her head in the door, as they both giggled and laughed while indulging in the sort of innuendo-fuelled cross talk that would embarrass the likes of *Kenneth Williams* and *Hattie Jacques*!

*

Other additions to the catering department over the years included Sally and Mary, two great cooks and terrific characters. Sally (who was known to some as Ms Snax) would eventually leave the BBC to embark upon a life on the ocean wave, as head chef on an ocean liner.

Mary left a little later after falling pregnant and then she later got married. Sadly Mary would pass away much too young, leaving a distraught husband and family behind.

*

Prior to the refurbishment, we also had working in the canteen, the near legendary mother and daughter double act of – Greta and Vera.

Not the kind of women you would want to anger, or upset.

Not unless you were looking to be thumped over the head by a rolling pin, or a frying pan.

Yet when Queen Street reopened in 1990 a brand new canteen staff would appear before us, offering up food from the gods (and goddesses) – but more of that, and them later.

*

Due to its upcoming refurbishment, 5 Queen Street was temporarily closed around 1987, and a farewell party was thrown in the canteen before everyone was finally decamped to the Thistle Street building for about roughly three years. This would be while the main building was being totally gutted.

The prospect of us all squeezed tight together like sardines within a small building such as Thistle Street, was hardly ideal. But, although it was a far from perfect arrangement, we just had to put up with it as a temporary measure. That was until Queen Street was up and running as normal.

So we all had to put up with it, although it felt sometimes like participating in that hilarious jam-packed cabin scene from the *Marx Bros'* classic comedy *A Night At The Opera!!*

Unfortunately, with me being on leave at that point, I completely missed the closing down party, from which I was told on my return, more than lived up to the rowdy reputations of past Queen Street parties! In fact, in some situations, it exceeded it!

There were, I believe, lots of drunken escapades, illicit liaisons and inhibitions freely cast to the four winds, as much drink was consumed and passions aroused as the evening inevitably wore on amidst much jollity.

Mac explained to me on my return regarding one particular incident that occurred on the night involving young Fraser and our "Boss lady" Bella.

"You should have seen that dirty wee bastard Fraser, lying on that couch over there with Bella. They were gazing into each other's eyes; all the while their hands were groping each other. Completely drunk out of their f*****g minds they were!" I was trying to visualise this bizarre scene in my imagination, but finding a little difficulty with it, as it made no real sense.

"What a f******g disgrace they were! And in full view of everyone as well," Mac added. "The two of them stretched out on that settee like f*****g Antony and Cleopatra!" At that torrid description, I suddenly burst out into loud laughter, as the image of them languidly feeding grapes to one another, while whispering sweet nothings into each other's ears in rich *Shakespearean* verse, worthy of *Burton & Taylor*, was absolutely priceless!

CHAPTER 8

Death At Broadcasting House

Life at BBC Edinburgh wasn't all fun-filled frolics and Carry On style capers – well at least not all of the time. It may surprise you to learn that hundreds of radio programmes and radio series, covering a wide range of important and entertaining subject matters were made within those walls, with many a lofty reputation built as a result.

But this chapter in particular, does not dwell upon any of that.

*

I suppose that you could say that it's an obvious, as well as an unfortunate part of life, that several of my colleagues would sadly pass away – some even in the most tragic of circumstances. Although I may have previously given you the idea that it was all laughs, there were a few tears and moments of genuine sadness during my time there that even today, made a deep and profound impact on me.

The first person that died only a couple of years after I started at the BBC was the celebrated Hearts and Scotland footballer *Jimmy Wardhaugh*. To those who remember him, Jimmy was (alongside *Alfie Conn* and *Willie Bauld*) one third of "The Terrible Trio" a name still revered many years later, by thousands of Hearts fans, for their combined skills and goal-scoring abilities.

Even as a Hibs supporter, I was aware of who Jimmy was

and remember my dad telling me about how special those three players were, and just how good the Hearts side was, that played together during the late 1950s. From my memory, Jimmy was a quietly spoken gentleman who worked as the BBC's Press & Publicity Officer (at a time when Edinburgh had one) following a time spent as a sports journalist with the Daily Express.

I liked Jimmy, and he was a modest unassuming guy, with no airs or graces or pretensions. Even though he had long retired from professional football, I recognised that he always kept himself pretty fit by playing a number of other sports. So it was a severe shock when I heard that he had suddenly died at the comparatively young age of 49. This was a real tragedy for a man still in the prime of his life.

Following his sad and untimely death, Jimmy's replacement in the role of Press & Publicity Officer would eventually be filled. In fact his first temporary replacement was an eccentric-looking character called *Dougie Stewart*. My first impression of him was that he already looked as if he should have been retired years ago! At first glance, he closely resembled someone who had enjoyed making a tidy living as a *Sir Harry Lauder* impersonator. Or even some crusty old actor who has just wandered off the set of *The Master Of Ballantrae*, still fully dressed in his historical costume as a geriatric Jacobite.

His usual attire consisted of a moth-eaten old bonnet, as well as an equally moth-eaten old kilt that looked as if it hadn't seen soap and hot water since the battle of Culloden!

It's no exaggeration to claim that in those days, 5 Queen Street seemed to attract baffling eccentrics like the kilted gentleman above like a magnet. However, the post of Press & Publicity officer would eventually be phased out in Edinburgh – never to return.

I became aware of a few other colleagues who would pass away during my time there.

There was Douglas Archer. Dougie (as everyone knew him) was another gentleman of the old school, who I am led to believe had been one of the longest serving members of staff in 5 Queen Street.

He had worked in the building a long time as an engineer, and could usually be found behind the main desk in the old control room.

Dougie eventually retired after many years' service, and I always found him to be an extremely likeable and friendly guy, and when I heard that he had passed away, not too long after retiring, I asked permission to attend his funeral.

Another tragedy I suppose was that of the young radio producer Martin Goldman, who was killed following a horrific train accident on the Glasgow to Edinburgh route. I must admit that I didn't know him all that well (if at all) but he hadn't long joined the BBC and again sadly died very young.

*

Then there were Pat Grieve and Edith Lamb. Pat was the BBC's cashier (when we had a cash office) and had been with the corporation for a number of years. Pat was another very likeable woman, with a quirky, dry sense of humour.

Unfortunately, when still quite young, she contracted cancer and was forced to leave work. Her last days were spent at St Columba's Hospice, and it was during her sad final days there, that Peggy and myself arranged to visit. We had decided to go as Edith (the canteen lady who had made us laugh so much in the past) was like Pat, spending her final days in the Hospice.

Peggy and I booked a taxi and went to visit Pat and Edith. We were a little shocked to see them at first, as Pat had grown so thin and was virtually unrecognisable, and Edith wore an eyepatch, as her cancer seemingly had spread to her eye. However, they both were so happy and glad to see us, that for an hour or so, we forget where we were, as we chatted and laughed and reminisced about the BBC, as you do in these circumstances.

I was glad that I went, and equally glad that I had the chance to say farewell to two remarkable women who gave so much to the BBC in Edinburgh.

*

Sad though those deaths were, they didn't quite prepare me for what would happen several years later to three other friends and close colleagues whose time at the BBC came to a shockingly tragic conclusion, that I still find it hard to comprehend all these years later. Their deaths still haunts many of us to this day. I am referring to Alex Colquhoun, Fraser Stewart, and Dorothy Laing.

Alex C arrived as the new handyman around 1985. He was replacing Tom who was due to retire and finally departing the building, taking his ever flexible and adaptable sonic screwdriver with him! However, Tom wasn't going to disappear entirely from our sight. Over the next several months, he was going to be employed – on a temporary basis as a driver – with the Commonwealth Games office that was being set up near Edinburgh's West End.

So Tom would still make frequent and welcome return visits to 5 Queen Street in his new position with the Commonwealth Games team. Although, if memory serves me correct, his screwdriver was nowhere to be seen!

Alex C had now started as Tom's replacement, and was a very different character, in so many ways. He was a small, wiry, dark-haired chap with glasses, who gave the impression that his energy levels had been bolstered by several Duracell batteries.

Alex C was an ex-army man, very efficient, very hard working and there appeared to be very little in the way of general handiwork around the building that was not beyond his considerable capabilities. What astonished me at the time was his work rate – it was simply phenomenal.

Alex could do more work in one day than poor old Tom achieved in an entire month – even with his flexible sonic screwdriver! Often after one job had been completed, he would sit down for five minutes, take out his small green Benson & Hedges tin that contained his tobacco and papers, roll himself a small cigarette, and then a few minutes later after he had puffed the life out of it, he would jump out of his seat, and be off to complete another task.

Initially, Alex C came across as a very brusque and blunt guy, and for a few of us at the beginning, he was a little difficult to fathom out. He got on pretty well from the outset with Mac, as they both shared in common a long military career, and they could discuss army jargon and stories of barrack room memories quite easily together.

Yet Alex C didn't hold back and made it pretty plain from the start of what he thought about many who inhabited 5 Queen Street. Usually describing a number of characters with the unflattering phrase of "Hooks, crooks and comic singers". Yet he reserved the majority of his ire for two particular individuals that he just couldn't abide – Hector and Sandy. He described them as "a right pair of f*****g twats!" and few would argue with him.

Alex C also gave off the impression that he was a bit of a misogynist, and he could be particularly scathing in his opinions of a few of the women who worked there. Unfortunately, it was our main receptionist Dorothy who came in for some of the worst of his verbal put-downs, as she couldn't understand why he was being so nasty to her at times.

Perhaps this was just part and parcel of Alex's abrupt personality, coupled with his many years of being indoctrinated within the armed forces.

To be honest, when I first got to know him, I wasn't sure whether I liked him all that much.

Perhaps it was mainly to do with the fact that I had liked and got on so well with Tom and missed his easy-going manner and presence about the building (with, or without his adaptable sonic screwdriver!) and it took a wee while to get to know Alex C, who was an entirely different type of personality.

Like myself, Alex C lived in Leith, although I could count on the fingers of one hand the amount of times that I might have bumped into him. Occasionally I might have seen him doing his Saturday shopping in Leith's old Kirk-gate, or the odd time that I spoke to him briefly in a couple of Leith pubs, but those occasions were few and far between.

Often, Mac, Stan, Fraser, and myself would attempt to tease him out on the odd night for a drink, just for the opportunity to get to know him a little bit better. We felt that lurking beneath his stern exterior was an altogether different guy, who would enjoy a drink and a laugh, as much as anyone.

Yet, invariably, he would turn us all down, stating that he was busy that night, or he was meeting some friends and had other arrangements.

We often got the impression that he simply just wanted to keep himself to himself, and not socialise with any of us. I suppose, looking back, that was just the impression he gave during those early days.

The first night that Alex C finally relented and decided to join "the gang" for a drink, occurred when the "BBC club" (Edinburgh was one of the very few, if the only station that did not possess its own club premises – but that's another story...) had organised a "Mexican Night" in a local bar just around the corner from Queen Street. Mexican drinks, Mexican food and Mexican music were on the menu that evening, with Mac and Stan particularly getting in the mood, with both of them wearing appropriate Mexican-style gear.

Stan had on his head a large sombrero, as well as what looked like an old colourful blanket that he was now using as a poncho, with a large section cut out of it in the middle. What with his dark swarthy looks, generous girth and drooping moustache, he looked the part to perfection. All that was missing from the image of a colourful bandit, was him snarling the lines from *The Treasure Of The Sierra Madre:* *"Badges, badges, we don't need no stinking badges…"*

Mac too had made a supreme effort on the night. He was wearing a smaller Mexican hat, along with a pair of tight fitting, black studded flared trousers that gave him that carefree "gay caballero" look! At least that's what many thought on the night.

Anyway, after a while once a few drinks had been consumed, guess who walked down the stairs into the pub – none other than Alex C.

All of us looked a little shocked and astonished as we were totally taken aback as to his surprised and unannounced appearance.

He was smartly dressed (it was the first time anyone had seen him without his working clothes on) and he was wearing a cravat – just like some dandyish lounge lizard. He walked straight towards the bar, produced a large leather wallet that was simply bulging with notes, turned to the barman and then said, "I'll have a large glass of dry white wine please."

All of us were still in a slight state of shock as to Alex C turning up, but we were also genuinely pleased that he had finally made the effort and decided to join us.

Many more drinks were consumed and laughs exchanged and it turned out to be a great night. Unfortunately, for me, the night ended a bit earlier than I anticipated. Alex C had decided to set up a number of tequila slammers on the bar for all of us to consume. I suppose with this being a Mexican Night, tequila was going to be readily available to sample. This was a drink that (on top of a few beers) made me feel very giddy, and after one too many, I felt my legs turn to rubber and then I collapsed onto the floor!

Soon after, I had to make my excuses and headed home, an evening that was soon to follow by a morning complete with an accompanying "Hangover from Hell – Mexican style".

From that evening on, Alex C became one of the gang and we all got to know him that bit better, with the result that all of us got to like him a great deal. Yet, I still felt that there was a part of him that he was keeping close to himself and not too ready to divulge with us all.

Not too surprising that he also got on pretty well with Bob, although they also indulged in a bit of good-natured insulting banter from time to time, with insults flying back and forth, usually accompanied by loud laughter.

One funny story concerning Alex C happened when we were due to depart 5 Queen Street with the building's refurbishment now almost upon us.

Good old Hector by this time had been working in BBC Glasgow in the position of a Foreman, and had arranged for a large BBC van to pick up some technical equipment from Edinburgh, that was then going to be transported back through to the west. By all accounts, Hector was now relishing his new position and status through in Glasgow, giving him the opportunity of becoming (at least in his imagination) a figure of monumental authority, as he undoubtedly issued countless orders and instructions to those poor guys working under him.

Once Alex C had got wind that Hector was sending through a van, his mind went into overdrive, whirring away with a fiendishly funny plot developing in his brain. I overheard heard him saying something along the lines of, "I'll fix that bastard Hector! He'll get more than he bargained for."

Alex's plan was simple and very straightforward. It involved shifting the entire surplus rubbish material, outdated engineering equipment, old furniture, large cables, and everything else that needed to be jettisoned (prior to the building's temporary closure) and back through to Glasgow via the van. In fact the majority of the items that Alex was cheekily sending Hector's way, were originally due to end up in a very large skip outside on the main street.

The arrival of the van was the perfect set-up for his ingenious plan to ultimately get one over on Hector. When the driver and his two assistants eventually turned up to lift, what they thought was only going to be a few bits of surplus equipment, Alex C moved into action.

"Hector asked for all this to go through as well," he said to the Glasgow guys, with a completely straight face, as he pointed towards all the excess furniture, boxes and sundry other large cumbersome items that were left lying and cluttering up the corridor.

The Glasgow guys were momentarily speechless. Alongside, Alex C, Mac and myself were around to view the proceedings, as we didn't want to miss this, all the time attempting to stifle a laugh at what was about to happen. "How are you finding Hector as your new boss?" Mac innocently enquired.

Without missing a beat, and with little hesitation, one of the Glasgow workers replied back with a snarl, "Hector? He's f*****g useless!"

His pal, while surveying with horror all the bulky and no doubt heavy items that were soon having to be loaded onto the awaiting van, further added for maximum effect, "That f*****g bastard Hector, he always gets it wrong."

Not surprisingly, they both now began to question Hector's overall qualities as an efficient Foreman. Then taking a deep collective breath, they started to load the van (cursing Hector at the same time) with all the rubbish that Alex had been looking to get rid of for weeks.

Suffice to say that it took them a hell of a lot longer than they anticipated, as they were well and truly physically and mentally shattered by the time they climbed into their van aching, bruised and sore, for the return trip back to Glasgow.

I don't think I had ever seen Alex C look so happy, with such a wide beaming smile on his face, and in such a joyful mood, as he was on that particular day.

I only think that what would have made him even happier, if he had managed to be a fly on the wall when the van eventually arrived back in Glasgow – complete with the shocked look on Hector's face (possibly followed by a loud cry of "Holy f**k!!") when the van doors were opened up in front of him!

Alex C dined out on that story for quite a while.

When we all moved along to the small offices in Thistle Street, Alex C came with us, although the potential for any real substantive work that he had been previously used to, had now greatly diminished. So when we eventually moved back around 1990, Alex was going to be busier than ever, with so much work to be done getting 5 Queen Street back up and running.

*

My last memories of Alex C are sad and tragic ones, and the memory still resonates with myself, many years later.

It was coming up to Christmas 1991 when we all decided to go out for a Christmas meal together and no doubt a few drinks afterwards. We had selected the restaurant above the Abbotsford pub in Rose Street for the venue. It was reasonably priced and the Christmas menu looked, well, good enough to eat.

If my memory serves me correct, there was Mac, Stan, Fraser, Alex, Eric (the heating engineer who had not long joined us) and myself. So it turned out to be an all-boys outing, with a guarantee of plenty of laughs, and much drink to be consumed, as we were all in the mood to celebrate the festive season.

Once the meal had been enjoyed and completed, we then decided to take ourselves along to, where else but the Beau Brummell for a few more drinks. Alex was adamant at first, that he had friends to meet that same night and would therefore be leaving us pretty soon.

However, after much coaxing, we managed to persuade him to join us for one drink at least, before he would go on his way.

This we did, and so Alex walked with the rest of us towards the Beau for that drink.

When we got there, Alex produced his wallet (like before, it was literally bulging at the leather seams with a multitude of very large notes) and bought us all a round of drinks. After about half an hour, he then said that he really had to leave, as he was meeting up with friends. So he said his farewells, wished us a merry Christmas, walked out the door and vanished into the night.

That was the very last that we ever saw of him.

*

A day or so later (think it was just after the Christmas) I received a surprising phone call at home one morning from Ian Cowie (a.k.a. Mr Snax) who had started out as a sound engineer and was now working in the newsroom as part of the newsroom film crew.

Ian proceeded to tell me the most shocking news imaginable. Alex C had been found dead in his flat in Sandport Street in Leith, with the entire evidence pointing to the fact that he had been brutally murdered in his own home.

I couldn't believe it. I was in shock, Alex dead.

It was just hard to take in, particularly since it was not that long ago that we had all been out together for a Christmas meal. The brutal fact was plain – he was gone and at the still youthful age of 51.

The news soon spread, and all of my colleagues who were with him that evening, were equally shaken up with the dreadful news. How could it have happened? What bastards would have done such a thing?

There was anger, there was fury, and there was sheer disbelief that someone we all knew, someone we all worked with on a daily basis, and someone we all got to like, was gone from us in the most horrific manner possible.

A dark cloud descended upon 5 Queen Street during that time, and it would be a dark cloud that would remain there over the next couple of years.

The story that later emerged was that Alex had gone to a gay nightclub in town, after he had left us earlier in the Beau Brummell. While there, he got chatting with two young guys who had clocked onto the fact that Alex was carrying a wallet bulging with cash. They then got a taxi back to Alex's flat in Sandport Street in Leith, where an argument ensued, and then a ferocious fight, with poor Alex coming out the worst. As luck would have it, a taxi driver soon identified the two assailants, with the police finally apprehending them. They were sentenced sometime early in the New Year.

During the police investigation, two officers of the CID set up office in 5 Queen Street in order to question not only myself, but also everyone else who was out that night with Alex before the Christmas. I remember being called into an office that was now being used as a temporary investigating room, and questioned by one of the officers (the other one said nothing, but just looked squarely in my direction). Speaking honestly, it was a very strange and uncomfortable experience to be in – coming face to face with good cop and bad cop.

I simply said (as no doubt did all the others) that we had all been out for a Christmas meal in town that evening then we all went for a drink afterwards. Alex was with us, bought one round, said his farewells and disappeared into the night. That would turn out to be the very last time that anyone ever saw of him.

The police officers thanked me for my statement and I then left the room.

*

I suppose it's natural to feel a sense of deep sadness when someone you know passes away so suddenly. But when it happens, the way it happened to Alex, you couldn't help but feel a deeper sense of loss, as well as a mystifying form of numbness that takes a long while to recede from your thoughts. Alex was, in many ways, a very private man who shielded a great part of his life from so many of us who worked alongside him at Queen Street.

Yet for all of his sometime surface abrasive personality, quirks and eccentricities, he was a good man, who I think of often and who – like the majority of the guys who were around at the time – once we got to know him a little better, we got to like a great deal.

*

Young Fraser arrived at 5 Queen Street to initially work on a temporary basis within the mailroom, and it turned out that he would be with us, more or less, over the next dozen years. Fraser was small, with dark hair and had the kind of smooth, boyish good looks that made him immediately popular with females of all ages.

Yet, at the same time, those dark pin-up features, would also attract equal attention and desires from a good few males as well – both in and out of the BBC.

Fraser was personable and friendly and easy to get on with. We struck up a good friendship there and then, and remained close pals during all that time.

We shared many a laugh together and many a good night, although it was often funny to see him succumb to the many girlish temptations placed in his path, as well as his attempts to evade unwanted advances from, well shall we say, gentlemen who should have known far better!

There was one occasion that Fraser found himself attempting to escape the amorous clutches of a guy (not, on this occasion one of the BBC staff I hasten to add) with the wonderfully flamboyant name of Pearson Abercromby-Smythe. This gentleman was, going by his demeanour, manner, and reputation, what you would accurately describe as being about as camp as an outside caravan site!

So it was during a lavish BBC Christmas party that Mr Pearson Abercromby-Smythe checked over young Fraser at the bar and then announced to all who were there at the time – "I think I'm in love!" He must have thought that all of his Christmases and birthdays had merged into one tiny cute male package! Suffice to say Fraser wasn't best amused when he began to follow him around the venue with his tongue hanging out, while gazing lovingly and longingly in his direction for the remainder of the evening.

He even followed him into the gents' toilet, in which Fraser (putting on a gruff and deepening edge to his voice) told him not to be so bloody stupid! When, on his return, he told the rest of us who were now sitting having a drink at a table what had happened, all of us in unison then burst out into loud laughter, which made Fraser just a little annoyed. Yet for him, being so attractive to both sexes was a pertinent fact of life that he was just going to have to learn to live with.

Taking all that into consideration, I never really found him immersed in any form of arrogance (unlike my earlier colleague Hamish) that the fates had blessed him with the smooth dark looks of a young *Colin Farrell* (whom he closely resembled). But in all the time that I knew him, he would never find himself short of female companionship – in one form or another.

"I know I'm cute, and I know that I don't have any

trouble attracting the girls," he once told me, as if trying to rationally explain it. I suppose it was just part and parcel of who he was at the time. He was also given a few well-chosen nicknames by a number of his colleagues during the course of his employment then.

Names such as: *"The Wee Man"*, *"Little Tiger"*, *"Tiny Timothy Tight-Bum"* (not quite sure who gifted him with that specific name – although I have a pretty rough idea!) and perhaps most bizarrely of all – *"The Official Ship's Cat"*.

That last moniker conjures up the image of a scruffy, mangy creature, a little lost and forlorn, skulking warily amongst the dark corridors of the building. In truth, Fraser wasn't quite as bad as that.

Although he could look somewhat the worse for wear on the odd morning he came into work after a particularly rough night on the drink!

One morning he did indeed come in unshaven, unwashed, wearing a long dark coat and all told, looking a bit scruffy and bedraggled.

You could say, that he resembled something the cat just dragged in. Then again, since he was known as the "Official Ship's Cat", maybe he was just dragging himself in??

Mac took one look at him and said, "What a f*****g state you're in you wee bastard! You look just like f*****g *Ben Gunn!*"

For those unfamiliar with the character of *Ben Gunn*, he was the lone sailor marooned for many years on *Treasure Island* (later discovered by Jim Hawkins), and was described as a scruffy and bearded eccentric, forever dreaming of cheese! Not sure if Fraser ever dreamt of cheese (vodka perhaps?), but– at least in Mac's eyes – he did on that morning bear a strong resemblance to *Robert Louis Stevenson's* character, nonetheless.

From very early on, Fraser had begun to attract the

attention of a couple of new additions to the audio crew. The two gents in question were the flamboyantly named Franz Reinbold, and the late Alan Stewart. When Franz first caught a glimpse of Fraser running up the stairs, his heart missed a beat as he inquired, "Who is that pretty little thing with the letters?" Fraser used to take quite a ribbing from many of us, as his presence seemed to bring out a lot of frustrated desires amongst certain males in the building. He used to say to me that he didn't do anything to encourage this form of unwelcome attention, but there was nothing much he could do about it.

Yet, a few of us who were standing around (myself included) attempted to wisely inform him that constantly brushing his (by now long dark hair) while preening himself in front of the mirror like a young *Joan Collins*, didn't exactly help his case!

Alan too made his intentions known to Fraser on a number of occasions, dropping several, oh so unsubtle hints, as to what they could get up to if he so wished. Fraser was having absolutely none of it – and told him so in no uncertain terms to forget it, and leave him well alone.

This didn't put Alan off, in fact he saw it as a bit of a challenge, as he tried to pursue Fraser during most of the time he was based in Edinburgh. It was a very amusing sight to see, as Fraser and Alan, appeared to be both taking part in a bizarre form of "chase me and catch me if you can" scenario.

I'm just realising after writing that last section, that I have now become acutely aware what Fraser was experiencing back then in the early and mid-1980s. It was quite possibly a form of sexual harassment. He wasn't the only one – I hasten to add – to have gone through something like this, but although he tended to laugh it off (most of the time) due to his boyish good looks, he probably experienced that kind of lewd and unwarranted attention, more than most.

*

Within a year, or so, Alan Stewart, alongside several others in the audio unit, would eventually move through to BBC Glasgow. Alan died quite young a few years later, following a prolonged illness.

Alan was quite an outrageous individual, who did, and said many a thing just to shock some of the staff.

We all knew what he was, and what he liked, and what he got up to in his private life (something he never hid), but in particular he enjoyed winding up some of the older staff members with the odd shocking announcement.

Like the time he informed Mona (one of the ladies on the switchboard, and a part time receptionist) just what he had been physically indulging in with another man the previous evening. On hearing this, Mona (who was quite a straight-laced lady) instantly froze with a look of startled horror on her face, while at the same time spluttering her cup of tea all over the reception desk. Alan laughed at her startled reaction and then walked down to the studio, to start his work.

One year on the lead up to Christmas, Fraser had received a Christmas card from a mysterious admirer. "Have a look at this?" he said as he passed an envelope on to me in order for me to have a look at. It had Fraser's name on the outside, as well as the address of the BBC at 5 Queen Street, Edinburgh. I didn't recognise the writing, so I was none the wiser as to who might have sent it.

I then opened up the envelope, and gave out a loud laugh at the image now staring back at me from the card's front cover. I couldn't believe (although in some ways, I should have) the image that now stared back at me. This was, you could say, a most unusual Christmas card. No Santa Claus, reindeers, carol singers, or Three Wise Men following a distant star. Pictured on the front was a well-muscled blonde hunk in a relaxed pose. Not sure if he was all that wise, but he did have a rather naughty smirk on his face.

He was stretched out on a long lounge chair, wearing nothing more than a pair of tight-fitting red shorts, bordered by some strategically placed holly and ivy, which must have been a little awkward for him to put on, and take off, I thought at the time.

In the background was a decorated Christmas tree, just to give the scene that extra festive feel. However, when I opened up the card, a mixture of laughter and shock now hit me. Inside it said: *Merry Christmas Fraser;* followed by the words *I'm Dreaming Of A Tight Christmas With You!*

There was no signature as to who had sent it, although both of us had a few select suspects in mind. "I can't show this to my mother!" Fraser told me.

After I had managed to stifle another giggle, I then replied, "Eh, no, I don't suppose you could. Any idea of who sent it to you?" I asked him.

"Who do you think?" he fired back at me.

I shook my head and then laughingly said, "Well, there are quite a few in here that automatically spring to mind." Fraser just nodded his head and then put the card away out of sight. I am led to believe that he never took it home to show his mother. And maybe just as well.

Fraser later admitted that perhaps the guilty party wasn't one of the BBC staff after all, but a character that was also known to hold Fraser close and dear to his heart at the time – Dave, the manager of the Beau Brummell pub. I had only met this chap on a couple of occasions when I popped into the Beau for a drink, but I was always aware that his eyes always lit up with excitement whenever Fraser arrived. I also happened to notice that, from time to time, he gave him that little bit of extra vodka in his drink. No doubt hoping for something that little bit extra in return.

One other suspect was Paul, the rather effeminate hairdresser who worked in the hairdressing salon, not too far from the Beau.

Fraser told me that Paul had also shown great interest in his wellbeing, and apparently loved to seductively run his fingers through his hair – whilst he was simultaneously cutting and styling it!

What it must have been for the poor guy to be so popular with so many, during that period?

Simultaneously, he became equally a magnet of attraction with yet another hairdresser – only this time a female. At first glance, she looked quite classy and attractive with a curvy figure and long, wavy blonde hair and she went by the name of Suzie. At Fraser's invitation, she turned up to attend a couple of the Queen Street parties back in the 1980s. Before I had got the chance to meet her properly, I asked Mac what she was like.

Without any hesitation, he then gave me his immediate appraisal of this girl's particular charms – "She's just his type – rough as f**k, with whore written all over her!"

As a joke, I then asked Mac if she was the kind of girl that you could take home to meet your mother. "You must be f*****g joking! She's got a tongue as rough as sandpaper!" he replied, leaving no one in any doubt as to her ideal suitability as a romantic partner. Oh dear. Not wishing to appear too ungallant, I reluctantly had to agree with him, for as soon as we were introduced, and she opened her mouth, all illusions were instantly shattered. She wasn't what you would describe as the chaste *Jane Austen* type.

On top of that, she gave the impression that she had never attended an exclusive, all-girls finishing school. "We had a f*****g right good night last night, didn't we Fraser?" she explained to the gathering, without a hint of any shame, or embarrassment. Fraser, with a bit of a naughty smile on his face, was now looking very much like a young boy who has just discovered all of his Christmas presents at the bottom of the wardrobe, meekly agreed.

I always wondered if they had been playing scrabble that particular night in question... then again, maybe not.

For a laugh, I later (with a strong sense of irony) dubbed her *"Suzie with the Golden Scissors"*, although she was far from anyone's idea of a "fairy princess".

In fact her rough-edged vocabulary would be extremely difficult to be found in any of the *Grimm Brothers'* writings.

Anyway, pretty soon, after several drinks were consumed, she was all over poor Fraser (although he wasn't particularly fighting her off) like a large bottle of hair conditioner. Causing the group who were sitting there at the time, to enjoy a right good laugh at his expense.

A little time later Fraser told many of us one morning that he harboured ambitions himself in taking up the trade of hairdressing. "A f*****g hairdresser?" was the shocked reply as his colleagues attempted to take in this sudden announcement. This also caused an almighty explosion of laughter from Mac, Dougie, Stan and myself – as poor Fraser now looked a bit stunned at our combined reaction. After the laughter had subsided following his shock statement, Fraser looked a little perplexed, as well as somewhat angry with his colleagues for taking the almighty piss!

"What?? How can you be a f*****g hairdresser, with f*****g hands that shake like that??" Mac asserted.

"Oh, just forget it!" Fraser replied back as he just walked away with his ambitions and ego slightly dented.

I suppose it was true in a sense, as often Fraser would arrive at work with his hands just a little shaky (a malady that afflicted many of the staff during this period, so Fraser wasn't exactly alone in that respect) following a heavy night on the booze.

Maybe with him mixing socially with a few in the hairdressing industry at that moment in time, the notion of taking up a comb and scissors had been well and truly "brushed into his psyche", in a manner of speaking.

But the prospect of him yielding sharpened scissors, along with the reality of his shaking hands, was a fact that meant it was simply never going to happen, and if he was honest with himself, he probably knew it.

Fraser often also boasted of several amorous encounters with slightly older women, who found his boyish looks just too good to resist.

One lady in particular worked in an office in Hanover Street and regularly drank alongside him on a number of nights at the Beau Brummell.

When his work pals cheekily enquired if his intentions were serious and honourable towards the mature lady in question. He smiled, then shaking his head, replied: "Nah, I'm just doing her a favour!" Well, that was hardly what you would describe as a *David Niven* style response. It was said with such casual indifference, as if he had just fixed a leaky pipe, or was helping her out with a spot of interior decorating!

There was yet another lady admirer he was "stepping out socially with" a couple of years later, whom he invited into Queen Street late one night, just to impress her, and show her around the building. There was no one around, and it was virtually empty, when during the tour, Fraser showed her the main switchboard. Intrigued by this, and while at the same time, Fraser was pouring them both a drink from his private stash of liqueur; the young woman concluded that this was an ideal opportunity to call up some old friends she needed to get in touch with. The only thing was, these old friends that she was eager to contact, all lived in Australia, Hong Kong and Singapore!!

I wonder what the phone bills were like on that particular month.

In between his attraction for frazzled and frenzied hairdressers, there was a period in which Fraser put aside his "tom-cat style antics" (well he was the official ship's cat after all!) and embarked on a real romance that for a period truly captured his heart.

This involved a lovely girl from Dingwall called Donna, and everyone could see that they made an ideal couple. Donna had been staying at Peggy's flat as her student lodger, and so Peggy decided to play Cupid by introducing them to each other. Physically they were about the same height, and from that first meeting they hit it off and inevitably, they soon became so happy in each other's company.

Donna was training at college, with her ultimate intention in becoming a beautician and Fraser was as happy as I had ever seen him.

During this period, anyone who spent time in their company, could instantly see they were both deeply smitten and simpatico in all things.

Unfortunately, this idealised relationship soon hit the bumpers, as the unending allure of the Beau Brummell (not forgetting the George Hotel staff club – a real den of vice and iniquity!) proved too much for the guy.

The relationship that looked so full of genuine promise for both of them, quickly soured and was now all but over. Donna finally left him to further pursue her ambitions elsewhere.

I don't think Fraser was quite the same guy after she left.

*

Fraser and I had become good pals and we socialised regularly outside of the BBC. One night we decided to go to the movies after work to see *Clint Eastwood* in the film *Bronco Billy*. The film was showing at the old ABC Film Centre in Lothian Road, and it didn't start until just after 6 o'clock.

We mentioned this to Bob, and he said that he would give us both a lift up the road in his car to the cinema.

Sounded good, however, little did we both realise that Bob

had other things on his mind, as he was planning (with both of us in the car at the time) to re-enact, on the city centre streets of Edinburgh, the furious car chase scene from *The French Connection*, with Bob in the guise of *Gene Hackman!*

Once we got into his car, and clicked the seatbelts, Bob's face began to look very different, almost like *Dr Jekyll* might have done, once he had supped that lethal potion!

He began to cackle wildly as he started up the car, and then before you could say go, we were speeding alarmingly along Queen Street, as if we had just robbed a bank, and were now being hotly pursued by the police.

I made the mistake of asking Bob if he might slow the car down a wee bit – wrong move. This just made him worse. Bob began to laugh again, as the car increased in acceleration, just as he was now turning up towards Frederick Street.

He was now combining the driving skills of *Frank Bullitt* and *Popeye Doyle*, as the car sped at a frightening rate up the road and then down, as it headed towards a very busy Princes Street. Fraser and I both looked at each other wondering if this experience was soon going to be our very last hours on earth, as the car just got faster and faster.

Once on Princes Street, Bob then gave us a further demonstration of his wild and reckless ability behind the wheel, as he began to drive *backwards – yes, you heard me correctly, backwards,* along a very busy Princes Street, dodging cars, taxis and buses, while laughing like an unbalanced madman – which he was giving a very good impression of at the time.

He then stopped the car midway, and with the loud sound of car horns blaring in his ears, he put his foot right down on the pedal and speeded back along the westward direction towards Lothian Road. He then drove faster and faster, as I began to imagine that I saw my past life flashing in front of my eyes, but not only that, he then took his hands away from the wheel, as the car, for a few fleeting seconds, was now seemingly driving itself!!

My heart was jumping all over the place, while at the same time Fraser had a look of abject terror in his eyes. Bob then drove the car up Lothian Road, and finally stopped just outside of the cinema.

"Hope you enjoy the film," he said to us as we emerged slightly shaking from the car.

"Eh, thanks Bob, see you tomorrow," I replied to him, as he then closed the car door, and zoomed into the night as if he were driving the Batmobile!

The film, as you can imagine, was a bit of a blur after that, and it became obvious that both Fraser and I were now in dire need of a large drink to calm our shattered nerves.

"Next time we decide to go the movies, we'll just take the bus," I said to Fraser, as he was still a little shaky, as he took a large gulp of his first pint of lager.

"Yes, I think after tonight's experience in Bob's car, that's probably a good idea."

*

For me, one of the most enduring highlights of my time working at 5 Queen Street didn't involve work, or the building itself, but rather what happened out with it. If that sounds a little confusing, well what I am attempting to convey is the enjoyment I felt about the Thursday night football match.

This "kicked off" (oops) around the mid-1980s, when a number of the newsroom and current affairs staff decided they fancied a weekly five-a-side game to be played on the all-weather pitches at Meadowbank Stadium. Included amongst the weekly line-up were the likes of *Kenny MacIntyre, John Milne, Colin Blane, Colin MacDonald, Kit Fraser, Neil Fraser, Simon Walton* and many others from the BBC.

Not forgetting myself, and (for the first few weeks

anyway) young Fraser. Soon others would join the merry group, and what started off originally as a five-a-side kick-about, eventually evolved into a seven, or even an eight-a-side game, with a diverse range of skills, as well as some terrific goals on display each week.

I hadn't properly kicked a ball since I left school about ten years previously, but was very keen to see if "the old ball skills" (or something closely resembling that?) were still intact and thriving, following a bit of a dormant period. Fraser too was all for getting on the pitch and running up and down the wing with the ball at his feet – at least in his mind. But what we were all looking forward to was having a game and recreating a period of our past boyhood that we had all felt was long gone.

As I can remember, all the guys from the newsroom and current affairs were pretty good players. *Kenny MacIntyre* may have been a bit slower, but he read the game well, and made some telling tackles and passes.

As did *John Milne*, who controlled the midfield with cool skill, and like Kenny was an astute reader of the game, who could split a defence with a clever and well-measured pass.

Simon (one of the audio unit, a heavy metal fan and someone who you could describe as being a bit of a character – but a good friend nonetheless) on the other hand, was what you would describe as "a wild card". Some nights he was good and others, well, maybe not so good. I suppose that could easily describe myself as well, although I often felt that with my legs now a little slower than they once were, my best position would probably be best served in the heart of the defence. I could view the game, while stemming numerous attacks from the opposition, and setting up new attacks for my midfield teammates. At least that's what I thought.

The memory of Simon's bone crunching, shin splintering, sliding tackles still – even after all these years – make me shudder and break out in a cold sweat. He seemed to particularly enjoy lining up opposite Kenny, and Simon would make his intentions known in bringing him down with an almighty thump during the course of the game. "Oh, for f**k's sake Simon! Oh, oh, oh, ma f*****g ankle!" was the usual painful cry of lingering agony, after Simon had left one of his opponents lying prostrate on the ground, as he rolled around like an potential Oscar winner!!

On the other hand, if Simon and Kenny happened to be playing on the same side, you would often hear Kenny's wails of disappointment, as a particularly skilful move would instantly break down with Simon at the end of it. "For f**k's sake Simon!" Kenny would yell in his direction, as the ball would either go spinning over the bar – or straight past the post.

However, Simon often redeemed himself whenever he picked up the goalie's gloves and took up his position between the sticks.

I have memories of some of Simon's goalkeeping performances that would make the great *Pat Jennings* green with envy!

Unfortunately, just following a simply incredible save that defied logic and amazed all who were standing there, Simon would then blow it by throwing the ball straight at the feet of one of the opposition, who would then go on to calmly slot the ball into the net.

This of course, would automatically make Kenny shout out, yet again towards his direction, "For f**k's sake Simon!! That's f*****g awful!!"

At the same time, Kenny would grow increasingly frustrated when a terrific move would utterly collapse, as the ball skidded over the bar, past the post, or straight at the keeper.

"Oh boys, boys, boys…" was Kenny's constant anguished cry, while simultaneously shaking his head, as he began to wonder with exasperation as to why his sharpened footballing brain wasn't being replicated by the blunted feet of his younger teammates.

We even managed to arrange a challenge match with some of our colleagues from BBC Glasgow. Lining up opposite us that night were the recognisable figures of *Chic Young* and *Rob MacLean*, as we looked forward to a terrific game.

Unfortunately, our deficiencies in attack and defence were glaringly shown up, as we were well and truly trounced. Yet, it was an all-round good experience as well as a salutary lesson in trying to get the ball away from *Chic Young's* quick feet!

Following a busted wrist and some twisted knee damage (absolutely nothing to do with Simon, by the way!) my footballing days inevitably came to a sorry end a few years later.

However, as a small tribute, my fellow team members presented me with a trophy that I still treasure to this day.

It features a small figure of a player with the ball at his feet and is inscribed with the statement: *"Player Of The Millennium"*. I must admit that I was very touched by the thought and the gesture. Even if the statement and description of my ball-playing prowess was a trifle extravagant – even for me!

When I told my dad he just shook his head, laughed and instantly came to the conclusion that they were all just winding me up, taking the piss and having a laugh at (what he perceived) as my lamentable efforts on the pitch.

Yet despite his opinion, and even to this day, it is still something that I am quite proud of.

*

So usually on the Thursday morning Kenny, in passing, would call out "Are you playing tonight, Lawrence?" I would nod my head and then reply that I would be there.

Later he would spot Fraser and ask him the same question.

"Are you playing tonight, wee man?" Fraser would say yes and Kenny would then arrange to pick him up that night and give him a lift in his car down to the stadium.

Unfortunately and unusually, Fraser's unique idea of a pre-match preparation would invariably involve two hours spent propping up the bar in the Beau Brummell beforehand, downing several large vodkas, before he would pop back round to Queen Street for Kenny to give him a lift.

Once the game started, Fraser would be full of running and full of enthusiasm. For the first ten minutes or so, with the ball at his feet, he could be seen careering down the wing like a young *George Best*!

Sadly, those rare moments of fleeting skill were over all too quickly. Usually after about twenty minutes into the game, Fraser was posted missing. I recall looking around the pitch and the surrounding area, to see where he had gone. I then noticed him a wee bit away looking not at all well, with his face almost as green as his Hibs top!

He then proceeded to be violently sick, which put an immediate halt to him having any further participation in the match. I remember him saying during a break in the game that he wasn't feeling all that great and was going to get changed and then go home. Although, I had a sneaking suspicion that he might well have been heading back to the Beau Brummell for a few more vodkas!

Fraser's footballing comeback probably lasted about a couple of months, before the lure of the pub and the vodka bottle proved to be a far more alluring enticement. Certainly far more than kicking a football up and down the wing at Meadowbank Stadium on a Thursday night.

One Friday morning I came into work and Fraser asked how the previous night's game had gone.

"I had a pretty good game, I must admit," as I was feeling a little pleased with myself. "I even scored last night!" I added with a flourish, as if I had been practicing my ball skills at Easter Road, or Hampden Park.

"So you scored then?" Fraser enquired. Then with a hint of a naughty smile that began to sneak up on his features he then said, "So did I!" I suppose we both had received a pleasant evening's entertainment – although in very different ways.

On one occasion Fraser and myself were invited out for a "Fun Night" with our good pal Ian – who became better known to everyone at the time as "Mr Snax".

Snax arrived at Queen Street about roughly a year after me and took up his post as one of the younger members of the audio crew. Over the next few years, he would amass a reputation as one of the most skilful and adroit sound engineers in the entire place.

His talent, when it came to sound mixing and editing, would soon lead him to move into television news and he would later became equally renowned for his ability behind a film camera.

Snax was one of the most colourful and outrageous characters I knew during my time at the BBC, and today he is still a good friend. His cutting remarks, sardonic humour and his outrageously indiscreet behaviour, regularly left me creasing up with laughter.

He loved a good night out, with a few (or perhaps more likely a lot) beers, usually followed by a hot curry, for if he loves anything – it is his food.

In fact, over a number of years he would organise the annual "Crazy Christmas Curries" in which several of the staff would descend upon a curry house of his choosing and then indulge in a good festive feed – with some not unexpectedly scandalous behaviour that went along with it.

Soon Mr Snax would gather a reputation (far away from the editing suites and television cameras) as a "bon vivant", "curry connoisseur" and ardent pursuer of attractive available women.

This, I must add, was a number of years before he would meet his future wife Sheena, who also worked at the BBC, and they would embark on a loving relationship that would ultimately lead to a happy marriage.

But many years before that and like so many of us around during those heady days, he was young and constantly on the lookout for some frisky fun.

The problem being that he appeared to be enjoying far more frisky fun than anyone else! Myself included.

But putting jealousy aside, we loved him nonetheless.

Anyway, Mr Snax mentioned to Fraser and myself about going out for a "fun night" that would involve a few beers, a curry and a game of 8 Ball Deluxe!

For those unfamiliar with the term, 8 Ball Deluxe was a pinball game played in a number of Edinburgh hostelries.

For this particular night, we set out first to *Khushies Curry House* in Broughton Street, where we enjoyed a good hot feed, that included a few cooling beers to calm down our now red-hot taste buds.

Then, we made our way down to the Phoenix pub where the pinball machine awaited us. Snax got the first round in and then settled himself to master the intricacies of 8 Ball Deluxe.

I stood alongside him with my beer in hand and watched him at work, all the while admiring his skill on the machine.

However, Fraser appeared to be distracted. He had settled himself down at the bar and began chatting to the young barmaid, who made no effort to hide her obvious attraction for him. I got the impression that they had met before, or maybe she was an earlier conquest, and it was time for an emotional reunion.

We stayed there for a couple of hours, drinking more beer, with Snax now glued to the pinball machine like pinball wizard *Tommy* from *The Who*'s rock opera.

Fraser and the barmaid where getting on like the proverbial house on fire, all giggles, smiles, and furtive whispers. They were oblivious to us, as they seemed to only have eyes for each other.

Too much drink now made me feel a little bit giddy, and I needed to get home, as I was working the following morning.

So I made my farewells to my two pals and headed down the road for the comfort of my bed.

The next morning, I experienced one of the worst hangovers I can ever recall. I struggled into work, feeling none too great, just hoping that the day would pass quickly and I could get back home and head for my bed and an early night.

Mac immediately noticed my pale and washed-out appearance and then began to raise the volume in his voice just to get a reaction.

"So, you had a fun night out then did you?" he bellowed in my ear. "Maybe we should all go out with Mr Snax and have a f*****g fun night out!"

By this time, he was thoroughly enjoying winding me up and making sure that my internal agony was increased tenfold. "F*****g Fun!" he was now adding with just a hint of sarcasm. "Wish I went out last night and had a F*****g Fun Night!"

Every time he mentioned the fun night, his vocal range increased in volume, as if he was back on the parade ground barking orders at his men, making my already tender and fragile head boom and echo with increased agony.

"Where's that f*****g wee bastard Fraser this morning? Did he not have a fun night as well?"

Fraser had as yet not showed up for work, and was by this

time almost a half hour late. Then Snax popped his head in the door beaming from ear to ear, wearing a light-coloured linen suit, complete with a wide brimmed Panama hat making him look not unlike a Malaysian tea planter from the 1930s!

He smiled in both our directions and then said, "Ah Yes!" and then went on his way briskly up the stairs. Considering he was drinking just as much – if not more – than myself the previous evening, was all a bit disconcerting, as he looked as bright and fresh as a daisy. Certainly not what I was feeling, I can assure you.

A few minutes later, Fraser finally arrived. He looked rough – boy did he look rough. Mac just gave him a withering glance, not hiding his disgust, and sternly walked away.

"How are you feeling this morning, as I feel like shit!" I asked him.

"What a night I've had!" he said, as he began to tremble a little, due partly perhaps of the drink, or something else that had occurred during the post-midnight hours.

"What happened?" I began to enquire.

"Well, you remember the barmaid from the pub?" he said. "I ended up going home with her and I'm all in pain." With this lurid confession, he began to take off his shirt and show me his back, shoulder and neck.

"For f**k's sake!!" I cried out at the horrific image that now stood before me. "You look like you have just been mauled by a wild animal," I said to him.

From what I could see, his back, neck and shoulder were bloodied, scratched, bitten and roughly marked, as if sharpened teeth and talons had been dug deep into his skin. "I'm in absolute f*****g agony," he said through gritted teeth. And going by the terrible state of his upper torso, I didn't disbelieve him. "We were in bed and then she began to scratch and bite and sink her teeth into my body!"

I lamely tried to make a joke of it by saying, "Was this

before, or after you had your cocoa?"

Fraser wasn't smiling; at least he was trying not to laugh, as it was bringing him so much pain. I then tried to again lighten the mood by asking, "I take it a second date with this young lady is permanently out of the question?"

"What do you think?" he fired back at me, as he groaned once more in obvious discomfort.

From his vivid description of the evening's proceedings, it became obvious that he had endured far more agony than ecstasy!

And it appeared that for one night only, young Fraser had foregone the sporting enjoyment of 8 Ball Deluxe, for the more primal delights of 2 Ball Deluxe! But it came at a heavy and painful price.

For the remainder of the day, both of us slowly walked around the building in anguish and discomfort.

Myself with the remnants of the hangover from hell, Fraser with the scarred memory of a night enjoying the wild and untamed attentions of cat-woman!

But I suppose in looking back, it had been a "Fun Night", in more ways than one.

Fraser's activities during this point always seemed to give me plenty of verbal ammunition for sarcasm. But nothing nasty, that wasn't my intention.

In fact he used to laugh and enjoy some of my barbed comments that I threw in his direction. I loved to quote the odd line from a film at him, one that suitably would match the mood of the occasion.

A particular favourite was some of the rich dialogue that originated from the 1957 classic *"Sweet Smell Of Success"*. On occasion, I would affect a *Burt Lancaster* style voice and deliver a line to him, as if he were *Tony Curtis*.

Such as: "You sound happy, Fraser. Why should you be

happy when I'm not?" Or, "Fraser lives so much in a moral twilight..." or, "Don't be a two-time loser Fraser – the penalty could be severe."

We would both laugh at this, although, maybe I was hinting at an element of truth in his own character, one that he readily recognised.

*

One of the strangest episodes where Fraser was concerned, was his burgeoning relationship with our lady boss, Bella. Yes, the very same one who memorably screamed "Holy f**k!" at the top of her lungs during the photocopier disaster.

Looking back, I'm not quite sure what kind of a relationship it was. Neither did anyone else within in the building, for that matter. Was it physical, emotional, a casual close friendship, a meeting of minds, soul mates, a shared love of strong drink? Or maybe it was a combination of all of those things, with a few extra bits and pieces thrown in for good measure.

Whatever it was, throughout the building it caused much mutterings of disapproval, startled bafflement, perplexity, and just downright amazement at the unusual sight of them together in extreme close harmony.

Regularly I would be regaled first thing in the morning with a selection of hilariously tawdry tales of the two "amours" from the previous night and their romantic trysts in the pub, from the likes of Mac and Stan.

It appears that after work, they usually would pop into (not too prematurely I hasten to add!) "The Climax Bar" (what an imaginative name for a pub!), and accidentally catch "the lovers" in full-blown action.

Both my working mates couldn't wait to fill me in on what had happened the very next morning.

"You should have seen the pair of them, cuddled up

together in a dark corner, ignoring everybody – including us! His two pals!" said Stan, none too pleased at being ignored on the night.

"What a f*****g embarrassing spectacle they both made!" added Mac in his own inimitable fashion. "Both of them with their arms and hair wrapped around each other, you couldn't see their f*****g faces. They were like a pair of f*****g praying mantises during the mating season!" He then added the coup de grace: "It was like watching f*****g Samson and Delilah on heat!"

I will be honest, and confess that I always got on ok with Bella. She was always pretty fair with me and I had no issues with her, either as a boss, or as a person.

But I always got the impression that she had made quite a few enemies in the BBC, with a few individuals who would have been most happy to see her come an almighty cropper.

Again looking back, I always laughed when (if she was in a particularly snippy and sharp mood) she would request her team to carry out a specific job, or task. After fully explaining the intricacies of what she wanted them to do, she would then finish her instruction by stating: "And I want it all done – f*****g now!" With her raised voice adding extra emphasise on the "f*****g now!"

Not sure if any boss, manager, or supervisor could get away with that today, but it was very funny at the time when she would utter (or splutter) those words towards our direction. Usually when following a long liquid lunch hour, with probably Fraser in tow.

For about four or five years, Fraser's drinking habits were becoming more and more noticeable. Not satisfied with just a normal couple of drinks after work, he would drink during the lunchtime, and then when his drinking began to really accelerate, he would be drinking even before he started his work in the morning.

He would quite happily tell all that he was frequenting a pub near the back of Princes Street called *The Penny Black*.

This side street haunt was usually found to be open for custom around 6 in the morning, in order to accommodate the thirsty postmen (the pub was only a stone's throw away from the old Royal Mail headquarters) after they had endured a long, dry night shift.

I was becoming acutely aware that drink was really beginning to dominate his life. Vodka was his favoured tipple, although he would drink beer as well and occasionally whisky.

Although after he had drunk whisky, it would visibly alter his personality and that could easily turn him a little aggressive and argumentative.

Usually whenever he was in a bit of a foul mood, or something, or someone had upset or annoyed him at work, he would normally confront such feelings by announcing to all that were present: "After work, I'm going straight round to the Beau, and I'm going to get absolutely f*****g plastered!"

I suppose this was his way of dealing with things, and for a few hours his problems would dissipate in a foggy vodka haze.

Physically he wasn't looking all that great as well. He was beginning to look thin and gaunt, and his face was taking on a grey and sallow appearance. He wasn't eating, missing out on meals in the canteen and heading straight to the pub to get his regular vodka top-up.

However, this constant alcoholic assault on his system was beginning to take its inevitable effect. He would often come to work doubled up in excruciating pain, as he clutched his stomach in obvious discomfort.

A few of us during that time, implored him to see his doctor, as the longer he ignored the symptoms and went on like this, the more agony he would be in. He would try to laugh it off, with his ready-made remedy being even more vodka, followed by a hot chilli kebab on the way home at night! This was a recipe for a disaster, and a ticking health time bomb that could very well explode at any minute.

Mac decided that he might know the perfect cure, so he brought in a bottle of Mallox, a medicine that is known to alleviate severe stomach pain. Fraser thanked him and then began to drink it when the pain worsened.

Unfortunately, he would tend to mix Mallox with vodka – a most unusual cocktail you could say, and certainly not what his doctor would have prescribed, and not something that would go to make his health situation any better.

One day his condition got so bad, that he was forced to make an appointment to see his GP, as he was in danger of collapsing. Mac was of the opinion that he was showing all the evidence of a potential ulcer.

Although Fraser just brushed this diagnosis off, as not worth even thinking about. He was much too young for that, and that would only interfere with his drinking.

Yet the daily pain he was experiencing was taking its toll. So eventually, he booked a doctor's appointment and readied himself to get some medical treatment for his ailment.

The following day he returned to work, as I asked him how he got on and what his doctor had advised for him. He looked straight at me, and with the hint of a smile he then told me his doctor's prognosis: "My doctor said that I should cut out the drink, cut out the cigarettes, eat regular meals, that included… boiled fish and milky puddings!"

I was a little speechless at first, but then said something along the lines of, "Well, if that's what your doctor prescribes, you better start now."

Going by the look on his face, it was as if he was going to reply straight back at me, "That will be f*****g right!"

The thought of Fraser giving up his smokes, his regular daily dose of vodka, his midnight kebabs, all for the calming pleasures of boiled fish and milky puddings, was just never going to happen.

I knew it and if he was honest with himself, he knew it. He was in the unyielding grip of something that was far stronger than him, and it wouldn't let go.

I would often see Fraser disappearing during the morning into the basement, where he had a personal locker, and it was in this locker that he kept a secret stash of vodka. This was to keep him refreshed before lunchtime and his inevitable visit to the pub.

He was on a sad, downward spiral that he just couldn't escape from.

*

After the return to Queen Street and following the studio and offices refurbishment, Fraser's days at the BBC were soon to be numbered. The Corporation was changing; this was a time of "Producer Choice" and the BBC's embracement of an entirely different working culture that was bizarrely using the BBC's very own resources and facilities in the style of an open market.

Fraser's position would become an unfortunate casualty of changing times.

In early 1993, his job was being phased out and he was now facing the inevitability of being surplus to requirements, coming as it did with the inevitability of being made redundant.

I must admit that, at the time, it did seem a bit harsh, considering that he was on a pretty lowly salary. A salary that was almost the equivalent of one of *Jeremy Clarkson's* evening meals!! While I am convinced that he could have been utilised and readapted in some form or another, somewhere else in the building. Yet the "powers that be" had made their decision. His job was going – and unfortunately, so was he.

To his credit (although I am convinced that he must have

been really gutted inside) he didn't make a song and dance about it, and reacted to it, in some ways, quite calmly, stoically and philosophically.

He made no bones of the fact that the BBC were handing him a pretty fair payoff cheque, and he even spoke of going on a lavish Mediterranean cruise with some of his money.

I felt for him, as so many others did. The BBC was his life, and he had worked with us for about a dozen years, more or less.

No doubt at first, he would feel a little lost and perhaps abandoned. Yet he refused to be maudlin about it and tried to look to the future with some cautious confidence – although I wasn't entirely convinced that he was feeling so optimistic about his future.

The "Official Ship's Cat" was soon going to be cast adrift and marooned on a desert island, and left all alone – ironically just like old *Ben Gunn*.

Prior to his final day, he had mentioned inviting a few of the staff along for a farewell drink that he was planning to have in a pub in Edinburgh's High Street. With his redundancy cheque not coming through for a few more weeks, he asked if he could borrow some money from me, to pay for his farewell do. "Sure, no problem," I said, as I knew that he would repay me when his money arrived.

Quite a number of the staff turned up and the evening went ahead ok, although it was tinged with some sadness, as he was now leaving. And deep down, we all knew that he didn't want to leave.

A couple of weeks after his last day at work, he called me to say that his redundancy payment had come through, and that he would pop in to see me and repay my loan.

When he turned up, he was looking ok, and looked in a pretty good mood, as he gave me my money back and we spoke about keeping in touch and going for a drink regularly together.

I asked him what he had spent some of his money on.

He told me that he treated himself to a new leather jacket – and a video copy of *Lethal Weapon*. That day would turn out to be the very last time that I ever saw him alive.

A few weeks later, I received a phone call at home from Mac, who told me the most shocking news imaginable.

Fraser was dead. I couldn't take it in, and I just couldn't believe it, considering that I had only seen him a couple of weeks earlier and that it wasn't that long since he had left the BBC.

The official line was that he had collapsed in his house and died from a perforated ulcer. He was just 30 years of age.

When the news reached the work the next day, the entire building and those close colleagues who had worked alongside him, were shaken and upset, to say the very least.

At the time we had a temporary Admin Officer by the name of Fiona, who had to deal with the obvious grief that was now being experienced by so many of us at that time. I kept thinking back to a few weeks earlier when he seemed to be ok and was giving us the impression that despite being coldly jettisoned by the BBC, he would embark upon a new life elsewhere. But those of us who really knew him, knew that leaving the BBC was in fact, cutting a vital lifeline for him, and that he would be one sad, lost guy.

Recriminations and bitter accusations began to be vocally aired among a number of his close colleagues. Particularly when aimed at certain members of senior management, who, you could say, were probably responsible for getting rid of him, and thus (considering his acute drink problem) indirectly responsible for his tragic demise. To those of us who knew him, the idea of handing him a large redundancy cheque was almost akin to handing him a loaded gun.

I'm not saying exactly that they had blood on their hands, but during those days following his death, quite a few in the building were giving air to such thoughts.

There was a sense of anger in the atmosphere at the tragic and unnecessary loss of someone so young, someone who despite his many flaws had been part of the very fabric of BBC Edinburgh over a long period of time.

During the last few years that Fraser worked with us, myself and all his friends at Queen Street began to realise that his life was unravelling and that he was in real danger of pushing the self-destruct button.

This had the potentiality of leading to a very sorry end for the guy. But we had no idea that it would have happened so quickly, so suddenly and in the end, so tragically.

*

Fraser's funeral occurred on a warm Saturday in May. A coach had been booked and arranged to pick up as many people as possible from Queen Street to the Morton Hall Cemetery, where the funeral was to take place.

My dad came along with me, as he had met Fraser on a number of occasions, and after everyone had congregated, we boarded the bus for the sombre journey to the crematorium.

Knowing how popular Fraser had been with so many people from both inside and outside of the BBC, I wasn't at all surprised to see so many people turn up. One individual, who was markedly absent, was his mother Margaret. In some ways I almost expected it.

No one could possibly fathom how she must have been feeling by going through the terrifying shock of losing her son at such a young age. The prospect of attending his funeral would, not surprisingly, prove to be just too unbearably painful for her to endure.

As we all slowly walked along the narrow path towards the funeral chapel, I became aware and alarmed that something had happened. A little up ahead, while walking towards the chapel, Dorothy Laing, our receptionist, had slightly stumbled, lost her balance and fell awkwardly at the side of the path.

She was obviously in excruciating pain, as several onlookers came to her aid and assistance. So an ambulance was immediately called for, with her being in such agony and she was then taken straight to hospital.

The funeral service was, as expected, a deeply sad affair, reflecting the still palpable atmosphere of stunned shock that we all still felt.

With the sun shining from the outside, the chapel was filled to the brim with many familiar faces and many friends. It was a moving and ultimately touching service that culminated in a moment that left many of us a little teary eyed, including myself.

As a small tribute they played in the chapel *Elvis Presley* singing *"American Trilogy"*. I would like to think that Fraser would have approved.

*

Going back to work the following Monday after the funeral was pretty tough. But what was to happen in the next few days was to prove even tougher.

Dorothy Laing our receptionist was a happy, cheery, friendly woman who first arrived to work as a receptionist sometime around the mid-1980s. She absolutely loved her job and she loved meeting and chatting with the staff and this made her very popular with everyone.

However, once we returned to Queen Street following the building's refurbishment, she seemed totally convinced there were secret plans afoot to force her to retire early.

Over the course of several months, the poor woman was beside herself with (imagined, or otherwise) deep worry that she was soon going to be ousted from her job – whether she liked it or not.

Often she would quietly confide in me regarding her

severe fears about her BBC future.

She strongly felt that there was some form of furtive plot – conducted in conjunction with the union and personnel – that was aiming to make her retire early. Not sure if Dorothy had been watching too many conspiracy thrillers, or if she had in fact obtained some form of concrete evidence regarding this? But she was totally convinced that something was in the air supporting her theory.

I attempted to reassure her as best as I could, but in all honestly, I wasn't sure what was happening myself, and had no real idea if her position was indeed under any perceived threat.

But all my calming words didn't help her, as she began to get more and more paranoid about her future job prospects.

On the Monday following Fraser's funeral the general mood about the building was to say the least, extremely low and downcast. People just couldn't fathom it out, as well as having difficulty in taking it all in.

Things were attempting to get back to some form of normality when we were hit by another more seismic shock that was totally unexpected.

While I was sitting down having a cup of tea in the print room, Fiona our temporary Admin Officer walked in. She looked a little shaken, as she sat down beside me and then proceeded to tell me some more dreadful and devastating news.

After Dorothy's accident prior to Fraser's funeral, she had been whisked straight away to hospital, where due to the awkwardness of her fall, she had been diagnosed as having some serious problem with her arm and shoulder.

An operation was called for, but something went drastically wrong. Dorothy had reacted badly to the anaesthetic and as a consequence of this, she died.

To say I was shocked when hearing this news was an

understatement. I felt numb, confused, and just couldn't get my head around how and why, this could have happened.

It was bizarre, it felt so surreal and there appeared no logic as to how such a seemingly freakish accident could have led to this horrible situation.

As you can imagine, it didn't take long for the sad news to filter throughout 5 Queen Street, and no doubt throughout the rest of BBC Scotland.

If the mood had been low and depressed beforehand – it was now quadrupled as everyone was trying to come to terms with it and to make of it some form of sense.

The following day Dorothy's husband and son turned up to see Fiona. I collected them both from the front door and took them through to see her in her office. Both of them understandably looked in a total state of shock. I don't think that I had ever seen two men look so sad and so lost. God only knows what they must have been feeling and thinking during this dreadful time.

Several days later, and with what you could only describe as the cruellest sense of déjà vu, the building's staff once again assembled to await being picked up by coach and then taken this time to Warriston Crematorium, to attend Dorothy's funeral.

It was another deeply sad occasion, perhaps even more so, considering how this horrendous scenario had played out within the space of only a few days.

It was an experience that I never hope to go through again.

*

It's now been more than 20 years since Alex, Fraser, and Dorothy passed away and there are times when I look back and think of all three of them with a great deal of fondness.

In some eyes their contribution to BBC Scotland and BBC

Edinburgh may have been considered a slight and minor one and not perceived as being at all that significant. After all, they only worked behind the scenes in various support roles and were not involved in the cutting edge of production.

Yet that is not to say that their work was unimportant and that they should be forgotten. I'm convinced that those of us, who knew them during this time, won't ever let that happen.

If the process of writing this book has been good for anything, it has given me the opportunity to briefly revive their memory, as well as the many laughs and good times that we all shared.

And despite the tragically horrendous way they were taken from us, I have attempted to remember them in these pages with a little humour and a degree of personal fond and profound affection.

They cannot die. They are with me still...real in memory as they were in flesh.

CHAPTER 9

Wine, Women & Song!

They cannot die.
They are with me still…. real in memory as they were in flesh.

There is strong evidence that BBC Edinburgh was responsible for many highly acclaimed, prestigious and award-winning radio productions down the decades.

What is much less known (apart from those who were there and can vividly remember) is that it was also responsible for producing many highly acclaimed and unforgettable party nights!!

We may have lacked proper club premises to hold social events, but we more than made up for it by utilising the buildings own internal premises for numerous colourful and zany parties!!

*

During my first few years there, I enjoyed and entered into the spirit of the many "Cheese & Wine" parties that either took place in the canteen, or occasionally within the Studio 1 lounge area.

These first few social gatherings amongst the chilled bottles of chardonnay and the old camembert were more often than not, calm and sedate affairs, with little opportunity for anyone to behave badly by attempting to replicate *Oliver*

Reed style antics!

That would all come to pass a little further down the line.

Everyone was well behaved (that would soon change!) and conducted themselves with the appropriate decorum suitable for such an occasion.

This was the perfect opportunity for the likes of producers, managers, secretaries, and audio engineers to mingle amiably and chat about current and upcoming programmes.

There were also a number of assorted others (that included myself) who turned up vainly attempting to look and sound intellectual, while sampling the free drink and the mix of strong and mild cheeses.

So you could say that the "Cheese & Wine" parties were merely the starter. The main courses were about to begin.

They included Christmas Parties, Halloween Parties, Valentine Parties, Cocktail Parties, Birthday Parties, Fancy Dress Parties, Tarts and Vicars Parties (with the emphasis on the Tarts! Enough to get even men of the cloth hot under the dog collar) Then there were the Outdoor Barbeques, the Beer & Skittle events, and so many (I've lost count) Farewell Parties etc., etc., etc.

More parties you could say than a pre-election television debate!

*

I am often reminded by a few of my old BBC chums about the kind of alcohol I would tend to bring to some of the parties. At the time, I thought I was bringing something different and unusual to the gatherings. Yet on looking back, perhaps not. I would scan the shelves of the various off-licences for something rare and not easily found and then bring the said bottles to the parties.

These legendary names including such exotic beverages as:

Charger Lager, Old Inverness Whiskey, Kentucky Gold Bourbon and perhaps best of all – *Jock Daniels Finest Malt!* I was always aware of my chums giving me strange looks as they collectively shook their heads at my exotic carryouts!

Then there was the legendary *"Cowie's Crazy Christmas Curries!"*

Further down the line they would later morph and transform into *"Crazy Cowie's Christmas Curries!"*

Yet either way, they were invariably the social event of the year, and produced a much-anticipated evening of fabulous food, lots of drink, much laughter and occasional naughty behaviour!

All masterminded, organised, and arranged yearly in his own unique and inimitable fashion, by none other than Ian Cowie, known to the world as Mr Snax.

*

In his time, Mr Snax has been variously described as a sound engineer, TV cameraman, culinary broadcaster and reviewer, food intellectual and all round bon vivant.

He is also one of the funniest guys I have ever met, with a razor-sharp sense of humour that accompanied an acute, biting wit that always went hand in hand with a ready quip.

For two years he was also voted the indisputable *"Curry King of Scotland"*, a title once adorned no less, by Scotland's former First Minister *Alex Salmond*.

Yet for me (and for all his friends and admirers) no man devoted more passion and attention to the love of a good hot curry, than Mr Snax.

All polished off with his instantly recognisable bowtie that completed the unmistakeable portrait of a man with a grand passion for food.

I remember young Richard telling me of one of his earliest experiences of working as part of the audio crew, and his first experience of sharing the studio with Mr Snax.

This went along with Snax telling Richard on regular intervals, whilst running around the confines of the studio splicing tape, "It's not a circus, Richard… it's not a circus!" Richard took this mantra and mark of profundity to heart, although he must have been left a little confused, considering some of the circus-like clowns he encountered over the coming years. Both in and out of the studios.

*

One memorable (perhaps for all the wrong reasons) *"Cowie's Crazy Christmas Curry"* occurred sometime in the mid-1980s when a large group of us were assembled at *Khushis,* in Broughton Street. This was an Indian establishment that always served up a marvellous selection of delicious dishes.

On this particular evening, one of the guests who came along was a loud, large, bearded, slightly arrogant journalist (now there's a novelty!) who prior to him turning up for the meal was pretty far gone drink-wise. So you could say that he was living up to the caricatured image, as well as making a bit of a show of himself, with his loud voice getting on the nerves of one or two of the others at the table. Then as the starters began to arrive, he proceeded to attempt at entertaining the assembly with his very own speciality party trick. This was simply to unzip himself, and then, in full view of the diners, plonk his "best friend" on the table, right alongside the poppadoms, lime pickle, and mango chutney!!

Suffice to say, this did not go down too well with everyone already seated, and he was promptly asked to leave. Which he soon did, as we all saw him stagger out the door.

*

Maybe just as well, as God only knows what he might have done when the main curry dishes, pilau rice and naan bread finally arrived??

One memorable beer and skittles event took place shortly after the completion of the 1986 Edinburgh Commonwealth Games.

A challenge match was arranged between a number of the BBC Commonwealth Games team (that had been based in office premises near Rutland Square) and a team from 5 Queen Street.

The venue was set in a pub near Willowbrae, a place that was familiar to us, as it had been used many times before. So a splendid night full of good fun, good sport, good beer, laughs and hot pies, awaited us all.

The Commonwealth Games team largely consisted of about a dozen loud, crude, rowdy, raucous females. Just looking at them that night, I felt that they wouldn't have looked out of place at a Newcastle weekend hen party!

Right from the off, they were making sure that their presence was being felt – and heard – with all appearing to be pretty fired up with a lethal combination of booze and a bawdy, naughty sense of fun. They all looked like they could handle, ahem, bowling balls with comparative ease.

So it was no great surprise that the noise originating from their table was of a very high decibel level indeed. Perhaps after many weeks and months working intensely at the games, they just needed to let off a bit of steam!

What made their collective voices really hit the ceiling with an explosion of laughter, occurred when Mac stepped up for his first turn at the skittle alley.

Grabbing the ball, he carefully looked down the long bowling route, as he was now about to aim for the skittle target that lay before him.

Then he quickly bent over to release the ball. However, almost simultaneously, all you could now hear was a very loud *riiiiiiiip!!*

It appears that with his trousers being just that little bit too tight, they now split from crotch to backside, just as the ball speeded down towards the awaiting skittles.

At the same time, all that was heard from the opposition's table was a loud expression – "Whoooooooaaaaah!!!" followed by much laughter and a generous helping of unsubtle sexist comments.

Yet this roaring sound was not intended as a show of appreciation for his bowling skills, but more to do with the fact that the girls had now received a bird's eye view of his split trousers – and more importantly for them, what lay underneath!

In fact it was very reminiscent of that memorable scene from *Carry On Teacher* when *Joan Sims* (as the splendidly named *Miss Allcock*) is participating in a keep fit demonstration in front of her class of young schoolgirls. As she bends down, we then hear the unmistakeable sound of *riiiiiiiiiiiip*, as her gym shorts split in a most embarrassing place.

Well, Mac found himself in a very similar situation and was simply red of face and black-affronted. What increased his overwhelming feeling of embarrassment was the lewd and crude reaction of the girls from the opposition's team.

It also didn't help that when he was attempting to survey the trouser damage, the roar from the girl's table just got even louder.

Then each time he stepped forward to take his appointed shot with the bowling ball, there was an even louder screaming noise coming from the girls.

When he next bent down again, the noise was simply deafening, as the girls received another unintended glimpse of his colourful underwear!

I was a little surprised, as going by their reactions, as well as listening to some of their conversation, they didn't exactly give the impression that the sight of a man's undergarments was new or strange to them – far from it, in fact.

"Whoooooooooooaaaaah!!!!!" they screeched once more, as Mac quickly retreated to his seat and took a swig of his beer.

"Look at the state of my f*****g troosers!" he exclaimed to us sitting alongside him, while he grimly surveyed the widening gap that was now unstitching and stretching widely for all to see.

I'm sure on that particular evening the Commonwealth Games girls would have happily presented Mac with his very own gold medal for displaying, well, more than he had originally planned to.

*

It was always fascinating to watch the match set up that existed between certain male members of the Audio unit, with several of the female secretaries, researchers, and production assistants during this time.

It was almost as if BBC Edinburgh had – by pure accident – started an unofficial dating site for the staff.

Romances, flirtations, one night stands and brief physical encounters, would all find their first blossoming and stirrings during the heat of many a recording studio session, as technical and production talent often coalesced into a physical and emotional oneness.

In general terms, they certainly possessed the required grasp of technical knowledge.

Yet it's also fair to say, that they equally had a firm grasp of carnal knowledge to go with it!

With that being the case, for some unaccountable reason, a few of the audio guys seemed to possess a certain mysterious allure and magnetism that made quite a few of the women in the building faint at their feet and fall into their beds!

Perhaps it was all down to that intricate skill they displayed with their hands? Especially when demonstrated in the pressure pot of the recording studio, when the act of simultaneously handling and editing audiotape, impressed many a fluttering female and usually clinched the deal for them.

Before setting up home at Queen Street, many of the younger audio guys had previously been to university or some form of technical college, and once being accepted as new starts, they then completed their audio and technical training down at Evesham in England.

This was the venue that gave them the required tools of their trade in order to work in the recording studios, alongside various taxing producers and accompanying production staff.

From what I am led to believe, Evesham was also renowned as a great place to get drunk!!

At least that's what I was told.

When arriving in Edinburgh, they appeared (for the most part) bright, erudite, enthusiastic, with one or two of them verging almost on the manic side of eccentricity. So you could say that they were an almost perfect fit to inhabit BBC Edinburgh.

Thinking back, the Audio crew were a pretty mixed bunch of eccentrically disparate characters. But in general, they also proved to be a very amiable group of multitalented studio craftsmen, who could also party hard when the occasion demanded it. Which happened frequently – both inside and outside of 5 Queen Street.

During the days and nights in which they plied their trade in the confines of the studios, they all became expert in the fine details of sound mixing, microphone positioning and tape splicing.

Despite each possessing their own individual quirks and odd ways (some a little more quirky and odd than others!) they could all wield a razor blade with the type of flamboyant practiced skill that would make even a Turkish barber envious!

Patience, calmness, intelligence, and a sound sense of humour were much required of them, particularly when dealing with pretentiously arrogant producers, seductively pouting secretaries and production assistants, not forgetting highly strung, temperamental actors and musicians!

In fact, I'm convinced that a rival publication focusing on the many adventures (and misadventures!) of the Audio crew throughout the 1970s and 1980s, would prove to be a far more amusing and fascinating read than the one you are currently divulging.

How about this for a possible title: *Razor Sharp Tales from The Editing Suite?*

No, that's much too tame.

How about this one then: *"Is That A Boom Microphone In Your Hand – Or Are You Just Fiddling With Your Faders??"*

Yes, being good pals with several of them, I think that the second title is far more apt.

*

One evening following a hectic boozy session, one of the female staff members was beginning to feel the effects of the night's drink, and as it turned out, was also beginning to equally feel the unravelling effects of wanton desire.

She walked out of the pub where we had all congregated for a post-work drinks bash, and then before several startled witnesses, stood motionless in the very middle of the road! Ignoring any oncoming cars, she looked heavenwards towards the bright moon and glistening stars and cried out in a decisively loud voice – "I need a man!!"

Startling perhaps, but a bit rich too, I thought, since (allegedly) she had already enjoyed the close intimate and exhausting attentions of several of the male staff already!

With (also allegedly) the Audio crew being a particular strong attraction for her. Whether in fact she did achieve her chosen desire that evening, or just ended up with a bag of chips on the way home, is still a mystery to me this very day!

*

One of the older and longer established members of the Audio unit, who was working there when I first arrived in 1974, was a lovely gent by the name of John Wilkie.

My very first initial impressions of John, was that of a soft-spoken, gentile chap, who possessed impeccable manners, and also dabbled in a spot of amateur dramatics.

In fact I recall one day sitting beside him in the canteen, catching him reading the *JB Priestley* play *When We Are Married* whilst drinking his cup of tea. No doubt this was to be his next dramatic effort on stage?

However, in truth, John could give Harry a decent run for his money for the much sought-after title of 5 Queen Street's very own "Town Drunk". A position that had, over the years, thrown up many worthy, drouthy-mouthed nominees!

What with booze-addled house staff, pissed-up producers, the odd staggering and collapsing engineer, and not forgetting the presence of numerous whisky-breathed journalists, it's a wonder in those days that we didn't have a direct connecting line from 5 Queen Street – straight to Alcoholics Anonymous!!

To be honest, not having to work closely alongside John in the studio, I never really came across this particular aspect of his personality.

Yet, from the multitude of stories I heard from a good many of his fellow Audio chums, he was a man with an almighty, unquenchable thirst!

Like Harry, he would turn up for work a little the worse for wear, but unlike Harry, he had the serious responsibility of working on radio programmes, making sure that all the technical and recording aspects were spot on.

They usually were, despite his excessive boozy habits.

It wasn't so unusual for one of the audio unit to walk into a studio and become quickly aware that something wasn't quite right. Particularly when the studio was empty and quiet, perhaps too quiet, yet they soon became aware that there was someone else in the room.

From below one of the desks, a hand now slowly appeared, followed by another and then a head. It was John. He had been lying almost comatose on the floor, slightly dazed and just recovering from a long liquid lunch! And now he was ready to record a radio programme? This was fairly normal practice back in the days when a heavy drinking session and several hours studio recording, went hand-in-hand.

*

Another esteemed member of the audio unit was the sharply clever and witty Christopher Lambton, who devised, just for a laugh, a non-existent BBC position called "Controller Fridges". This was Chris's amusing way of highlighting and showing up some of the more ridiculous and ludicrous department names then were then being bandied around the BBC in general. In fact some deluded souls within the BBC actually thought there was an entire department devised and set up to soley promote and advertise a multitude of fridge-freezers throughout the Corporation.

The question remained, why stop at fridges? Perhaps we should have also had departments full of such outlandish titles such as: Head of Buckets (not to be confused with head in buckets!), Head of Hoovers, Head of Bin Bags, and Head of Toilet Rolls. Happy days!

*

Did I ever mention the mysterious case of the missing wine box?

This tale of skulduggery and parched throats would have baffled the combined brains of *Sherlock Holmes, Dr Watson,* and *Inspector Morse!*

With the mystery still unsolved more than 20 years down the line!

The story behind this torrid tale, concerned a regular drop off at the building of a box of 12 exclusive bottles of wine.

This had been organised by the former Odyssey producer *Billy Kay,* and was intended for some of the production staff that had placed an order with him.

From what I learned the wine was something really to savour and enjoy.

However, maybe it wasn't the wisest move to leave unattended boxes of wine lying around the building, with so many thirsty members of staff (and as I've already related there were quite a few of them) all eager for their next free drink!

As normal, Billy would drop the wine off, to be collected and uplifted later that day for their eventual destination. Yet on this particular day, they had been left lying along the corridor from reception and near the lift.

It was drama production assistant *Joan Raffan's* husband Alistair who arrived to collect it – only to discover that the wine box was missing, gone, vanished??

A major investigative search was mounted to track down the missing wine – but to no avail. The entire box had gone, never to return.

Its eventual destination was most likely going straight down the throat of an exceptionally thirsty member of staff, who no doubt, saw an ideal opportunity, and a chance going a-begging and then took it!

Not surprisingly, angry words were banded about, with accusations of outright thievery aimed at whoever the guilty party may have been.

As I said, it was a mystery that remains unsolved.

No doubt the mystery guzzler had taken the wine box, then threw a party to celebrate his (or hers) unexpected good fortune.

*

One time during the mid-80s, BBC Edinburgh's club organised a picnic outing one night to Beecraig Country Park, near Linlithgow in West Lothian.

A coach (in fact it was a double-decker bus!) was booked to take everyone from 5 Queen Street to the park. Here there would be an outdoor barbeque, with lots of burnt but tasty offerings and equally lots of drink waiting upon us. Probably just as well, considering how warm it turned out on the night – and how that fact made everyone there just that little bit thirstier.

Attending the outdoor jamboree included the likes of Mac, Dougie, Fraser, Alex, Bob, myself, and of course, so many others. So there was quite a large crown gathered and it proved to be a popular evening for all who travelled by bus for the night's festivities.

Unfortunately, quite a few got just a little bit drunk (must have been the warm weather) with one or two of the partygoers losing their balance, staggering and then accidentally slipping into a nearby pond!

Alex (after consuming a great amount of beer and wine) also lost his balance at one point (after comically arguing with Bob) and collapsed, as his legs became a little rubbery.

However, it was poor Mac who came off the worse. Not so much to do with the drink (although, like us all, he enjoyed his fair share that night) but he came under constant assault by the dreaded midges!

The little blighters proved a bit of an unpleasant annoyance throughout the evening, but they saw in Mac's head, an ideal feeding ground.

They attacked him without mercy, as his forehead quickly turned bright crimson red – just like a socialist flag.

They just never let up, ruthlessly targeting his vulnerable and exposed forehead, like so many Japanese zeros as they zoomed and swooped into *Pearl Harbour*!

"Look at the state of ma' f*****g heed!" Mac loudly stated as there was every indication he would be severely suffering the next morning.

*

It might surprise you to learn that BBC Edinburgh once had its very own house band!

It was called *The Tilsbury 373* (not to be confused with another band called *The Tilsbury 123* – or was it *The Tilsbury 321??*)

The band members included a number of the audio crew such as *Richard Kent, Doug Ring, Ian Hunter*, as well as glamorous lady vocalist, by the name of *Carol Strachan*.

Occasionally, they were even joined by a guest singer – the one and only *Simon Walton*, who, I have been told, took the art of rock singing into an entirely new dimension and stratosphere.

Their very first gig took place at the Fringe club, but that night was generally acknowledged to have been an absolute disaster.

Maybe they had forgotten to take their instruments with them? Or maybe the gathered audience weren't too chuffed with their choice of *Hue & Cry* covers? However, with studied practice, this went a long way in helping them to eventually bond as a proper band.

What also helped and assisted was (I think?) their lack of clashing artistic egos. So in time, the band slowly blended and began to achieve the odd engagement – as well as a formidable cult following among serious music fans.

They would also be called upon to perform at the occasional BBC party and function – and pretty good they were too. I suppose that it made for a refreshing change to see them playing music while tuning their instruments, instead of fine-tuning and playing with the affections of some love-struck PA!

Eventually, the band would split, although like a phoenix rising from the musical ashes, another band would later replace it. This time going by the name of *Midnight Media*, and featuring the slow-hand guitar playing of one of Ba'head's finest, *Martin Griffin*. A man whose passion for the guitar, was only superseded by his passion for Tennents lager!

With a new change in musical direction, the need for a raw-edged, bone-shaking singer like Simon, proved to be not exactly high on their list of priorities.

*

Getting back to the party nights in Queen Street, there was one lively affair that once we had all returned back after the refurbishment, occurred in the newly revamped canteen.

During a lull in the celebrations, I nipped downstairs to the ground floor loo, and on my return back up the stairs, I instantly became aware of the newsroom door slowly opening. There standing before me was a young, blonde-haired partygoer (someone's friend or guest on the night?) looking a little dishevelled.

She wasn't someone I instantly recognised, but she had obviously been scooping up the wine, going by her glazed look and unsteady gait. Her blonde hair was tousled, as she began to adjust her skirt and then button up her blouse buttons.

She looked not unlike the image of a young, innocent serving wench, who had just been chased, caught and debauched by the country squire.

A little bleary-eyed, she looked straight at me and then

slowly turned her gaze back towards the closed newsroom door with a look of distaste. She then turned her attention back to me, and then began to speak in a slurred voice. "He's f*****g useless!!"

With that particular pronouncement about the mysterious individual still lurking behind the door of the darkened newsroom, she then carefully walked back up the stairs towards the awaiting party.

I stood there for a few seconds, not sure what to think and half wanting to open the closed newsroom door to discover who, or what, lay behind it, but decided under the circumstances that discretion was the better part of valour.

Or, in other words, let sleeping journalists lie...

*

Just prior to the move out of Queen Street, the then Controller decided to throw caution to the wind and threw a lavish and extravagant bash in Studio 1. This however, wasn't for the benefit of the staff, but for a large gathering of specially invited guests.

This was a night that went down in BBC legend and was alternatively described as either "The Night Of A Hundred Stars", or (perhaps more accurately) "The Night Of A Hundred Disasters".

For this prestigious occasion the Controller particularly wanted the studio to be at its absolute best. He also wanted extra staff to be on duty, in order to facilitate and pander to the many needs of his guests.

So with that being the case, I found myself "volunteered" for the evening – or more accurately, roped in to help out.

In truth, I was happy enough at the time to assist, as there was some Saturday overtime going a-begging. As well as the prospect of a free feed – once the party proper had finished and the guests departed. The menu didn't look too bad either (smoked salmon as the main course, with rich chocolate profiteroles as a dessert) so it would be worth coming in for that alone.

The studio floor was thus going to be washed, waxed, and polished until it almost gleamed in the dark. This was smartly done and I don't think I had ever seen the Studio 1 floor look as good.

However, much merriment soon became evident when Stan and Fraser were attempting to move and position a number of the chairs and tables in the studio, before the main event began and the guests arrived.

With the floor being so highly polished, their footing was, you could say, a little all over the place.

They began to slip and slide and glide (as well as lose their balance at times) all over the floor.

All that was missing from Stan and Fraser's ballroom antics was the old rock & roll classic *Slippin' & Slidin'* or the strains of *Ravel's Bolero,* booming out in the background!

Perhaps the Controller was unaware that apart from providing a sumptuous feast for his guests, he was also literally providing a slippery floorshow as well!

I remember quipping that they resembled *Jane Torvill* and *Christopher Dean*, as they were performing on the ice rink!

Bob was watching this entire happening before his eyes, and he started to laugh. "Look at those two f*****g idiots! What a f*****g state they're getting themselves into!"

It became fairly obvious that the floor had indeed been wax polished to such a degree, that it began to resemble a vast ice rink.

Stan and Fraser continued as best they could with the furniture manoeuvres, but their feet just kept slipping and sliding, with both of them at great risk in causing themselves some serious damage.

When the guests were ushered into the studio, the

prepared food was sent down from the canteen in long trolleys. There before us was the tantalising sight of fresh, red smoked salmon and profiteroles covered in thick chocolate and stuffed with cream. It looked magnificent, and would no doubt taste magnificent.

Myself, along with the rest of the team, collected the trolleys and moved them carefully towards the Studio 1 lounge area. Yet, wouldn't you know it, Bob was seen pushing his trolley at such a speed, that all of a sudden a large silver salver of red smoked salmon skidded off the top of the trolley and landed all over the carpet tiles.

Not only that, but it was quickly followed by a large plate of chocolate profiteroles that sped off the trolley at an alarming rate and landed right beside the salmon.

What a mess! "For f**k's sake Bob, what are ye daein'?" cried both Mac and Harry as the combination of fish and chocolate cream dessert now lay on the floor in an inedible pile for all to see.

Bob then ran off and a few minutes later, arrived with one of the hoovers. He then switched it on and began *hoovering* (yes, that's right) the smoked salmon and profiteroles. We all watched dumbfounded, as Bob was hoovering like a madman and then all of a sudden, not surprisingly, the carpet began to turn a rich deep pink colour, as well as highlighted around the edges with an extra blend of chocolate brown. Bella appeared to see what was going on and tried to have the mess cleaned up before the Controller got to see it. I am sure that I heard her mutter the immortal phrase, "Holy f**k!"

As luck would have it the Controller was too engrossed with his guests to have noticed Bob's accident and subsequent artistry with the hoover – as well as the new colourful patterns that were slowly emerging on the carpet.

Yet all of Bob's efforts just made it worse, as it became noticeable that the salmon was also getting well and truly stuck and was now jamming the main function of the hoover.

And it was making one hell of a funny noise into the bargain.

So out came the brush and shovel! Bob was now on his hands and knees sweeping up the leftover salmon and profiteroles into a black bin bag.

He then left to deposit it outside. All that was left was a very large pink and brown coloured stain that was going to be there for an awful long time.

Not long after that, Bella was getting into a rather heated debate with Bob and Harry's other working partner on the night – big Barry.

Here was a guy who was known to some as "Big Bazza", or alternatively as "that Big Bastard". Depending on whom you spoke to of course.

Well, angry words appeared to be exchanged between the two of them about something or other, which prompted Barry to take off his jacket, throw it straight in Bella's direction and tell her (in no uncertain terms) to "Away and f**k off!!" He then walked straight out the front door, without as much as a backward glance.

Everyone standing there was a little stunned and mostly felt that Barry's days as a BBC Edinburgh employee were now numbered. Yet a strange thing happened.

Within two or three minutes since his departure, he walked straight back in the front door.

"It started to rain, and I didn't have my jacket with me, so I just thought I'd come back." What do you say about that? In any other company, he would have most likely have been severely disciplined, and quite probably even have been instantly dismissed for showing such aggressive disrespect towards his supervisor.

Under today's more stringent working conditions, Barry would have found himself fired straight down the Job Centre, quicker than you could say – *Iain Duncan Smith!*

Yet he just wandered back in as if nothing had happened. I don't think he even got as much as a slap on the wrists. What a night!

*

One memorable Halloween party was once thrown in the canteen that included the usual assembly of staff individuals, with much music, food, and drink thrown into the bargain.

With a couple of diverse highlights that made it stand out:

One had our very own Boy George from the canteen. He decided to come up with a plan to make a grand macabre entrance, close to the witching hour.

The lights dimmed, the crowd hushed and then, all of a sudden we heard part of *Andrew Lloyd Webber's* distinctive music announcing something a little grand and operatic.

A spotlight shone towards a distant corner of the room and then, slowly emerging from the darkened shadows, appeared George.

Capturing the spirit of the occasion, he was all dressed up just like *The Phantom of the Opera!*

I must admit that he did look the part, what with wide-brimmed black hat, black cloak and a bizarre mask. However, he never said anything. He just stood there for several minutes with his arms outstretched, basking in the dark limelight that enveloped him.

But he said nothing – he just stood there, awaiting some form of applause?

A few began to mutter that he at least should have given us a quick burst of *"Music Of The Night"* or *"That's All I Ask Of You"*, but nothing burst out of his vocal chords.

As everyone began to shake their heads and head back to their drinks awaiting them on the tables.

*

George and Kevin were quite a double act during their time working together in the canteen.

Their camp and sometimes bitchy interplay, whilst serving up the lunches, was always entertaining to observe and overhear. No wonder in certain circles they soon became better known as a kind of culinary *Hinge & Brackett!!*

On one occasion they had been instructed that they had to wear new hats while working in the kitchen. I thought at first glance that it made them look a little like a pair of Thunderbirds puppets!

However, at a particular lunchtime, Kevin had decided this new headgear just wasn't for him.

I was lining up in the queue when the dialogue went something like this:

George: "Where's your hat? You're supposed to wear it every time you're serving behind the counter."

Kevin: "I didn't like wearing it, as it made us look too much like *The Andrews Sisters!*"

George and Kevin – Queen Street's very own Boogie-Woogie Bugle Boys!

*

The other memorable event of that party evening, involved Suzette and Bella (both giving a fair impression of *Miss Hannigan* from *Annie* – the musical), having a right old blowsy barney at the back of the canteen.

This all came to a head after much wine had been consumed, and then their vocal ranges began to reach an extremely high level.

Not quite sure what sparked it all off, but they were now engaged in a fearsome row that everyone could hear.

What made it quite amusing for those of us sitting within earshot, was that apart from shouting and screeching, they were also now thrashing and banging about among the pots and pans and various utensils in the cooking area. What a racket! Someone then cheekily quipped – "I wouldn't venture through there – it's like the clash of the titans!"

This cacophony of noise prompted one quick-witted partygoer (it may well have been Dougie) to say that the noise reminded him of the scene in *Jurassic Park* that involved the two marauding velociraptors as they banged and crashed their way at the back of the kitchen!

There was another party evening where a large inflatable whale made an entrance, causing several drunken revellers to attempt either a wrestling bout with it – or a mating ritual!

*

Christmas was always a time when 5 Queen Street sparkled with boozy revelry and many a Yuletide party that brought all the staff and departments together to enjoy in unison.

However, during our final decade in the old building, there was also the much-missed "Christmas Howff Parties". These gatherings took place down in the House staff's rest room, way deep into the basement.

Small and intimate they may have been, but it was always amazing just how many drunken Christmas partygoers could easily cram themselves into the place.

The likes of Stan, Dougie, Lorraine, Suzette, Dot, Scott, Eileen, and myself all pitched in to buy some booze and nibbles.

We then set up the tree, hung a few decorations, brought in some Christmas songs and we were all set. It was an open and friendly invitation for all the staff to join us.

The meagre price of admission to such a bacchanalian gathering, was simply one bottle (or two) and heaven help anyone arriving empty handed!

Yet (surprise, surprise), there was always the odd tight-fisted, miserable, freelance journalist who when hearing the laughs and chat of merrymaking, turned up bereft of bottle, but full of thirst, hoping to sneak in for a free drink!

But they didn't counter on Stan's formidable presence though.

Unknown to them, our Stanley had in his youthful days, been an accomplished wrestler, going by the names of either *The Cat*, or *Mr Scotland*. And he wasn't a man to rile or get in a bad mood, as he had the large physical presence that would soon have you in a firm and unshakeable grip, one that would easily separate the men from the boys!

"Oh you're having a party?" the two young journalists joyfully announced as they attempted to walk into the room – empty-handed and hoping for some free festive booze, without bringing as much as a packet of mince pies with them.

Stan clocked them right away. "Have ye brought a bottle with you?" he gruffly asked.

"Eh, no, but from what I can see, you've got lots of drink on the table," they stated, as their eyes popped out with excitement, while glancing upon the combination of beer and wine that was nestling beside the Christmas tree.

"Well, you can f**k off right away!" Stan glowered at them both, giving them the kind of look that he would normally give to an opponent after two falls and a submission, followed by an agonising thump as they hit the canvas in pain!

The two thirsty journalists quickly scuttled back upstairs, not with a flea in their ear, but more likely the memory of Stan's dragon-like beery breath, for they didn't hang around long enough to experience Stan's almighty wrath, or wrestling prowess, first hand.

"A right pair of f*****g miserable gits!" was Stan's opinion as he casually picked up his bottle of lager for a quick swig.

*

During the course of the Christmas Howff parties, once several drinks had been poured down numerous throats, secrets and desires began to be shared amongst the group.

Young Kevin (one of the canteen staff) started the ball rolling when he expressed and bemoaned the lack of genuine love and affection that was sadly missing currently in his life. Sitting among a group of the generally sympathetic female staff, he swooned and sighed and divulged his innermost thoughts:

"All I want to do is to be cared for and to be happy. I want to find love, sing happy *Doris Day* songs, because I'm all alone, as I'm still looking for my *Rock Hudson*!"

Well, what can you say about that? Apart from "Enough of this pillow talk."

It was somewhat unavoidable but however lively and fun-packed the evenings usually were, the parties always tended to end with some solemn and teary secretary, or female production assistant, bawling her eyes out over some torturous broken romance.

"But I love him!!" went the routine cry, as many breathed an almighty sigh while inaudibly mouthing the expression "For f**k's sake!" as several eyebrows were soon raised towards the ceiling.

No wonder the floor was almost awash with tears.

This demonstration of a wine-induced emotional outpouring, led many to gradually move out of the away, while seeking solace with yet another bottle of beer and a festive mincemeat pie.

*

There was also the team Christmas night out to contend with each year.

About two or three months beforehand, we would attempt to book some venue that would suit everyone's tastes.

For the last few years at Queen Street, it didn't always turn out that easy.

The assorted group of potential partygoers included several members of the House and admin staff, the canteen staff, the odd cleaner, and sometimes even the occasional welcome (or more likely unwelcome?) guest that would all head out on the town for a night of festive fun.

Nevertheless, many weeks before we would put on our Christmas glad rags to enjoy a meal and some drinks, the bitter accusations would soon come bubbling to the surface like bubbles in a cheap bottle of plonk!

"Well, if he's going – I'm not going!" Or alternatively, "I'm not going if she's going!"

Not forgetting, "There is no way that I'm f*****g sitting beside her all night!!"

I'm sure you would agree that it's hardly what you would describe as being in the finest traditions of the Christmas spirit.

Just to think that thousands of years ago, three mystic astrologers from the east, wearily travelled across the hot, burning desert to follow a bright star and celebrate a new birth. If only they knew that many centuries later, this would prompt the kind of mean, petty and uncharitable attitude shown by some of my colleagues at Christmas time.

With this in mind, I'm convinced that the three wise gentlemen would have halted their journey, turned their camels around and headed straight back home!

*

Then there was the equally much missed and rightly lauded Christmas lunches.

These events took place in the canteen and were presided over by the Edinburgh catering staff, who from all my time there, always put on a gargantuan feast that everyone generously lapped up.

Not surprisingly, the lunches were always memorable and thoroughly enjoyed, by everyone who attended.

You could also bring in your own wine to accompany the meal, which tended to make the lunches very high-spirited affairs.

To my recollection, they usually turned out to be truly epic, some lasting almost as long as *Gone With The Wind*!

Menus usually included the likes of – soup, prawn cocktail, turkey, roast potatoes, vegetables, stuffing, and bread sauce. Not forgetting Xmas pudding, sherry trifle, coffee and mince pies, all readily consumed and washed down with countless bottles of white and rose wine!

During my last ten years at 5 Queen Street, it was funnily enough, our table that contained most of the wine – and the giggles!

Aside from myself, Lorraine, Suzette, Eileen, and the fabulous Dot Gregor, usually all brought in at least two bottles each. So we were really going to enjoy our Christmas lunch, and the hell with anyone who thought otherwise.

Dot really came into her own when (on more than one occasion) our table would be approached by a few tight-fisted producers who noticing our wealth of vino displayed in front of them, decided to chance their luck.

It always amazed me that considering the kind of salary the majority of the producers were on, they couldn't muster up four or five pounds to buy a bottle of wine to share with their colleagues, sitting at the same table.

It was Christmas after all, but a number of the producers were giving a fair impression of a man known to all as *Ebenezer Scrooge!* I often glanced at some of the adjoining tables and all you could see before you were a dozen or so diners, with about a dozen empty wine glasses – and only one bottle between them! No wonder they all looked over towards our table with much thirst-driven envy.

So, while we had uncorked our bottles and we were wishing each other a Merry Christmas, one clearly embarrassed producer gingerly approached our table to sneakily ask for a glass of wine.

"Have you no' brought any wine with you?" Dot sternly asked.

"No, I forgot to buy some, but I was just wondering if you could spare a couple of glasses?" the producer meekly asked.

Dot then didn't hold back and with a look of fury, she really let him have it, and she was a woman who never held back when angered.

"No! You can bugger off!" Dot replied just as the producer squirmed back to his table that was full of Christmas crackers – but very little Christmas wine.

"What a f*****g cheek! It's Christmas time, and he couldn't even put his hand in his f*****g wallet and buy a bottle of f*****g wine!" Dot asserted, just as she was filling her large glass with even more white bubbly and settling down to enjoy her Christmas lunch. Suffice to say all our bottles would soon be empty by the end of the afternoon. What a woman!

The post-Christmas Lunch canteen singalongs, usually began after the staff had scoffed their final mince pies and departed from the room. Then the kitchen staff – exhausted, but relieved – settled down to enjoy their own Christmas lunch.

Once again, numerous bottles (not of the soft drink variety) began to be quickly opened up. While simultaneously, they also began to open up their lungs and vocal chords!

One particular shining chanteuse was Queen Street's answer to Blues legend *Bessie Smith* – Margaret Davis!

Margaret could belt them out with the best of them.

And by late afternoon, the massed cacophony of singing styles (ranging from the lyrically sublime – to those of a wounded beast in its final death throes) soon began to drift out with the canteen confines, towards the descending floors and corridors below.

*

As I said, the magnificent Dot (who was also known to belt out a song along with the canteen girls) was a terrific character, and she instantly made her presence felt when she first arrived in Edinburgh sometime in the 1980s with the News & Current Affairs gang. And she stayed with us right up until the building finally closed. Dot loved a party, loved a drink, loved a laugh, and loved to enjoy herself.

She had a particularly caustic sense of humour and turn of phrase that often made me regularly crease up with laughter.

For example, during the early 1990s, when the policy of "Producer Choice" was spreading its unwelcome tentacles around the Corporation, a new unit was formed and soon to be based at 5 Queen Street.

This specially chosen team was one that would look after the finances and budgets of a number of the production departments, making sure that they didn't overspend, or waste finances.

The very idea! As if producers would dare do such a thing?

Anyway, once Dot got wind of this set-up, she couldn't believe her ears.

"You will never guess what's happened now," she exclaimed to a few of us during lunchtime. "They have only set up a new department called Business Unit Managers!!"

She then further added, "Can you imagine that? And can you imagine the f*****g salaries they'll be on?" Dot was raging at this new initiative. "F*****g Business Unit

Managers! What does it stand for – BUMS F*****g Bums!"

I had to admit it, the way that Dot colourfully described them, was pretty funny.

Trust Dot to put it into its purest and most basic terms.

I also particularly recall one boozy night as a group of us where enjoying a few drinks. Dot was in fine fettle, but her face soured a little whenever anyone brought up the name of one particular producer. Someone she didn't particularly care for, as she let us know about it on a number of occasions.

When this happened, her face lost its good-humoured smile as if she had been sucking on a lemon (perhaps it was the very same one that had been planted in her glass of gin and tonic?) and then she glanced at the gathering before her. All during this tirade she was firmly gripping her seventh (or was it her eighth?) G&T. She then gave her individual assessment of the producer's uniquely personal and creative qualities.

"What a complete f*****g arsehole!" Yes, Dot was a one-off, who rarely suffered fools – or for that matter, certain BBC producers.

Dot also loved to belt out a song or two when the mood took her, with a couple of songs that figured prominently in her repertoire.

When she was full of laughter and fun (as well as, what else, gin and tonic) she would give out with that old *Gracie Fields* favourite – *'Wish me luck as you wave me goodbye…'* just as she awkwardly slipped off the table during a riotous dance routine.

However, if feeling a little melancholy following one or two many glasses of this time, white chardonnay, she would moodily sing (and then inevitably screech) another one of her hits: *'I'm nobody's child, I'm nobody's child…'* No party in Queen Street (or Thistle Street for that matter) was ever quite complete without the glorious *Dot Gregor*.

*

I also enjoyed (if that's the correct term?) yet another Christmas night out that almost turned into an *Agatha Christie* murder mystery, as a dozen festive diners were left mystified as to who hadn't paid their part of the bill.

Looking back, I am chuckling at the thought of it, but believe me at the time, it was no laughing matter.

After the meal was consumed and we were handed the final bill, something was obviously amiss and not quite right. We all looked intently at one another, as the bill was checked, rechecked, double checked and triple checked!

But the evidence was overwhelming – someone had oh so subtly, not paid their share.

Everyone sitting there was adamant that they had put in their money, but after a while suspicions began to be aroused. One individual had (with a great deal of possibly well-practiced skill) hoodwinked everyone sitting at the table.

I must admit it was cleverly done, as we all sat intensely staring at each other like characters straight out of a *Sergio Leone* spaghetti western.

But the guilty party was not forthcoming, so we all had to input that little bit extra to cover the shortfall.

So, not only is there such a thing as a free lunch – there is (particularly on that evening) equally also such a thing as a free Christmas dinner!

CHAPTER 10

The party's over, so on the way out, please switch the lights off and close the doors behind you...

I do hope that you have enjoyed travelling down my own personal journey through past Scottish Radio Days. And I equally hope that you did not find its raw, rude, racy and irreverent tone, too off-putting.

Believe me (and despite what many of you may think); I can assure you that I didn't make any of it up. Well, not much of it anyway!

*

So, after much deliberation, it is time to finally sum things up, by asking myself after all these years – what does the BBC mean for me now?

Before answering that burning question, I suppose there will always remain the lingering thought of what might have been. Of unfulfilled ambitions and opportunities missed. Of being bypassed and sometimes ignored, as I found myself being often sidelined in preference of others. I sometimes looked upon some of the so called "intellectuals" who turned up to work within the building and I came to the conclusion that from what I could see their grasp of intelligent thought and expression, was, well, a little bit shaky at best?

Yet, I don't consider myself too bitter or in any way

cynical about my time there.

The cards fell a certain way for me and as a consequence, you often find yourself walking down a very different road that you never originally intended to.

That's just me getting a little philosophical… for what it's worth.

I guess I got stuck doing a fairly mundane and routine role, while all the time watching from the sidelines while numerous others blazed a glorious (or more often an inglorious?) broadcasting trail.

Maybe I lacked the confidence, the drive, or the ambition to fully delve in and involve myself deeper towards other things. That is something that I do regret; yet for all that, it's all a lot of water under the bridge now, and times have moved on.

When anyone used to ask me what my job entailed at the BBC, I tended to reply that I did a bit of everything. Which being honest, was more or less the truth? I saw myself as a bit of a jack-of-all-trades, encompassing everything from printing scripts and documents, ordering stationery, audio and computer consumables, running the mailroom, the tape-store, taking ID photos, setting up remote studio interviews, doing the odd PR request etc., etc., etc.

Being part of the "support and back room staff", I always found it amusing, in a strange way, that some of the producers, or journalists, tended to ignore, or walk straight past, without any form of friendly acknowledgement.

However, when they required you to do something for them, or if they felt you could supply them with something they desperately needed or wanted, all of a sudden, as if by magic – they greeted you like a long lost pal! Isn't that funny?

All during this time, my department went through various incarnations, name changes and numerous transformations.

One minute it was Administration, then House & Office

Services, and then Administration & Resources… What a merry-go-round! No wonder my head was often spinning with so many changes.

This usually happened when BBC Scotland was (for want of a better phrase), internally "reinventing itself", such as the time around 1978 when Radio Scotland was first announced and then came to the fore.

But what's in a name? I suppose it was all the same to me!

*

When telling people that I worked for the BBC, quite a few were visibly impressed. Even I was impressed occasionally, not sure why.

"Wow! That sounds great – bet you get loads of perks!" was the usual line pointed towards me. They were in for a surprise!

"Perks??" I replied with amused puzzlement. This was then usually followed by a look from me of curious confusion, as I tried to figure out exactly what "perks" they might be referring to? Maybe they were under the deluded impression that we all received free television sets, as well as having all our TV licences paid!

In fact in all the years that I worked there, the only "perk" that immediately sprang to mind, was receiving a free copy of the *Radio Times!*

Although, from my earliest days there, the *Radio Times* was only supposed to be issued to club members and retired staff. Not handed out to every Tom, Dick and Harry – or visiting scrounger, of which there were many.

Well that ruling soon fell by the wayside, as the staff now expected and indeed demanded, their own copy – each and every week. Christmas time was the worst, with the Christmas edition of the *Radio Times* becoming a much sought-after item. In fact there was often grand theft afoot when several copies went missing. Not just the odd one or two, but whole batches of them.

I often wondered if the "Radio Times Thieves" were selling them around the pubs?

This fact tended to irritate Lorraine, who when discovering this massed thievery uttered the following: "Bunch of feckin' thieving bastards!" was one of her kinder descriptions of those few individuals who took more than their fair share of the magazine. In their eyes, it was free and going a begging, so what did they care?

Towards the end, it got to the point that the *Radio Times* (whether Christmas, or otherwise) was now kept severely under lock and key.

By this time, Lorraine had taken over as the grand dame of the reception desk.

Sometimes known in certain quarters as *Lala, The Blonde Bombshell, Quiche* (as in Lorraine), *Tour-Guide Barbie,* or even *Miss Polly Kettle,* Lorraine returned to Edinburgh to fill the position following the sad passing of Dorothy. Lorraine had originally worked at 5 Queen Street a few years earlier, then manning the old switchboard. But then not long after, she found herself being transferred through to BH Glasgow.

That move followed yet another department restructure.

Yet despite the tragic circumstances that prompted her return, it was good to have her back, for she was always full of good fun and plenty of laughs. Something we badly needed after the recent tragedies.

*

One humorous story concerning Lorraine happened when our good lady boss Bella, requested her to work at an official function, where she would be meeting and greeting numerous VIPs.

As a prelude to this, Bella stressed the importance of the evening by saying to her, "Now I want you dressed smart for the occasion – and ditch the pelmet!"

In case you are wondering, the pelmet was Bella's somewhat cheeky, if not downright rude reference to Lorraine's preference for wearing extremely short skirts that had a tendency to show off her long, slim legs.

When she fully took in this specific dress-code instruction from her boss, Lorraine was, you could say, less than amused. In fact she was boiling mad! "Feckin' cheek! Dress smart she said! Have you seen the feckin state of her lately?" Lorraine was fuming at this criticism of her dress style, coming as it did, from someone who was, well (putting it politely), slightly less smart than she was.

"Feckin' cow! She wouldn't know the meaning of the word smart!!"

Lorraine, you could say, had a special way of expressing herself, by using particular Anglo-Saxon words that came out uniquely all her own.

Her usual war cry, whenever she came into work (following a heavy night on the tiles), was, "Stodge, stodge, I need feckin' stodge!"

Which implied to all around that she desired a cooked breakfast. This usually involved fried sausages on a roll, with the occasional tattie scone thrown in for good measure – covered in thick sauce!

*

By the time we returned from our exile in Thistle Street, the days of the security men (and the old world style Commissionaires) was now well and truly over. It didn't take a genius to work it out that this was unquestionably down to the simple fact of economics – with the wonders of modern technology thrown in for added measure.

So Queen Street would be wired up with a modern alarm system that made it unnecessary for 24 hour a day manned security cover.

The men with the spreadsheets had finally vanquished the men in black.

An electronic entry system was also installed at the front door. This was placed there ostensibly to prevent unofficial entry. So whoever was on duty at the front door, simply buzzed staff or visitors in when recognised.

However, this didn't prevent the odd cheeky staff member attempting to circumnavigate and bypass the front door security system, by sneaking through undetected like a brazen Calais migrant!!

Much to the chagrin of Lorraine, who cursed them with her usual refrain of "Feckin' cheeky bastards!" as they slipped through the security gate and disappeared into the corridors above, below, and beyond.

*

From time to time, there was the odd occasion where I would find myself being asked to provide some substantial film research material for one, or two radio programmes (in the pre-Google days!) whenever they required it. Finally, I would get the opportunity to work on a number of programmes.

I was aware that a few of the resident producers recognised something in me that so others failed to notice regarding my film knowledge. So, at last, after 20 years or more, I was finally getting the chance to become more creatively involved in programme making.

Not surprisingly, it turned out to be something I really enjoyed doing, and being honest, was the prime reason that I wanted to join the BBC in the first place.

Not long after we moved back to Queen Street I became involved in a one-off radio show that was hoping to be further commissioned for a series.

It was called "The Big Picture Show" and recorded before a live audience in Studio 1.

The presenter and the producer were two good friends – *Iain Agnew* and *Colin MacDonald* (one of my Meadowbank football pals).

Iain was an actor, writer, and broadcaster who added a humorous edge as the presenter of the show; while Colin was a news journalist who has since branched out successfully as a writer of film, TV, and radio.

I was approached to come on board as the main question compiler and researcher – which, as you can imagine, I didn't require to be asked twice!

The show turned out to be a movie-quiz with two teams of local celebrities battling it out.

Among the guest participants included the then Scottish Rugby Union captain *David Sole*, acclaimed and popular stage and TV actress *Eileen McCallum*, and children's author, actor and former comedian *Jonathan Meres*.

The show went well and the audience lapped up the light-hearted quiz, that included music, soundtrack excerpts and various questions covering a wide range of movies.

We were hoping for it to be commissioned – but as luck would have it – it didn't quite come off. Which was a great pity, as I could easily see some potential in it, and it would have given me the opportunity to do something much more creative than what I was doing at the time.

A job that in all honesty, could have easily been done by a trained monkey!

*

Despite my rare and occasional foray into radio creativity, for the majority of the time, the BBC tended to prefer using young graduates just fresh out of university, than someone already on the staff.

I got the impression that quite a few of them had received their automatic production passports into a position in Queen

Street, due to some form of a nepotistic connection. At least that was how it looked at the time. Who knows?

If that was indeed the case, it was no great surprise, as it was generally known to exist and was a fairly common practice in most industries.

At least, it used to be, not too sure about today?

*

Talking of missed opportunities, one particular and very prominent scenario came to dominate the majority of my time at BBC Edinburgh. This was simply the elusive and illusory promise of a brand new broadcasting centre for Edinburgh. And illusory was what it eventually turned out to be.

I lost count of how many times talk was generated on all levels of the BBC regarding the building of a new broadcasting house for Scotland's capital city.

Over a great number of years, the staff was promised a building that was going to be "state-of-the art", possessing all the most modern technical advancements available.

A plush new reception, luxurious office suites, a top-class restaurant and most important of all, a number of superb recording studios that would make the entire BBC throughout the rest of the UK, simmer and boil with envy.

Yet this wasn't always the case. Almost from my very first day at Queen Street, the general talk was that the building was eventually going to be closed down, with everything (and everyone) being shunted through to Glasgow!

These rumours continued to persist over the next few years, with the general thought being that Edinburgh was somewhat irrelevant and always going to be regarded as a poor second cousin to the main headquarters at Queen Margaret Drive.

However, with the shadow of devolution slowly creeping over the Scottish political landscape, it soon became a pressing issue for BBC Scotland that Edinburgh would and should, require a much more substantial centre for radio and television broadcasting, in order to fully cover this likely and probable happening.

As it transpired, the BBC had in their possession a large area of land positioned not too far from the top of Leith Walk and extremely close to the city centre.

This plot was ideally situated at Greenside Place, and it soon became popularly known amongst all the staff as, not surprisingly, "The Greenside Project".

Which made it all sound a bit like the title of a *Robert Ludlum* novel!!

However, despite some twisty plot developments and an atmosphere of possible political machinations clinging to it, this sorry and costly tale would not ultimately enjoy anything like a happy ending.

To begin with, it all sounded grand and good in theory. The fact that we would all be moving into a brand spanking new building, with all mod cons, was leaving the majority of the staff salivating with eager anticipation. Yet even amidst all this pent up excitement, dark clouds of doubt began to gather and then be emotionally expressed.

Mac in particular was especially vocal in his suspicions that all was not quite right with the entire enterprise.

"A complete f*****g waste of time and money, as it will never get f*****g built!" he firmly and regularly stressed, to anyone willing to listen.

Not sure if he was gifted with mystical second sight (like a bearded Mystic Meg, perhaps?), or he was just winding up certain figures in senior management to see what reaction he would get. Perhaps it was a bit of both?

His assertion that the building's true foundations was more of mud and straw than brick and mortar, was strongly condemned and shouted down by a few senior figures, who were not best amused by his claims.

As a rebuff, they answered his scepticism and doubting words with a firm promise to all staff stressing that it would *indeed* be built.

They also subtly warned him that it was perhaps not in his best interests to verbally cast seeds of doubt upon the project.

He told quite a few of us at the time that this amounted to him being almost threatened to keep quiet – but this had no effect – and he just continued to spout his opinions by loudly casting suspicious doubts on the entire credibility of the project.

As it eventually turned out, and with the benefit of hindsight, it would have been far better if they had just said nothing, and subtly threatened no one, rather than ultimately embarrass themselves in the longer term.

Thinking back, the designs of the new building were mightily impressive. It certainly did look good, and indulging in a little wish-fulfilment fantasy, we could all see ourselves happily working within this "broadcasting Brigadoon" (as it eventually turned out) within a few years.

During this period of the early 1980s, all the staff excitedly attended numerous presentations of lavish and expensive plans and designs.

We saw slideshows, endured long detailed question and answer sessions, viewed intricate scale models, etc., etc. With the general feeling that the architect's fees alone on this prestigious project must have been astronomical – and by all accounts, were increasing by the hour!

There was even a time when one of the intricately scaled models of the new broadcasting centre was left on display in the main boardroom for all to see.

This was a fabulous opportunity so that the staff could examine it in greater detail. I remember looking at it and trying to visualise (I suppose like all of us did) the finished structure, and where we would eventually find ourselves situated within its walls.

During those days, the future did indeed look very bright for the BBC in Edinburgh, but (in the poetic words of *Jim Diamond*) we should have known better!!

*

One day, Mac, ably assisted by Tom the handyman (without his flexible sonic screw-driver on this particular day), had been asked to carefully remove the model from the manager's boardroom and then to be taken down to the ground floor.

For some reason both of them had been afflicted that morning by a fit of the giggles and when they turned up in the manager's office, they found it difficult to contain their decorum, as they were unsuccessfully fighting back tears of laughter.

Catherine (the manager's secretary) was not at all amused, as she vainly attempted to maintain her sense of dignity amidst the hilarity, while issuing them instructions as to the model's new destination.

Yet she found herself a little disturbed as each time she spoke, both Mac and Tom couldn't look at each other without bursting out laughing!

Then between them, they began to carefully lift the model, only for their combined giggles having a knock-on effect, by knocking over a few of the figures and parts off the model.

Catherine wasn't smiling at this untidy treatment of the new broadcasting centre, as its shape and form was now beginning to resemble a shaky *Thunderbirds Tracy Island* after a wild dog had gotten a firm grip of it!

Still laughing fit to burst, Mac and Tom eventually deposited the now crumbling model down the stairs, where it was going to be uplifted and returned to the architect's headquarters.

Perhaps in hindsight, the loose and unsteady structure (now with bits and pieces of it beginning to fall apart) served as a comical metaphor for what would eventually happen, not that far down the line?

Yet it was also a funny thing, that each time the staff were gathered to view and discuss the proposed new building, I swear, the scale model appeared to be shrinking!

The talk now bubbling among some of the staff focused upon what was now looking suspiciously like the "Incredibly Shrinking Broadcasting Centre!"

Something was seriously amiss, as scepticism about the final outcome was now beginning to infect the staff like a plague.

When will it get built? Will it ever get built? Will we be long retired and picking up our Pension when it eventually gets built?

And what will it eventually look like, considering it was markedly reducing in size from its original design and conception?

All the time, there was still the distinct mutterings that all was not well and the reality of the planned new broadcasting centre was (in the words of *Dad's Army's Private Fraser*) frankly doomed!

When the "Greenside Project" eventually collapsed (just like the model!), you could say the staff displayed a rich range of (not altogether happy, or positive) emotions and opinions.

Many felt a sense of anger, frustration, disappointment and deep betrayal that all those hefty promises (as well as very expensive architect's fees!) came to absolutely nothing. In fact, the general consensus was that Edinburgh had been well and truly cheated. We all fell for a building that was all smoke and mirrors, with little or no substance.

No wonder we were all mightily (no, not *Mitiely*, that came much later!) pissed off.

Mac, in particular, felt rightly vindicated that his forecasts of the building's demise before a brick was even laid, turned out to be correct in the end.

*

So why was the plug finally pulled? The real answer no doubt had something to do with the mounting financial cost of erecting the new building. Perhaps Glasgow (and by implication the power brokers in London?) just got cold feet and decided not go through with it?

Although there were many (particularly amongst the union members) who felt that the entire withdrawal had the distinct smell of implied political interference.

Perhaps not – maybe after all, it was just a simple case of economics?

But I guess that we might never know the entire truth of it.

However, once the news was announced, the union soon got themselves into gear and decided to do something about it, by raising public awareness to the BBC's failure to go through with their promise.

They mobilised their efforts by contacting the press and gathered support from a number of high profile Scottish MPs at the time that included the colourful representative from Leith, *Ron Brown*.

This was the very same man who once swung the ceremonial mace high above his head in the House of Commons, making him (along with a certain *Oliver Cromwell*) one of the select few who have actually done this.

With that extravagant act alone, he certainly put Leith on the political map!

A press photo-call was arranged near the top of the undeveloped Greenside Place plot, in which our union rep and several staff (including myself) stood holding placards in defiance of the BBC's unwise decision. This was followed by

313

a press conference that took place in the *King James Hotel*, in which the union strongly put forward their case.

The story (with accompanying photo) hit the newspapers the next day.

Unfortunately, even after all that gallant effort, it wasn't meant to be, as the BBC refused to alter, or bend on the issue and the "Greenside Project" became history.

What happened as a consequence was that the land was subsequently sold off to Edinburgh Council and the proceeds went towards the refurbishment of... wait for it... 5 Queen Street.

There were many groans of disapproval at what the majority of the staff felt was ultimately a cheapskate compromise. Thus denying them the chance to work within a brand new building they could be proud of. Maybe we really shouldn't have been all that surprised at the eventual outcome.

We were reluctantly remaining within our spiritual (albeit slightly antiquated) home. Although not quite straightaway. The planned refurbishment of 4, 5, and 6 Queen Street (which would take up to three years to finally complete) would necessitate the staff to be decanted to alternative accommodation for the duration.

This turned out to be the somewhat cramped quarters in Thistle Street, which would turn out to be our base for the next three years, or so.

It's fascinating to speculate just how things might have turned out for BBC Edinburgh and its staff, if the proposed new building at Greenside Place had gone ahead as originally planned.

Was it a missed opportunity?

I suppose considering how the Scottish political landscape would alter and take on an entirely different shape over the next 30 years, having a modern broadcasting centre in

Scotland's capital city could only have been a good thing. But, I suppose it is something that we will now never know.

Before they could embark upon the massive program of refurbishment, there came the tricky problem of purchasing the part of Queen Street that didn't actually belong to the BBC!

It did seem rather odd to me at the time that the central part of the building, covering the main reception area, was actually owned by – a bookmaker! But that indeed, was the bizarre scenario back then.

No doubt realising just how desperate the Corporation were in purchasing that vital and integral part of the building, the "gentleman of the turf" probably, and wisely held out for an extremely generous price, with him either laughing all the way to the bank – or rushing towards the nearest racecourse!

So, as it turned out and after many, many years 4, 5, and 6 Queen Street was now safely back in the hands of the BBC.

*

You could say that my time as an employee with BBC Scotland was roughly split into three separate stages:

1974-1987 – The early years at 5 Queen Street.

1987-1990 – Being decamped to Thistle Street during Queen Street's refurbishment.

1990-2002 – The final years before leaving just prior to the building's eventual closure.

I was also duly aware that there existed six (very) different Director Generals who each held office, while simultaneously attempting to guide the BBC through some very choppy political waters.

And here are the gentlemen in question:

SIR CHARLES CURRAN, SIR IAN TRETHOWAN, SIR ALASDAIR MILNE,

SIR MICHAEL CHECKLAND, SIR JOHN BIRT, GREG DYKE

Roughly around the same time, we also had a number of BBC Chairmen.

And here are a trio of the most prominent:

SIR MICHAEL SWANN

MARMADUKE HUSSEY

SIR CHRISTOPHER BLAND

It was *Sir Michael Swann* whose lavish Edinburgh shindig during the 1970s caused poor Bob L to lose control of his faculties (as well as his trousers) while provoking a small controversy into the bargain!

Lord Marmaduke Hussey and his good lady stepped into Thistle Street one day on an official visit. Apparently it was his contentious background presence that caused Mr Milne to experience many a sleepless night, which eventually forced him to eventually step down.

*

It wasn't all that unusual to receive the occasional all-important visits from whoever the Director General was at the time.

The DGs were invariably viewed as remote, elevated figures that caused mixed emotions among their staff. They provoked an entire range of feelings such as: awe, reverence, sympathy, respect, and more often than not, bitter, cold indifference. Depending on whom you spoke to, of course.

For the bulk of the 1980s, *Sir Alasdair Milne* would pop in whenever he was back in Scotland. So he became a reasonably familiar face around the place – both in

Edinburgh and in Glasgow.

However, I don't think that his immediate successors (that included the distant and controversial *Sir John Birt*) made themselves as cosily welcome north of the border during his tenure.

The only time I ever saw Sir John was once during one TV Festival, when I caught a brief glimpse of him sitting in the back of his car, while it was parked just outside of 5 Queen Street.

Maybe he felt he was just too good for the old place. But I don't remember him popping in, shooting the breeze, cracking jokes, or chatting merrily to any of the staff!! From my viewpoint, he looked very busy and preoccupied, while scribbling away about something or other, while sitting on the back seat of his car.

Perhaps following a burning hot tip that was given to him by one of his acolytes, he was maybe writing out his racing bet that day?

Or maybe he was just finding a bit of "me time" and began writing out his Christmas cards that a little bit early?

At least his eventual successor, the more approachable *Greg Dyke*, made the effort in walking around Queen Street and having a brief chat to a number of the staff, before the place finally closed down.

*

During their individual tenures, the DGs in question, championed and defended the need to retain the licence fee at all costs, maintaining the traditional core values of the Corporation, while battling away any form of external interference. Particularly when it emanated from 10 Downing Street.

Although one or two of them courted huge controversy, much division and deep resistance, they valiantly tried to mould the BBC into a very different kind of entity. This was in order to confront the massive changes in technology and broadcasting that lay not too far up ahead.

I suppose that the roughest passage occurred during the bulk of the 1980s, which (surprise, surprise) just happened to coincide with the full ferocity of *Margaret Thatcher's Tory Government*.

The general whispers that were permeating throughout the corridors of the BBC during this decade, concluded that we weren't exactly top of her pops – to put it mildly.

This was brought home during one staff meeting I attended, in which the then Operations Manager stressed to all of us who were seated, that the cosy, comfy, easy days were now well and truly over.

To quote *William Holden* once more: "*Those days are closing fast…*"

He further added (the Ops Manager – not *Bill Holden!*), that if we (meaning the BBC) didn't put our own house in order, by making massive savings and implementing a radical reorganisation, the Government and *Mrs Thatcher* would then step in and kindly do it for us.

No beating about the bush there, then!

So we all became immediately aware that there was brewing intense political pressure heading our way.

The BBC was very much within Maggie's sights, and from what we could gather, she was determined to dismantle aspects of the BBC that she perceived as politically and ideologically subversive.

The BBC (in Scotland and no doubt elsewhere) was eventually going to become (whether it liked it or not) a much "leaner & fitter organisation". This term ("leaner & fitter") was regularly rammed down our throats in order for us to make sure that we all got the inevitable message.

The times, indeed, were soon to be a-changing.

When they first started to repeat it (leaner & fitter, leaner & fitter…) over and over again, I had this horrific thought that what they were really trying to tell us, we should all be running up the stairs, four or five times a day.

Either that, or cutting back on fruit sponges, apple crumbles and bread and butter puddings that were being served up at lunchtimes in the canteen!! Yes, I'm just funning!

*

Another similar phrase was soon added to the new expanding BBC Scotland lexicon – "Multi-functional". This began to be uttered more and more by the beginning of the 1990s, amongst senior managers and usually aimed direct at the staff.

When the expression of being "multi-functional" was being uttered on more than one occasion, I first thought of some type of miraculous kitchen appliance that could be used to make soups, sauces and casseroles?? Or maybe they were describing old Tom's equally miraculous screwdriver? How wrong could I be?

In purely BBC terms, the word multi-functional was very simple in its execution:

Less staff, doing more work, for the same money!

Yes, that's all there was to it – pretty effective and very simple in practice it was too.

I always wondered whose multi-functionally inventive brain came up with that theory.

*

During the early 1990s *James Boyle* arrived as the new Head of Radio Scotland. You could say, that he came complete with a large broadcasting sweeping brush.

Out with the old and in with the new, was his mantra, as several long-established shows and accompanying presenters could now see their entire futures writ large on a large wall.

And it didn't look all that good for them!

Some shrugged their shoulders, mumbled a few dissenting words and inevitably accepted that their former glory days enveloped within the bright sunshine of Radio Scotland, were now coming to an end.

However, there were a few others who refused to go quietly and mounted a media campaign to get themselves reinstated – while strongly criticising the new regime. It was to no avail. Their days in front of a BBC microphone were truly over and it was soon apparent that it was time to move on.

The New HRS had a vision of how he wanted to see the station to progress and he wanted to see that vision mature to fruition.

I suppose you could equate it to a new manager arriving at a modest football club – one that was happily sailing along comfortably, but not competing as it should be, for the big prizes. This would soon change, as our new boss ditched some players, brought in new ones and then totally changed the team's tactics and playing style in the process.

So a group of new shows and new presenters soon made their mark, while quickly bedding in to the new BBC Radio Scotland structure. While at the same time, the station now looked as if it was speedily ascending on an unstoppable upward trajectory.

The station's newfound confidence was confirmed when it would go on to triumph in the Sony Radio Awards, winning National Station of the Year, no less.

The kudos would come thick and fast, as the station (and the HRS) positively glowed in the spotlight.

This would turn out to be possibly the station's finest hour, with BBC Edinburgh standing proud as a major part of it and basking in the glory.

However, to take that footballing analogy a step further, Mr Boyle would soon find himself lured and enticed to "a bigger club" down south – BBC Radio 4.

You could say it was the equivalent of leaving the likes of Celtic, or Aberdeen for Manchester United or Arsenal.

Once again he would arrive with his large broadcasting sweeping brush and almost straightaway change players and tactics. And once more, he would meet a degree of resistance and some opposition while doing so. Particularly from the likes of *Lord & Lady Ha Ha* from the Home Counties, who exactly didn't appreciate the thought of some unruly Scot from across the border, altering the programme line-up of their favourite radio station.

Eventually his changes to the prestigious station's output and structure would soon become grudgingly acceptable. But his brief time down south would eventually come to an end and he would eventually leave the BBC.

Yet, looking back, his time as the HRS, during the first half of the 1990s, is often looked upon now as initially controversial, yet ultimately it turned out to be a particularly creatively productive and golden period in Radio Scotland's history.

*

Anyway, back to more mundane affairs.

By the mid-1990s I was introduced to the joys and wonders of the monthly business resources meetings. These were mind-blowing (or should that be more mind-numbing) events that some 20 years down the line, I still haven't fully recovered from.

In fact, you could say, that they amounted to several hours of my life that I will never, ever get back!

I realise that under certain situations having team/group/department meetings can have a constructive and positive effect, offering up the opportunity with the valued exchange of ideas, differing opinions, and how to constructively improve your working environment.

Unfortunately for me, the majority of my own personal experiences tended to be more an exercise in enduring pure unadulterated waffle. With the odd verbal gem thrown in just to keep you awake!

The meetings usually took place in the boardroom and were presided over by the technical resources manager, who travelled through from BBC Glasgow to impart and update us all on what was happening throughout BBC Scotland.

Whatever that may have been?

My first post impression of these meetings was my urgent need for a strong glass of something to stir me out of my stupor. *What the f**k was all that about?* I thought to myself as I slowly stumbled down the stairs from the boardroom in a bit of a disturbed daze.

For me anyway, I really felt that it was a complete and utter waste of time in attending. I did try numerous times to get out of any future ones, but it was impressed upon me that it was imperative that I attend.

So, unfortunately for me, I continued to do so – but under some duress.

Lunch was provided (that made the meetings just a little bit more palatable) that included tea, coffee, a selection of sandwiches and some chocolate and plain biscuits. Not too bad considering we weren't paying for it.

Yet I suppose we were paying for it in another less enjoyable way.

To be perfectly honest (and if my memory is not confusing me with this?) 99% of the discussions dealt primarily with technical/engineering/audio issues that rarely – if ever – touched upon things that had any relevance, or importance to my specific job.

During the course of these meetings, the manager kept describing obscure technical terminology such as "plant" and "kit", which meant nothing to me and went way over my head. I thought at one point he was describing the workings of the *Beechgrove Garden!!*

In fact around the same time there appeared in conjunction with these meetings, a regular internal publication entitled – *Kit & Caboodle.*

After browsing through this monthly magazine, I came to the astonishing conclusion that I had inadvertently discovered an instant cure for insomnia!

So, heading back to the meetings. All during the manager's talk, I tended to concentrate more on regularly filling my empty coffee cup and pondering on just how many biscuits and sandwiches were left on the plates, in order to satisfy my hunger pangs.

Yet, even if I, and a few of my non-engineering colleagues gamely attempted to give the meetings the almighty elbow by making any excuse to get out of them ("I've got a compelling newspaper I want to read at lunch time!"), we were (how should I put this?) oh so gently coerced into attending.

As if our presence made any real difference at the end of the day.

So, as a result, every month we trudged reluctantly and painfully up the stairs towards the boardroom, waiting on the inevitable 90-odd minutes of verbal turgidity. While at the same time, I closely examined the wallpaper and the carpet for some kind of divine salvation, and maybe even some spark of philosophical enlightenment! None was forthcoming.

I only wish that the likes of Bob and Mac had been around during those days. Just to add a little diverting fun to the meetings.

Mac could have showed his withering contempt by staring out of the window all throughout the meetings duration; while Bob could have banged his fist with frustration on the table a couple of times, just to keep everyone awake, as well as warble the odd swinging jazz tune to liven things up!

These meetings should have prepared me for what would soon lie up ahead, for the days when I eventually left the BBC, further down the line.

Then I would find myself embarking upon a brand new "career" in the banking and financial industry. One full of "memorable moments" (don't ask!) managerial one-to-ones and a surprise special gift from one specific bank (the same one that would feature in many a scandalous media exposé) for doing record business, that included a whopping great profit running into millions. So what did we all get?

A gingerbread man! Just a little something that we could dip into our tea while we were in the process of helping to make even more millions for the senior banking executives. You just couldn't make it up!

Within that heady environment, you would be called upon to sit in on meetings, after meetings, after meetings.

A lot would be said, but not a lot would be understood – at least by me.

Yet I suppose it offered me greater opportunity to examine the varied colours decorating the walls, as well as the elaborate designs and patterns emblazoned on the carpet.

*

One curious episode involving the BBC occurred for me around early 1983 when I actually could have been a television star. Yes, you heard me correctly!

At that time, BBC 2 was producing a TV quiz show entitled: *"Film Buff Of The Year"*, a programme aimed at movie buffs and "geeks" like myself, with varied questions covering all aspects of the cinema.

The show itself was being made with Manchester-based producer *John Buttery* at the helm, and presented by *Robin Ray*, a well-respected arts broadcaster and son of comedian *Ted Ray*.

As an avid viewer of the show, I secretly harboured desires to appear and test my knowledge amongst contestants from all over the country.

So how to go about it without making it obvious that I was a BBC employee?

What made the whole situation a little ludicrous in my mind was the fact that many might imagine that working at BBC Scotland would have gained me some kind of unfair advantage. If they had ever wandered into the building at 5 Queen Street they would have observed that there could be no obvious tangible advantage weighted in my favour, whatsoever.

For the fact was that what we were dealing with here was a comparatively small radio station. So there was absolutely no film department, or archive present (holding books, magazines, film-related literature of any kind) that would have gained me an unfair advantage. Certainly not to be found in Edinburgh!

So anyone thinking that just because I worked for the Corporation, this would gain me easy access to all the correct answers, was simply barking up the wrong tree!

What knowledge I did possess was totally down to myself, following years of personal study, by reading and watching, learning and assimilating knowledge and information without assistance from anyone.

So, further stressing the obvious, my efforts with my chosen subject, involved no secret help, or furtive guidance whatsoever, from anyone at the time, within the corridors of "Auntie Beeb"!!

Well, glad I got that off my chest.

Anyway, I decided to give it a go and try to see how far I would get with the show.

Part of the deal was to phone up their production office number and do an initial question and answer session down the phone.

If my memory serves me correct, the question master asked my name and address, but at no time (and this is crucial) did he ask me where I worked. So in essence, I was not lying, or doing anything illegal or amiss.

As luck would have it, I passed the telephone round with flying colours and was then told that they would soon be in touch to invite me for a proper preliminary round at some future date.

I now really felt excited at the prospect of testing my knowledge to its limit, as well as seeing just how far I could go in the show before I was eventually "rumbled". A few weeks later I received an official letter from BBC Manchester, inviting me down to Newcastle to take part in the elimination heat.

I mentioned this to one or two of my colleagues (including Mr Snax) that I was going, so I took a day's leave and journeyed down to Newcastle, full of anticipation

I arrived at the venue, which turned out to be a large palatial hotel, just placed directly across from the Newcastle railway station. Which was nice and handy.

No sooner had I arrived, I was introduced to my fellow contestants, the production team and *Robin Ray* himself, who was a most charming man.

They had hired a large meeting room and set it up to resemble a TV studio, providing the ideal atmosphere and giving us all a taste of possible things to come, if successful.

I would find myself far ahead in the quiz, coming out on top and finally winning. It was a great feeling and everyone was extremely kind and gracious, as they congratulated me on the day.

I left for my return train back to Edinburgh with a feeling of real and not imaginary elation. However, progressing to the next stage might prove to be a little tricky.

Not long afterwards, since I had been one of the successful participants, I received another letter inviting me to go down to the BBC Manchester studios to take part in the actual recording of the show.

What to do now? was the question praying on my mind.

That decision was somehow taken out of my hands. Not sure how she found out, but it appeared that my boss, Miss Wilson, had cottoned on to the fact that I had entered for the show, and being successful, I was now due to appear on television – BBC 2 no less!

She called me into her office and we had a heart-to-heart discussion about it. While she could understand and in some ways, sympathise with my predicament, she stressed that my participation in the show could arouse press suspicion, and ultimately cause a great deal of public embarrassment both for me, and the BBC in general.

It could also cost me my job, which at the time, I had to take into serious consideration since I had not long obtained a mortgage.

I fully understood where she was coming from, and so reluctantly I went along with her, and decided to step down from the show.

I called to speak with the producer *John Buttery* himself, and he was a little stunned at first, as I explained to him that I just happened to be a BBC employee.

He understood and regretfully accepted my decision, further adding that despite the potential embarrassment it may have caused, I had achieved one of the highest scores in the early rounds!

No doubt from then on, they would scrupulously check the employment details of all future applicants.

I must now hold my hands up and confess to a little fraudulent activity during my final years at 5 Queen Street. Hold on, before you jump the gun, I can assure you it was nothing in any way criminal, or illegal, or even faintly immoral, just a little incident that happened to tickle my particular sense of humour. Whilst at the same time, showing up some of the absurd practices that were then prevalent during the 1990s in BBC Scotland.

*

Around this time we had to endure an overabundance of excessive official propaganda thrown in our direction about providing "excellent customer service" to our, well, customers.

Or, you could put it in more straightforward layman terms, our colleagues who just happen to be working in other departments – as they had done for years.

What a complete waste of time, energy and, I suppose, expense. I guess this was just another glowing example of the changing culture that was now gripping the BBC in the wake of "Producer Choice".

The term of "Producer Choice" was yet another phrase that first came into light during the early 1990s.

A rough translation of this was that each department became primarily responsible for their own budgets, while shopping for BBC facilities in an open market style format. No wonder many of the older and long-established staff confronted this dramatic alteration in their normal working procedures with a cry of "Eh? What??"

While overhearing several of the production staff discussing this, I learned that they all generally viewed it as totally bizarre, wholly unworkable and a complete waste of time.

For example, it was now going to cost the individual departments a fee to borrow music from the sound archives to include in any future programmes.

So instead of strictly adhering to this nonsensical set-up, quite a number of the producers just went out and purchased a CD from a local store. This was rather than go through an overly complicated (and costly) process of borrowing the very same music from the BBC sound library.

To quote yet another line from *"The Bridge on the River Kwai"* – "Madness… Madness."

As a result of this, we would now find that our daily working life was frequently and unnecessarily getting all tangled up in a plethora of useless jargon and unnecessary obfuscation (just love that word!).

After all, for over 20 years the majority of my colleagues (including myself) had always provided the very best of service whenever required, to whichever department we were dealing with.

Call me stupid, but wasn't that what we were always doing?

We certainly didn't need to be patronised by faceless bean counting accountants (a term much favoured by the tabloid press at the time) and middle managers, constantly harping on to us about the importance of "customer service", as if we were employed by the likes of *Sainsbury's, M&S,* or *John Lewis?*

It was like preaching to the converted. But I suppose they had to do something to justify their expanding salaries.

"Producer Choice" and "Customer Service" – what was all that about?

That's not what I regarded as core principles of the BBC.

Well, that's me had my say on the subject, so I'll get off my soapbox now.

*

Once upon a time there was announced a new initiative whereby the entire BBC staff could nominate a member of the Resources/Admin department, who in their humble opinion, had gone "above and beyond the call of duty", in providing an "excellent customer service experience!!"

That word again.

This wouldn't be my last encounter with this tiresome

kind of working practice. As I discovered to my cost a few years down the line, when I would find myself working for the Standard Life Bank Mortgage department. But that, as they say, is another story…

Come to think of it, that very phrase (excellent customer service experience) often reminded me of Bob's frequent and enjoyable visits to a certain "house of ill repute" while visiting Edinburgh's new town!

*

While I was in the newsroom one day, I overheard some of the journalists discussing (in humorous and none too polite terms) the ridiculousness of this set-up and how it was ripe for comical exploitation.

I later found out that a few of them had even filled in a few of the nomination forms themselves, that would include such well deserving staff names as: *Mickey Mouse, Donald Duck*, while not forgetting *The Lone Ranger* and *Tonto!!*

I recall discussing this subject one night with my then partner, jokingly saying that, at least, I should receive a nomination for this pointless honour. As a joke, she said something along the lines of, "Well, why don't you just nominate yourself then? Who's going to know?"

This is what is commonly known as a "lightbulb moment!" So with that in mind, I decided to follow her instruction, and I did exactly that.

After all, not only did I think (due to my lengthy years of loyal service), that I deserved it, but I also wanted to highlight the fact that there was an obvious deep flaw in the overall nominating process. This was something I was about to cheekily expose to my own advantage.

A few weeks later I received acknowledgement of my successful nomination that included an invitation to accompany my fellow nominees (from all over BBC Scotland) down to London for the award ceremony. This included a generous slap-up lunch, which I was very much looking forward to.

During the ceremony itself, our senior departmental boss (where the hell did they get these rather dour-looking characters from?) individually called us up to the stage to receive our winning and much deserved "certificate".

When I mounted the podium, he grimly smiled at me (like some chillingly haunted figure straight out of a terrifying *Edgar Allan Poe* tale) while shaking my hand rather limply.

From what I am led to believe, the gentleman in question who presented the awards, would controversially depart the BBC not that long afterwards!

What an absolute farce!

*

Around 1994 my good friend *Iain Agnew* (actor, writer, and broadcaster) approached me about doing some radio work. Iain had at one time, been a stalwart contributor to many of Radio Scotland's schedules.

He had appeared in radio dramas, co-presented the popular *Travel Time* programme, as well as providing regular theatre and film reviews for the various arts shows.

Unfortunately, Iain had become one of the "casualties" during the station's brand new look (courtesy of the new HRS), and his radio work in BBC Edinburgh was slowly drying up.

However, he had been approached to become a late-night presenter with a brand new commercial radio station that was being set up down in my own backyard of Leith. In fact right down at the Docks.

It was called *Scot FM* and it had been started to provide a balance of music, sport, chat and news. It sounded great and Iain came up with an idea.

He asked me if I would like to come on his show as an

occasional guest and do a bit of a light-hearted film quiz. As well as chat about new film releases and all manner of film stuff. I didn't have to be asked twice.

The only quibble was (well there was two), the show started about midnight on the Saturday and I suppose I would have to check with my boss (Bella at the time) if broadcasting for a rival station was permitted within my contract.

This wasn't going to be a problem as there was no real clash of interest and it was after all at a weekend. So it was all systems go.

The studio complex was all brand new and as I said, based right down at Albert Docks in Leith. Iain would pick me up by taxi just after 11pm and we would head down to the station.

I wasn't nervous and for the next two hours or so, Iain and I just had a laugh and enjoyed doing the programme. We opened up the phone-lines and allowed any listeners to try and beat me live on air with a movie question. If they did, they would win free tickets to the cinema. Of course, considering the show was going out live over the post-midnight hour on a Saturday, we did get the occasional drunk phoning in, but it was all part of the fun factor in doing a live radio show. We had our usual listeners and callers who liked to phone up for a chat and discuss not just films, but other things as well. And Iain was an experienced and accomplished broadcaster who helped make the show go smoothly with a lot of laughs along the way, and I looked forward to making my appearance with him every weekend.

When I mentioned this upturn in my fortunes, a few of the BBC production staff I mentioned this too, were, you could say, a little snooty in their attitude to commercial radio, regarding it as not quite the real thing and just a bit of a circus with very little intellect and substance. True, it wasn't quite Radio 4, but for me, it was a terrific learning experience – as well as just pure great fun.

One Saturday, my dad asked if he could pop along, as he was curious as to how we did the show. Iain was more than happy for my dad to be there.

However, my dad had enjoyed a few drinks that evening (he wasn't drunk, just a little relaxed!) and while sitting in the studio with us, he began to laugh at some of the questions being asked. Iain found it a bit funny too and explained to the listeners, "Tonight folks, we have a special guest in the studio with us – Peter, the Laughing Painter!" With that, my dad just laughed even more. But his biggest laugh came when somebody called up with a question regarding the old Hollywood film *Tarzan And His Mate*. Well, my dad just couldn't stop laughing at this, but the show turned out well, and my dad felt well pleased at his radio debut.

*

Another of *Scot FM*'s presenters (in fact he was probably its highest profile one) was a character called *Scottie McClue*.

In fact that wasn't his real name – just his showbiz one, but he turned out to be the station's very own late-night *Shock Jock*. I met him a couple of times while being at the studio and I also vividly recall listening to one of his shows. On that specific evening Scottie had received a call from someone (let's call him Jimmy) with a particular grievance.

The conversation flow went something along like this:

"Hello Scottie. Is that you Scottie?"

"Aye this is Scottie McClue. What can I do for you Jimmy?"

"Scottie, I've just got one thing to say to you"

"What's that, Jimmy?"

"Scottie – yer' an absolute bampot!!" and with that Jimmy slammed the phone down.

Scottie McClue would soon leave the station (like so many others) and what started out as a brave new venture in commercial radio, soon sadly dissipated into acrimony and disillusion.

Iain would eventually leave as well, and as a result, my first real adventure into live radio would come to an end.

Eventually, *Real Radio* would soon swallow up *Scot FM*, with the old studio building at Albert Docks now long gone. Yet, although it turned out to be but a brief moment in my broadcasting life, I still look back upon with warmth and great fondness.

*

Around 1992, my same acting chum *Iain Agnew* had been approached to present a proposed one-off TV programme called B-ZARRE. A show that would hopefully be later commissioned as a series.

No, just in case you were wondering, it wasn't a look inside the comings and goings on at 5 Queen Street. That kind of a show would have more likely to have been called *Bizarre!*

So, the content of the show was going to be a weekly look at the world of horror, science fiction, and fantasy in the cinema. Come to think of it, that could well have described some of the "characters and personalities" that I had *Bizarre* "close encounters" with at Queen Street!!

Anyway, back to more serious matters. Taking into consideration the vast, passionate worldwide following those particular genres had, it couldn't fail to hit its intended target.

Iain asked me to come on board as consultant/researcher, so I provided him with sufficient material for the programme's pilot episode that was filmed in a studio in south Edinburgh.

Unfortunately, the idea failed to be picked up and commissioned. A great pity, as we could all see the enormous potential such a show possessed.

*

Aside from my enjoyable weekend stint with Scot FM, around the same time, I also finally received the opportunity to work on some BBC programmes. With them destined for both BBC Scotland, as well as BBC Radio 4.

This was all down to the invitation of the late arts and features producer – Ian Docherty.

The late Mr Docherty proved to be yet another fairly divisive figure during this period (there were so many!). He was much admired for his intellect and his audacious choice of program material, yet he was also a figure viewed with much suspicion in certain quarters.

Sadly, he also turned out to be yet another of the never-ending list of Edinburgh staff, whose profile came complete with a strong and unstoppable adherence for the demon drink.

I first casually met him when he was in one of the opposing teams, when my dad and I attended the monthly Film-House film quizzes. The ones that we usually won most of the time, as we carried home in triumph lots of bottles of beer as our main prize!

Speaking personally, I always got on fine with Ian Docherty. Particularly as he was the only producer at that time who showed a degree of confidence, belief and faith in me and recognised that I might have something worthwhile to add to the content of a programme.

Yet I was also aware that he wasn't everybody's cup of tea as a person.

Aside from that he was well versed in film history, and came up with quite a few good ideas for programmes that he was hoping to commission.

After a discussion we came up with an idea for a short series on Radio Scotland that took a look back at the Scots film pioneers who made an impact during the early years of Hollywood.

We then planned to include such names as: *Donald Crisp, Frank Lloyd* and *Mary Gordon.*

Donald Crisp would be the first project to work on and one I was looking forward in tackling.

I did my research diligently, by reading up as much as I could.

I also contacted the American Film Institute, the Academy of Motion Picture Arts & Sciences, and the New York Museum of Modern Art. Not forgetting keeping in contact with Hollywood actor *Roddy McDowell*, who had worked with Crisp several times and had some amusing memories and stories of him that he kindly shared with us.

The bulk of my research regarding Crisp had all pointed towards the small Perthshire town of Aberfeldy, as the place of his birth. I had also been touch with a number of people in the town, who kindly provided me some valuable background info on the man.

With the programme beginning to take shape, Ian Docherty suggested to me that I should nominate *Donald Crisp* for one of the new Blue Plaques that were being erected around the country. These were issued in celebrating numerous individuals who had made a telling contribution to the art of film.

Crisp was a prime and (as I thought at the time) appropriate figure to honour, considering that he was an Oscar winner for the *John Ford* film *How Green Was My Valley.* Yet taking aside the fact that he was one of Hollywood's longest serving character actors with a string of classic films to his name – he was also an accomplished director.

A man who had worked with *DW Griffith, Buster Keaton, Douglas Fairbanks Snr, Lillian Gish* and so many others during the genesis of the Hollywood film industry.

At this moment I seemed to be on a roll.

The first programme on Donald Crisp had been made and

was well received. I was then encouraged to write a follow-up article about Crisp and pitch it to the *The Herald* newspaper. This I did, and it was duly published.

It was for me, a tremendous thrill to see my words and name printed for all to see in a national newspaper. On top of that, I was invited to attend the official unveiling of the Blue Plaque in memory of *Donald Crisp*.

This event that was going to be held in Aberfeldy and doing the unveiling was none other than one of the biggest names in Scottish show business – *Jimmy Logan*.

I met and chatted cordially away to *Jimmy Logan* before and after the occasion (there was a lavish lunch provided, courtesy of the town council) and he gave me the impression that he felt duly honoured to have been asked to preside over the unveiling. However, a few weeks later, following all the publicity surrounding both the programme and the plaque unveiling, something happened that threw everything a little bit up in the air.

A local researcher had been digging away, only to discover that *Donald Crisp* hadn't exactly been entirely straight about his background.

Not unusual there, as many an actor and actress who headed out to Hollywood during the same period tended to doctor some of their background and origins.

Yet would you believe it? Mr Crisp wasn't born in Aberfeldy, he wasn't even Scottish – he was a Londoner! Born not too far as it happened from Bow-bells!

Well, I felt slightly cheated and just a little embarrassed for perpetuating what turned out to be a bit of a fraud.

Yet, hand on heart, in all my research both here and in the USA, all the evidence pointed towards *Donald Crisp* being a true-blue tartan Scotsman who hailed from Aberfeldy! He even used to talk warmly and fondly about the place during his lifetime.

Maybe he and his wife had just visited the place on holiday one time and fell in love with it. With such things myths are born.

For the remaining programmes in the short series, I stringently checked and re-checked all the facts – particularly those concerning birthplaces.

Didn't want to be caught out again.

Although, to be honest, it wasn't unusual for birth dates and birthplaces to be a bit all over the place, with so many discrepancies emerging and floating to the surface, years later. After all, in the many books that I had read about *David Niven* he often claimed Scotland as his place of birth, only for this theory to be quashed and finally disproved.

Donald Crisp was just one of many.

The other programmes profiled Oscar-winning director *Frank Lloyd* and veteran Glasgow actress *Mary Gordon* – best known for playing *Mrs Hudson* in the *Basil Rathbone Sherlock Holmes* films.

Talking of *Sherlock Holmes*, a couple of years later, Ian Docherty once again asked if I would be interested in working on another proposed Radio 4 programme entitled – *"The Druid's Blood"*.

This was going to be a forensic (no pun intended) look at the various screen (both film and TV) incarnations of the great detective. Plots and stories that hadn't originated from the writings of *Arthur Conan Doyle*. It turned out to be a different slant in looking at the great detective, one that was far removed from the author's original conception.

A little later, *Ian Docherty* further approached me in doing some other work for him in the role of film-researcher/consultant with a new project he had been commissioned to do for Radio 4.

This was to be called *Mr America*, in which he had also invited the Canadian actor *Angus MacInnes* to write and present.

For those unfamiliar with the name of *Angus MacInnes*, well, for an entire generation of movie lovers, he will be forever known as *Gold Leader* from *Star Wars: A New Hope*.

He had also appeared in numerous film and television productions, including him featuring opposite *Harrison Ford* in *Witness*, and *Sean Connery* in *Outland*.

So Angus was the ideal man to work on such a programme.

What *Mr America* was all about, was a detailed look at the evolving figure of the American leading man in the cinema.

So we examined such important and towering personalities as *Gary Cooper, John Wayne, Henry Fonda, James Stewart, Gregory Peck*, right up to the likes of *Sidney Poitier, Clint Eastwood, Harrison Ford, Tom Cruise, Denzel Washington*, and *Tom Hanks*. For me it was a terrific programme to work on, and it later led to a follow-up with Radio 4. This was called *Beautiful But Deadly*, an investigative look at the impact of the femme fatale in the cinema.

This highlighted the likes of *Marlene Dietrich, Rita Hayworth* and *Lana Turner*, going right up to the likes of contemporary sirens such as *Sharon Stone*.

So another great programme to get my researching teeth into, as I selected sound clips and interviews to feature within the structure of the programme.

I also was asked to do some film work for the then fledgling film page on the BBC website. On that occasion, I simply answered as many questions that were offered up online, regarding the cinema. And guess what, I also get paid for it too!

On that very subject of being paid (and again, in thanking *Ian Docherty* for this), it was he who made sure that I received the full and proper payment for any work that I did on any programme that I was involved with. Not something that was usually forthcoming by one or two in the building, who regularly tapped into my brain for information and offered me... nothing. I suppose nowadays they would just log onto their laptops and Google whatever it was they wanted to find out.

*

Ian Docherty left the BBC just prior to me leaving and began working as a freelancer particularly in the USA, on programmes that attracted great attention and not a little controversy.

He passed away in 2009 at the relatively young age of 47.

Not meaning to sound disrespectful, but I expect that Mr Docherty (alongside so many others) is propping up the bar in the great "BBC Club in the Sky."

Yet, I have much to thank him, for he alone gave me a chance to vent my creativity (however modest) that was denied me by so many others.

By a strange quirk of fate, some ten years after leaving the BBC I would find myself placed within the position of writing, producing, and presenting my very own live radio show.

Not only that, but I was also approached to write online film and theatre reviews during the Edinburgh Film Festival, as well the Edinburgh Fringe. Certainly something that never occurred for me during my entire 28 years as a BBC employee.

Granted, this task was performed for two separate local community radio stations *(Leith FM* and *East Coast FM)* but the opportunity and experience this presented me, was invaluable and immensely enjoyable.

It brought back to mind the words from a former colleague of mine as he once explained to me: "It is often recognised that the BBC is renowned for unfailingly ignoring and dismissing genuine talent that's hidden right under its very nose." I rest my case.

How it initially happened was that I popped into the Leith FM offices one night to enquire about the possibility of volunteering in some capacity, when I happened to mention my previous employment with BBC Scotland.

The board members seemed slightly impressed – even though my original position within the Corporation was hardly that of a writer/producer/presenter.

However, despite this, and to my great surprise, they offered me my own radio slot.

My imagination went into overdrive, as this was a real dream come true. My intention was to present a film-music programme that profiled and highlighted many of my favourite composers, as well as a selection of the finest film-music – both past and present.

In fact earlier that year (following the death of Oscar-winning composer *John Barry*), I listened to a somewhat lacklustre tribute show about him on *Classic FM*. So disappointed was I with the show, that I fired off an e-mail expressing my disappointment and then finished up with words along the lines of: *"I could have done a far better job myself…"*

Well, flash forward some three months, and there I was sitting in a small, intimate radio station in Leith waiting to go live on air with my very own tribute show to *John Barry!*

*

I would like to add that this was all my own effort. Even though my BBC background helped to prise the door open and helped get me the slot in the first place (with me having no formal radio studio training), on this occasion, I did it all on my own steam. So my former employers really deserve no credit.

*

For almost two years I presented two shows live on air. The first was modestly called – *Lawrence's Magnificent Movie*

Music. This was a gilt-edged opportunity to play great music from films past and present, as well as impart information (not forgetting the odd laugh or two) to the late-night listening audience in Scotland's central belt. I also wrote and presented a companion show called *The Night Of The Singers*, which was a celebration of the great vocalists and song stylists of the 20th century. I would like to think that particular show was a small tribute to my parents and the music that they both loved. Suffice to say, it turned out to be another marvellous experience.

At the same time, I regularly shared the presenting chores on the Saturday morning show.

First with a colourful character called *Jimmy Rainbow,* in which in between him playing the music, we discussed the latest film releases, funny stories in the newspapers and our weekly Leith Quiz.

Much fun was had, and many laughs were generated as we did the show for a full three hours on a Saturday morning.

After a while, Jimmy stepped aside and was replaced by *Ricky Callan.*

I didn't know Ricky all that well, but I later found out that he was a multi-talented actor, writer, and broadcaster – as well as being an enormously funny man.

In fact Ricky was also, as it turned out, a comedian of enormous quick wit.

The Saturday shows that we did together were amongst the most enjoyable that I ever did – with us striking up a good friendship into the bargain.

Unfortunately, due to health issues (as well as his deep disillusionment at how the station was being run) Ricky stepped down from the Saturday show and gave up his broadcasting.

I felt sad, as I always looked forward to doing the Saturday morning show with Ricky – if only for the fact that we had such a great laugh doing it.

But it all came to an end, more's the pity.

*

At the moment the station (which later evolved – if that's the right word – to Castle FM) is, I believe, still broadcasting. Although all of the original presenters have left, and the station has – over these past three years – been engulfed in controversy involving court cases and legal wrangling.

*

One offshoot of my time as a community radio broadcaster, has been kickstarting me as a writer of sorts. This began when I wrote a short article and pitched it the *The Leither* magazine. They duly published it, and since then I have written quite a number that have all been published.

Among the subjects I have written about include:

A look at the cultural impact in the cinema during the year of 1962

Elvis Presley's film career

The comic legacy of Benny Hill

A light-hearted nostalgic look back at the old Leith Cinemas

The traditions of the American Crooners

The Scottish Footballer and how that impact has affected soccer in England

A tongue in cheek look at my family's potential inheritance

Two separate articles looking at two great film composers: Miklos Rozsa & John Barry

The controversial court case of Errol Flynn

And not forgetting a short article about my memories of working for BBC Scotland

That last piece went a long way in preparing me for embarking on this very project that you are reading now.

*

If you are at all interested in reading any of the above, you can no doubt go the The Leither's website, which I am sure will point you in the right direction.

http://www.leithermagazine.com/

http://www.leithermagazine.com/2014/02/24/benny-hill-elephant-room.html

http://www.leithermagazine.com/2014/09/24/the-last-picture-show.html

http://www.leithermagazine.com/2015/04/23/the-man-with-the-midas-touch.html

http://www.leithermagazine.com/2015/02/17/can-take.html

*

When my time at Leith FM/Castle FM came to a close, I would still find myself involved in some minor capacity with local radio. This time with East Coast FM, a community station based out at Haddington in East Lothian.

Only this time my efforts were not placed before a microphone, but on a PC, as I became one of their film and theatre reviewers during the Edinburgh Festival.

Again, if you have any desire of reading some of my reviews, please find a selection in the link highlighted below:

http://ecfm107.co.uk/reviews-2/frank-sanazis-das-vegas-voodoo-rooms

http://www.ecfm.co.uk/2013/08/nosferatu-the-jazz-bar/

http://www.ecfm.co.uk/2014/08/the-hollywood-ten-the-space/

http://ecfm107.co.uk/reviews-2/the-usherettesthe-space-at-surgeons-hall/

http://www.ecfm.co.uk/2014/08/the-genius-of-charlesdickenssweet-grassmarket/

http://ecfm107.co.uk/reviews-2/the-canterbury-tales-studio-1-greenside/

http://ecfm107.co.uk/reviews-2/bondthe-zoo-at-the-pleasance/

http://www.ecfm.co.uk/2013/08/the-complete-history-of-the-bbc-in-60-minutes-abridged/

http://ecfm107.co.uk/reviews-2/the-cabinet-of-dr-caligarijazz-bar/

http://www.ecfm.co.uk/2013/08/macbeth-the-cheshire-actors-youth-theatre/

One show I watched, reviewed, and wrote about two years running at the Fringe was funnily enough called – *The Entire History Of The BBC – In 60 minutes!*

A breathlessly energetic and comedic run through eight decades of the BBC's finest and most celebrated moments on radio and TV.

Although, from my recollection, Edinburgh barely elicited a mention, so no great surprise there I suppose. But it didn't spoil the enjoyment as it turned out to be a good show nonetheless.

*

At the time of writing, there are at least three of my former colleagues still working in BBC Edinburgh (The Tun) – Dougie, Stan, and Lorraine.

However, although they are still working *in* the BBC, they aren't exactly working *for* the BBC.

If that sounds a little complicated, this is down to the fact that once 5 Queen Street closed down, certain departments and individuals became what is commonly known as "outsourced".

A rather cold word that meant their contracts and terms and conditions came under the auspices of another company. A harsh, unfeeling and crummy way to treat loyal and long-serving staff, I felt at the time, and I still do – so there!

I suppose if you look at it simplistically and dispassionately, this was purely a way to save money. And it wasn't just a large organisation like the BBC that decided to go down this particular road in recent years.

A far cry from how things used to be, I suppose?

*

So, do I feel at all bitter at my lack of anything resembling a successful BBC career?

No, not really, as time has softened and mellowed any frustrations I may have felt.

It was a different time and a different place and things have certainly moved on.

In spite of its many flaws, faults, errors of judgement, and occasional unavoidable crassness, it was in hindsight a privilege to have worked for such an organisation as BBC Scotland.

So it's safe to say that in summation, its many virtues outweighed its occasional deficiencies.

*

As I near the conclusion of my story, it appears that – once again – the BBC stands at an important and crucial crossroads, in which its very existence is possibly at risk.

Yet it's not surprising considering all the recent bleak media coverage concerning the BBC's future that dark, ominous clouds of gloom are gathering once again on the horizon.

It's really quite funny (as well as ironical), that the BBC has been guilty of turning its inquisitive gaze inwards towards… the BBC and all that it entails.

No wonder everyone is slightly bamboozled!

Massive job cuts, departmental decimations, efficiency savings and implied threats to the survival of much of the TV and radio output, do not bode well.

For some considerable time now, the BBC has been coming under the public and governmental microscope like never before. The questions that are raised (igniting furious debate) about where it's heading in the 21st century, just never appear to let up!

Even the thorny question (or should that be thistly question?) regarding Scotland's position within the BBC's unified structure has recently been raised, particularly with the idea of having a separate BBC Scotland channel and an extra radio station.

So then the varied questions begin: Should it be this – should it be that?

What are its primary broadcasting responsibilities?

Is it totally impartial?

How can it survive under its current shape and form?

Are the public getting proper value for money?

Should they be sacrificing their more popular entertainment output, for more serious and intellectual subjects?

Do we really need a licence fee? And if not, what replaces it?

Maybe by the time I reach 75 and receive my free TV Licence (if it, and me are still around), the situation will hopefully be much calmer and a clearer picture (no pun intended!) will have gradually come into focus.

After emerging severely damaged from a series of high-profile scandals (the Savile controversy?) the Corporation looked to have regrouped and appeared to be sailing in smoother, calmer waters. Even finding time in having a side glancing chuckle at their own beaurocratic excesses with the sharply written and performed BAFTA winning comedy series *W1A*.

Although, it doesn't always pay to be too complacent, as you never know what other once deeply hidden ghastly secrets and stories could well be unearthed further down the line. Hopefully nothing contained within these pages.

I'll just consult my lawyer!!

However, intense debate over the upcoming Charter renewal continues to grow ever louder.

But if that was not enough, following a recent election, a new Government is now settled and sitting comfortably with ease in the House of Commons, bringing with them a confident swagger, as they flex their renewed and rejuvenated political muscles, given to them by the majority of the electorate. Although, not all that surprisingly, from the people in Scotland.

No doubt this new grasp of power will bring extra-enforced vigour, as they attempt to tackle, tame and chastise "good old Auntie Beeb" over its still unsure future, as well as questions over the licence fee.

With today's vast array of digital channels, and multimedia gadgets, all readily available for watching everything and anything, at any time of the day, or night, the old reliable TV Licence has found itself stuck in an unfortunate time warp.

Maybe that's why some of its more vicious critics have been known to accuse its programming content of taking "a jump to the left" once too often? Well, whatever.

The BBC, the licence fee, the Royal Charter, the value and integrity of its programming output, not forgetting its very existence within the broadcasting universe of the 21st century, will soon be resolved – one way or another.

One thing however is for sure; in the near future it will look far different to the one that we have all been used to.

"It's the BBC Jim… but not as we know it!"

*

After all that naval gazing, I don't think it's too much of an exaggeration to state that the BBC I knew no longer exists.

Yet (hoping not to appear too pessimistic), I do feel that it would be an extremely sad day if (a few years down the line) that turned out to be the permanent case. I really and sincerely hope not.

So even after going through what amounted to a "Broadcasting Botox job" in the wake of the Thatcher years, another reinvention, or more likely a regeneration worthy of *Doctor Who*, could well be on the cards.

Watch this space as undoubtedly even more fascinating days lie ahead…

*

My last day at 5 Queen Street was set for Thursday March 30th 2002, and one not surprisingly, filled with a mixture of emotions: sadness, humour, regret, anticipation, nostalgia and uncertainty.

After spending close to 28 years working in the same place, it almost felt like my second home.

So, it was natural in feeling a growing sense of loss at the unreal prospect of no longer walking through the same doors each morning, seeing the same faces, or drinking the same tea in a much-treasured BBC paper cup!

I received a leather-bound autograph book filled with signatures, amusing comments (the odd artistic drawing), and kind good wishes from so many of my soon-to-be former colleagues.

On the cover was etched my name, alongside both my starting and finishing date: *10/06/1974 – 31/03/2002*

This was an extremely touching memento, covering the

time that I had spent working there.

My colleagues kindly threw me a farewell party in the canteen, in which the bulk of the staff attended. I recall being deeply moved at their generosity, friendship, thoughtfulness and warmth throughout the entire evening. A fact that, up until then, reflected just how grateful I was, to have spent much of my working life amongst them.

There was food, drink, and music supplied and at one point in the evening, I even got up and made a farewell speech.

Yet this was not some off-the-cuff spontaneous act, as I had only been working on it for over a week!

But just how do you encapsulate the experiences of the past 28 years in a few pages of typed out notes?

A tough one, but I had terrific material to work with. It was just more of a case of what to leave out. However, I think I didn't do too badly, as I attempted with some ironical humour, to give everyone a brief impression (as well as the odd laugh) of my time at 5 Queen Street.

And as you will see below, here are a few extracts from that very same speech:

It does seem strange – though not altogether unusual – that after 28 years, I am now looked upon as "surplus to requirements", or is it "excess baggage"? Anyway, I don't want to hang around too long or I may end up in one of the skips that are due for outside the building, so I think I'll get out now while the going's good. The ship is slowly – no, it's rapidly – sinking, and I want to grasp the life raft that awaits me before I get engulfed.

I promise not to shed too many tears this evening, though if the BBC manages to bugger up my redundancy cheque, that may be reason enough for a good greet…

I could relate a few stories and anecdotes about this place and some of the people who have worked here over the years that would make *"Sodom & Gomorrah"* look like *"Disney-Land Paris"*!! And some of the characters who have worked here with the situations they created, wouldn't go amiss in a Carry-On film, or a Marx Brothers comedy!

When I think back to the very beginning, my initial introduction to working at BH Edinburgh was akin to being thrust totally unprepared into the midst of a wacky Christmas Pantomime! Talk about *"Watch out he's behind you!!"*

It was a totally strange environment, more lurid and grotesque, than artistic and creative.

A range of strange, colourful and offbeat characters inhabited it, including good guys, bad guys, and idiotic clowns. As well as gentlemen of – how can I delicately put this? – ambiguous sexual orientation? Everything from sceneshifters – to shirt lifters, you could say.

It was certainly a heady brew for a fresh-faced teenager, arriving as I did straight from school – young, stupid, gullible and very naïve!

So my very first years at the Beeb are coloured by memories of drunken religious bigots, raving psychotic madmen and self-deluded fantasists with overactive imaginations, who came complete with a tendency and desire to play pocket billiards, regardless of who was watching!

It was like I was venturing tentatively into Narnia, or the merry old land of OZ – full of *"wicked witches"* in one form or another! With some of the individuals I encountered either stretching the imagination – or leaving very little to the imagination!

You can take your pick?

We've had everything from embezzlement to exhibitionism – enough ingredients and material to fill out a very bad soap opera…

Anyway, that was all a long, long, time ago in a broadcasting station far, far away, with the place now a little more bland and soulless by comparison – more's the pity. It seems that the laughs have all dried up and faded away, finally disappearing into the night.

Well, I suppose it's now time for me to *"pick up my chips and find myself another game".*

So once more, I just want to thank you all, for every good thing that has come my way these past 28 years. And I truly believe that this time, I am witnessing the end of an era.

So in closing, and to quote the words of the great Spencer Tracey in his final film appearance: "…the memories are still there, clear, intact and indestructible and they'll be there if I live to be 110…"

So after all those years, my time had finally come to leave, and so I left and soon embarked upon a new road in my life.

However, about a couple of months later, I received an official invitation to attend *"A Farewell To Queen Street"* party, in which so many former friends and colleagues attended.

This was a real glorious last hurrah before the few remaining staff were eventually shunted down to The Tun in Holyrood Road, and the doors of 5 Queen Street were finally set to close for the very last time.

The farewell bash proved a most enjoyable and entertaining evening, where I met up with a few old pals and familiar faces that I hadn't seen in a long time.

Entertaining the crowd live on the stage of Studio 1 were our old friends from many a past BBC Edinburgh Fringe show, *That Swing Thing* (or otherwise known in certain circles as – *Swing That Thing*).

However, I think for that particular evening, they were generally known as the former, rather than the latter. Perhaps just as well, since the latter name would more than likely cause more than a few eyebrows to raise skywards, due, no doubt, to a later police enquiry involving an Internet scandal, where the very fact of *Swinging That Thing (*not this time in front of an audience but in front of a PC screen), could get you into all kinds of trouble!

There were also quite a few individuals who were supping

YOU CAN'T DO THAT HERE! THIS IS THE BBC!

up the drink and munching away at the free food, that I had never ever met before, and I found myself puzzled as to their BBC connection, and just how they had been invited in the first place? Particularly as there were quite a few former BBC faces I noticed were missing from the assembly.

Perhaps they had in fact been invited, but for reasons best known to themselves, decided to give the entire shindig an almighty body swerve?

There was one guy in particular, who looked not unlike the old 1940s Hollywood actor *Sidney Greenstreet (Mr Gutman in The Maltese Falcon)*.

He was of a similar shape and build, wearing a pinstripe three-piece suit, while wearing a black bowler hat on top of his head and carrying an umbrella! Perhaps he was an actor in costume? Though I suppose it was quite apt that he was there that evening to preside over the closure of the building, as in some eyes it possibly represented *the stuff that dreams are made of…*

There again, he may well have just been someone's special guest for the night? But he did made a few heads turn, as well as offer up the odd baffled question – "Who the f**k is that big bloke in the bowler hat?"

Apart from that, it was altogether a good night, and a good way to finally say farewell to the old place.

*

There was quite a lot of genuine regret and sadness when the BBC decided to finally move out of 5 Queen Street.

We all knew that the building was expensive to run (and was getting ever more expensive by the minute!), but it had a drama studio second to none that was the envy of most, with many a superb production originating from it.

So taking that alone into consideration, the whole notion of abandoning our broadcasting spiritual home just didn't make much sense.

But the decision had been made – and sadly, there was no going back.

*

As there was no real equivalent to my job in Glasgow, I was given the redundancy option, which under the circumstances, I decided to take.

The BBC was being somewhat generous, and this would give me the opportunity to embark on a brand new career – somewhere else.

In my imagination I possibly thought that someone in radio production might have come up with the blinding thought that I could still be of some use. I felt (and still do) that I possessed some talent and it seemed a bit of a waste to let me walk out of the door without giving me a proper shot at something.

I think I did apply for some position in Glasgow as a researcher, or something like that (my memory regarding the details of this is a little sketchy) but I was again overlooked. So I grabbed my cheque and eventually departed.

A few weeks before I left, a colleague said to me that I wouldn't truly appreciate the BBC and what it really meant in working there, until I had actually left it and went to work for a completely different company, or organisation.

And do you know what? He was right.

You could say that once you have spent some considerable time working within the Corporation, its looming shadow stays with you – and refuses to budge – wherever you eventually land up!

"Once a BBC man, always a BBC man… "

*

Well, with the BBC's very future existence seemingly up for grabs, what will Edinburgh's place and position in broadcasting terms look like in years to come?

One thing's for sure, it will never be as colourful, as entertaining, as crazy, as manic, as dangerous, or as downright debauched, as it has been in the past!

*

Flash forward a few years, and I found myself recently wandering along Queen Street one Saturday afternoon, and couldn't help myself in standing, for several minutes outside of the old building, just looking... and remembering.

It was a strange and unsettling feeling, thinking that I had spent close to 28 years working there – almost half my life. While at the same time, wistfully recalling happier, funnier – and crazier times.

As I gazed at the doors, windows, and basements, I was momentarily caught up in my own thoughts.

I then peered with curiosity through the doorways, noticing that there are obviously parts of it that have altered and now, not with any great surprise, look very different.

Although the outside facade still sends out a well-worn statement that it was once an important building, full of prestige and noble creative efforts. Nothing less than a solid and reassuring presence that in times gone by had creatively blended the austere with the aesthetic.

Well, at least we can be eternally thankful that it wasn't turned into some ghastly, tasteless and abominable bingo hall!! What a disaster that would have been!

Like so many of the large older properties situated in Edinburgh's Newtown region, the building has undergone yet another refurbishment, finding itself split and divided to accommodate a number of new smaller companies.

Yet, while continuing to look, I also humorously wondered if any of the newer owners and occupants was aware of its colourful past as a former radiobroadcasting centre? And had anyone ever been disturbed, or distressed, by any strange and spooky goings on? Or even experienced other worldly sights and sounds late at night?

No, not coming from the First Aid Room! That room, with all its dark, devilish and wicked secrets, is now sadly long gone!

But more particularly in the rooms, tucked away out of sight and remotely placed near the very top towards the attic space?

I am convinced it still has its share of ghosts and phantoms, but ones that should reverberate and echo with raucous laughter, and of joyous times now past.

I took one long, last look at the old building, then turned to walk away, leaving memories of friends and colleagues, as well as the prime years of my youth, now far behind me…

The drama is done. All have departed.

AFTERWORDS

The Final Roll Call Of Honour...
or something like that

With the book project finally completed, I decided one evening to give my memory an elaborate exercise, by adding that little bit extra element of panache, that could only be described as a truly Herculean task. Phew!

This was simply to write down as many names that I could possibly remember in one go who were (in one way, or another) around during my 28 years as an employee at BBC Edinburgh!

Considering that I did not in any way contact the BBC Scotland HR department, or utilise any search engines, databases, or websites (you may not be all that surprised to learn that there is absolutely *nothing* that covers this particular subject currently on the internet!!) I think that I didn't do too badly under the circumstances.

Who knows, perhaps during this extensive "brain clearout", I may have inadvertently started an entirely new Wikipedia entry??

Unfortunately, you may also find that there might be the odd name missing.

So many, many apologies if I have accidentally omitted anyone. This was certainly not intentional. If the "windmills of my mind" have temporarily blown certain names away, once again I can only apologise profusely. After all, a man's brain can only hold so much information at one time!!

Hopefully, this fact will be properly corrected, rectified, and updated if a future edition of this book is ever reprinted.

*

You might also notice that certain names have been left out of the gathering.

This is due to the fact that several of them feature and contribute – in one small form or another – to the thrusting narrative of my tale!

So, as you will see, it's not quite a cast of thousands – but I suppose, it's pretty close to it.

In saying that, a special mention must go to my old BBC chum *Richard Kent* for coming to my rescue and assisting me in filling in a few of the name gaps, as well as correcting some of the original name spellings. Yes, it's always good to have someone on hand that was around roughly during the same time frame as yourself, to help and guide you in such matters.

When I first showed him the long list of illustrious names, Richard initially looked closely at the pages and then gasped with a mixture of surprise, incredulity and shock at the memories (both good, bad, and perhaps even a little ugly) that simultaneously stared back and stirred within him, whilst he was reading the exhaustive name list.

"OMG!!"

"F***k me – and to think that I went home with her one night!!"

"Scary Woman!"

"Strange Guy!"

"What an absolute bastard he was…"

These were just a few of the surprised expressions that emanated from Richard's lips, whilst he was taking in this brain-stretching literary trip down memory lane.

We also discussed some of the quirky nicknames that used to be unknowingly attached to a few of the individuals on the list.

Wonderfully bizarre and descriptive names such as: *Fluffy Bunny, The Tree Fairy, The Bunny Boiler, Old Jock, Mokit Drawers, The Diva, Mr Honky Tonks, Miss Frosty Knickers, Green Boots, Halloween Cake-Face, Darth Vader, Tits Ahoy* and *The Back Scratcher?*

You will now discover listed below, in alphabetical order, without alluding to importance, status or merit – a fair selection of some of the many individuals who – between the years 1974-2002 – happened to work, visit, annoy (a few likely suspects there!), inhabit (or just occasionally staggered and wandered around?) the confines of the studios, offices, rooms, canteens, toilets, lounges and corridors of BBC 5 Queen Street, Edinburgh – whether briefly, or otherwise.

The vast majority of those listed were (for the most part) friendly, approachable, and agreeably good-humoured, versatile, talented and all in all, thoroughly decent human beings. With quite a number of them possessing unimpeachable integrity, allied with an ennobling work ethic and commitment to quality in the best traditions of BBC Scotland. This combination added a formidable and rare distinction to the stations output on television and radio over many decades.

However, you may also discover one or two individuals mentioned below whose overall contribution to the activities within BBC Edinburgh, that might well be regarded as somewhat suspect, dubious, and questionable at best.

No names – no pack drill! Well, I suppose nobody's perfect!

Everyone who recognises, or encountered those distinguished (or less than distinguished?) individuals will undoubtedly have his, or her, own personal opinions already formed in that direction.

So, with that being the case, I can only present the evidence and let my readers make up their own minds as regards to that.

As for me, well, I couldn't possibly comment...

And Here They All Are:

ABEER MACINTYRE

AILEEN CLARK

AILSA MACINTOSH

ALAN DOWNIE

ALAN GRAY

ALLAN JACK

ALAN MACKAY

ALAN MELDRUM

ALLAN HUNTER

ALASDAIR MCARDLE

ALASDAIR MACLEOD

ALASTAIR CLARK

ALASTAIR HETHERINGTON

ALASTAIR MACDONALD

ALEX BURDON

ALEX GIBSON

ALEX MCLEAN

ALISDAIR DUNCAN

ALISON BELL

ALISON BROWN

ALISON CHERRIE
ALISON GILLIES
ALISON HARLEY
ALISON MCLEAY
ALISON PERRY
ALISTAIR MCCABE
ALYSON MITCHELL
AMANDA HARGREAVES
ANDREW BARR
ANDREW BRITTON
ANDREW LOCKYEAR
ANDY DAVEY
ANDY WEBB
ANGELA BARNETT (ROBERTSON)
ANGELA MACLEAN
ANGUS MACINNES
ANN CONNELL
ANN DICKSON
ANN GALLIVAN
ANN MCKELVIE
ANNIE WOOD
ANNA BENSTEAD
ANNA HURSTHOUSE
ANNA MAGNUSSEN
ANNE DIACK
ANNE FALCONER
ARCHIE LEE

ARCHIE MACPHERSON
ART SUTTER
ATHOLL DUNCAN
AVRIL MORTON
BARBARA MACRITCHIE
BEN FOGG
BETH NAIRN
BILL CARROCHER
BILL JACK
BILL MACINTOSH
BILL MASON
BILL MILLIGAN
BILL TAYLOR
BILLY GORDON
BOB CRAWFORD
BOB DICKSON
BOB HOOKER
BOB WARRILOW
BRIAN INNES
BRIAN MORTON
BRIAN PENDREIGH
BRIAN SUTTIE
BRIAN TAYLOR
BRONWEN TULLOCH
BRUCE YOUNG
CAROL KIRKWOOD
CAROL STRACHAN

CAROL WIGHTMAN
CAROLINE ADAM
CAROLINE BECKETT
CAROLINE KING
CATHERINE CAMERON
CATHERINE SMITH
CATHY MCDONALD
CATRIONA WATT
CHARLES NAIRN
CHARLIE CAW
CHRIS ARMSTRONG
CHRIS IRWIN
CHRIS LOWELL
CHRIS WORRAL
CHRISANNA KENNEDY
CHRISTINE MACLEOD
CHRISTOPHER LAMBTON
CLAIRE FERRIER
COLIN BELL
DAN BUGLIS
DAN MEIKLE
DAVE AYLOTT
DAVE BATCHELOR
DAVE HAMILL
DAVE MCEWAN
DAVE MELDRUM
DAVE QUINN

DAVID CALDER
DAVID CAMPBELL
DAVID DORWARD
DAVID GLENCOURSE
DAVID JACKSON YOUNG
DAVID MCMEEKIN
DAVID MILLAR
DAVID NISBET
DAVID PAT WALKER
DAVID PORTER
DAVID ROBERTS
DAVID STENHOUSE
DEBBIE CUMMING (MCPHAIL)
DEBBIE RIDGEWAY-MCDONALD
DECLAN LYNCH
DELLA MATHIESON
DENISE PRESSLEY
DEREK ABRAHAMS
DEREK BATEMAN
DESMOND CARRINGTON
DICK SILVER
DOLINA MACLENNAN
DOMINIC BLACK
DONALD GUNN
DONALD IAIN BROWN
DONALD MONRO
DOREEN STEWART

DOREEN TAYLOR
DOROTHY GRACE ELDER
DOT GREGOR
DOUGIE DONNELLY
DOUGLAS ARCHER
DOUGLAS KYNOCH
DOUGLAS MCLEOD
DOUGLAS RING
DOUGLAS STEWART
DR MARINELL ASH
DUNCAN KIRKHOPE
EDDIE MAIR
EILEEN PHILIPS
ELIZABETH CLARK
ELIZABETH PARTIKA
ELIZABETH QUIGLEY
ELKE WILSON
ELLIE BUCHANAN
EMMA CADZOW
ERIC WOOD
ESME FRAME
FATHER BILL ANDERSON
FATHER WILLIE MCDADE
FIONA CAMERON
FIONA CLARK
FIONA CROALL
FIONA HENDERSON

FIONA MCLELLAN
FRAN MORRISON
FRANCES ALLAN
FRANCES BARBOUR
FRANCES BROWN
FRANCES STEEN
FRANK FORBES
FRANK HEDLEY
FRANK MUNGALL
FRASER FALCONER
FRED MCAULEY
FREDA BORTHWICK
FRIEDA MORRISON
GAIL CLARK
GARETH WARDELL
GARY FERRIGAN
GARY LUGTON
GAYNOR MCFARLANE
GEOFF BASKERVILLE
GEOFF BROWN
GEOFF CAMERON
GEOFF WEBSTER
GEORGE BRUCE
GEORGE HUME
GERDA STEVENSON
GERRY FORD
GERRY MCKENZIE

GILL DONALDSON

GILLIAN CHARLES

GILLIAN IRVINE

GILLIAN MCLEAN

GINA CAMPBELL

GLYNN HENDERSON

GORDON CHALMERS

GORDON CRUIKSHANK

GORDON EMSLIE

GORDON LEISHMAN

GORDON SMITH

GRAHAM COLLINGE

GRAHAM POVEY

GRAHAM TAYLOR

GRANT STOTT

GREG RUSSELL

GREGOR GRAHAM

GREGOR ROBERTSON

GRIGOR STIRLING

HAIG GORDON

HARRY SMITH

HAYLEY MILLER

HAZEL MARSHALL

HEATHER BOWNASS

HEATHER SUTTIE (RINGLAND)

HELEN HENDERSON

HELEN ROSS

HOWIE FIRTH
IAIN ANDERSON
IAIN HUNTER
IAIN MCWHIRTER
IAN ALDRED
IAN DOCHERTY
IRENE BAIN
ISHBEL MCLEAN
ISOBEL & DANNY (A.K.A. D-BOY!)
ISOBEL FRASER
ISOBEL MITCHELL (MCNEILL)
JACK REGAN
JACKIE GRANT
JALDEEP KATWALA
JAMES BOYLE
JAMES MALLOY
JAMES RUNCIE
JAMES SPANKIE
JAN FAIRLEY
JANE FOWLER (GARDEN)
JANE HOUSTON
JANE MACLENAHAN
JANE NOAKES
JANE SUTHERLAND
JANICE FORSYTH
JAY FLETT
JEAN RIMMER

JEAN ROBERTSON
JEAN THOMPSON
JEANETTE COUTTS
JENNIFER CHRISTIE
JENNIFER COLLIE
JENNIFER MADDOX
JESS KING
JESSIE BARBOUR
JIM GALBREATH
JIM HUNTER
JIM ROSS
JIMMY OLIVER
JO MACDONALD
JO WHEELAN
JOAN RAFFAN
JOAN TOWNEND
JOANNA BUCHAN
JOE BARNETT
JOHANNA HALL
JOHN ARNOTT
JOHN BOOTHMAN
JOHN EASTON
JOHN FORSYTH
JOHN GRAY
JOHN KERR
JOHN KNOX
JOHN MACNEISH

JOHN MCCORMICK
JOHN MILLAR
JOHN MILNE
JOHN RUSSELL
JOHN SCOTT PATERSON (JASPER)
JOHN SOWREY
JOHN STIRLING
JON KEAN
JONATHAN AITKEN
JOYCE MACMILLAN
JOYCE NICOL
JULIE CORCORAN
JULIE FRASER
JULIE HUNTER
KAREN BELL
KAREN MACKENZIE
KATE COPSTICK
KATE MASON
KATHLEEN REID
KAYE ADAMS
KEITH ALEXANDER
KEITH HALDEN
KEITH MUIRHEAD
KEN BRUCE
KEN CARGILL
KEN MACQUARRIE
KEN STEWART

KEN SYKORA
KEN THOMAS
KENNETH MACDONALD
KENNETH ROY
KENNY CAMPBELL
KENRIS MACLEOD
KEVIN FAGIN
KIRSTEEN CAMERON
KIRSTEN LOCKE
KIRSTIE LAMONT
LAURA MACINTOSH
LEE MCPHAIL
LESLEY DRENNAN
LISA SUMMERS
LORRIE FAY
LOUISE BATCHELOR
LOUISE BEATTIE
LOUISE DALZIEL
LOUISE SMILLIE
LOUISE WELSH
LOUISE YEOMAN
LUCINDA WITHINSHAW
LUCY CONAN
LUCY HETHERINGTON
LUCY WILSON
LYNSEY MOYES
MACK COUPAR

MAGGIE CUNNINGHAM
MALCOLM TORRIE
MALCOLM WRIGHT
MARGARET DAVIES
MARGARET HARPER
MARGARET KRYZNOWSKA
MARGARET MAGNUSSEN
MARIA DUDZIAK
MARILYN IMRIE
MARION MENZIES
MARJORY CALIKES
MARK COUSINS
MARK CROSSLEY
MARLENE MCCALLUM
MARTHA FAIRLIE
MARTIN GIBSON
MARTIN GRIFFIN
MARTIN SMILLIE
MARY BRENNAN
MARY CALLUMKEIRIAN
MATT SPICER
MAUREEN BEATTIE
MAY MILLER
MICHAEL CALDER
MICHAEL COLE
MIKE CRYER
MIKE LLOYD

MIKE MCLEOD

MIKE SHAW

MING ROBERTSON

MO MCCULLOUGH

MOIRA BOWMAN

MOIRA DOW

MOIRA FIRMAGE

MOIRA SCOTT

MONA WILSON

MONISE DURRANI

MORAG KINNIBURGH

MYRA MACPAKE

NEIL BURNETT

NEIL DALGLEISH

NETTA FORBES

NETTA PETERSON

NEVILLE GARDEN

NEVILLE TURNER

NICK BALNEAVES

NICK LOW

NICK WEBSTER

NIGEL ROBSON

NIGEL SHEPHERD

NOBLE MCPHERSON

OLIVE MARR (MILLIGAN)

PAM WARDELL

PAMELA HURST

PAT CHALMERS
PAT GRIEVE
PAT MACSHANNON
PAT RAMSAY
PATRICK RAYNER
PAUL DENVER
PAUL MACINNES
PAUL MITCHELL
PAUL SUMMERLING
PAULA WHITEHEAD
PENNY BARR
PENNY TAYLOR
PETE COLE
PETER CLARK
PETER DOBIE
PETER EASTON
PETER MACRAE
PHIL AIKMAN
PHIL TAYLOR
PIP WHITEHOUSE
RAB NOAKES
REEVEL ALDERSON
RENTOKIL RAB
REV DOUGLAS AITKEN
REV JOHNSTON MCKAY
REV STEWART LAMONT
RICHARD ATKINSON

ROBERT LIVINGSTONE

ROBERT DAWSON SCOTT

ROBERT SPROUL CRANN

ROBIN AITKEN

ROBIN RICHARDSON

ROBIN WYLIE

ROGER MORTIMER

RON WILD

RONNIE GUILD

ROSE MCGILL

ROSEMARY BINNIE (TAYLOR)

ROSEMARY RAEBURN

ROSS ANDERSON

ROY GREGOR

SALLY MCNAIR

SANDY FRASER

SHAUN O'ROURKE

SHEENA COWIE

SHEENA MACDONALD

SHEENA STEWART

SHEILA HAWKINS

SHEILA MACK

SHEILA NOBLE

SHELAGH CLAPPERTON

SIMON WALTON

SIOBHAN DONNELLY

SIOBHAN SYNNOT

STAN TAYLOR
STEVE ANSELL
STEVE HORNE
STEVE KYDD
STEWART CONN
STUART GREIG
STUART PAULEY
STUART SPENCE
SUE INNES
SUE MEEK
TINA MCIVER
TOM HUNTER
TOM KINNIMONT
TOM MORTON
TONY NEILSON
TRACEY SMITH
TREVOR ROYLE
UZMA MIR-YOUNG
VAL PIKE
VICKY DAVIDSON
W. GORDON SMITH
W. SINCLAIR AITKEN
WENDY ASHWORTH

P.S. As a final, final word, I almost forgot to present you with a sort of bonus disc of *BBC Edinburgh's Greatest Hits*.

So here below are a mixed list of programmes that were once proudly produced within the studios, offices, and walls of 5 Queen Street Edinburgh.

Scottish radio nostalgia buffs will no doubt come over all excited and beside themselves with unfettered joy at the mere hint of a mention of their much-loved titles. Then again... maybe not.

GOOD MORNING SCOTLAND

TWELVE-NOON

TRAVEL TIME

THE BEST OF SCOTTISH

THE MUSICAL GARDEN

QUEEN STREET GARDEN

CHINESE TIMES

THE USUAL SUSPECTS

MOVIES & SHAKERS

TIGHT LINES

THE BRIAN MORTON SHOW

KILBRECK

TAKE THE FLOOR

COVER STORIES

TRAVELLING FOLK

THE MUSICIAN IN SCOTLAND

RYTHYM & NEWS

ODYSSEY

THE DAILY SKETCH

ROCK ON SCOTLAND

CHECK THIS

THE ARTS IN SCOTLAND

LAWRENCE P. LETTICE

LUNCHTIME REPORT
CHURCH NEWS AND VIEWS
NICKETY NACKETY
HOME FRONT
HOPSCOTCH
TUESDAY REVIEW
DIG THIS
FOCUS
SPEAKING OUT
KANE OVER AMERICA

Printed in Great Britain
by Amazon

87140139R00231